U.S.
WAR
DEPT

10ᵗʰ RODMAN

RODMAN GU

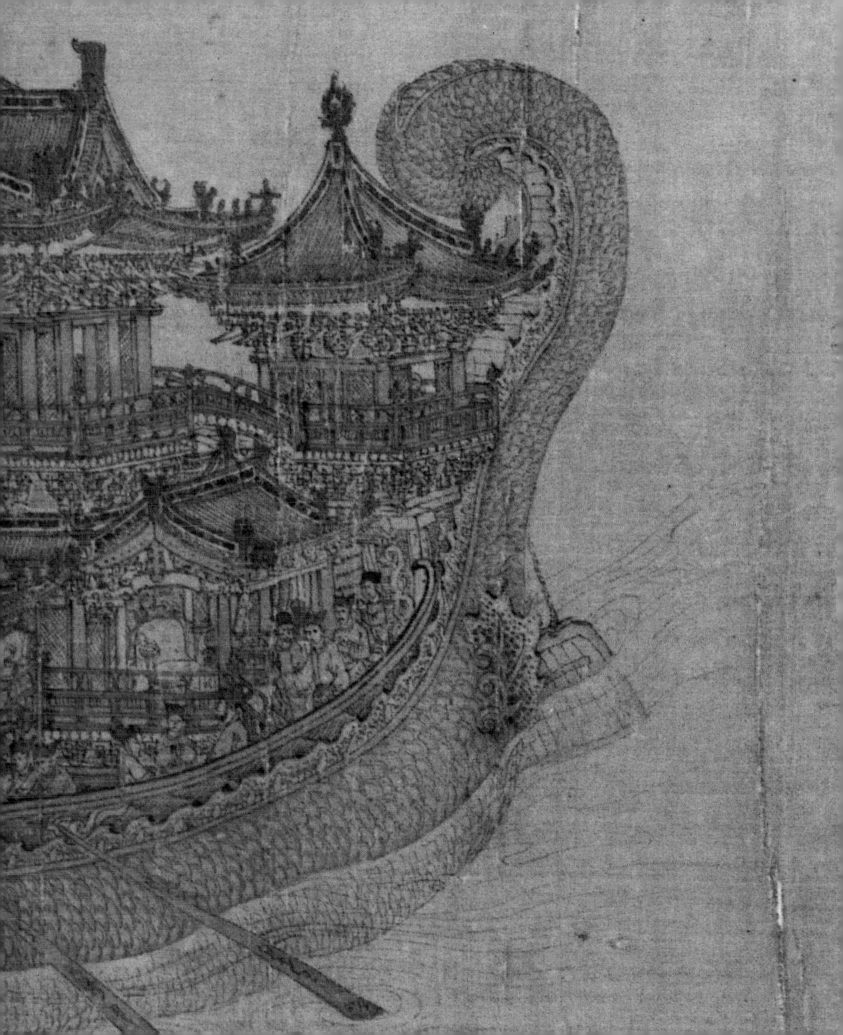

The
Smithsonian Book
of Invention

Smithsonian Exposition Books

Distributed to the trade by
W. W. Norton & Company
New York, N.Y.

Contents

Smithsonian visitors witness the origins and impact of invention. Ships, cannon, uniforms, and a model fort crowd the flag-bedecked Arts and Industries Building's "1876: A Centennial Exhibition," page 1. At the Museum of History and Technology, the great Foucault Pendulum sweeps across the floor, pages 2-3. A Chinese conception of a great dragon-boat floats out of the past, *pages 4-5; a painting of the first U.S. textile mill reminds us of industry's debt to early invention, pages 6-7. An 1890s drawing reveals women demonstrating for recognition of their inventions, patents at the old Patent Office (now Smithsonian's National Portrait Gallery), page 8. Viewers stare down the business end of a 10-barreled Civil War Gatling gun, opposite.*

The Smithsonian Institution
Secretary, S. Dillon Ripley

SMITHSONIAN EXPOSITION BOOKS

James K. Page, Jr., Director
Russell Bourne, Senior Editor

Editors: Alexis Doster III, Joe Goodwin, Jane M. Ross
Production Editor: Ann Beasley
Research: Caren Keshishian
Copy Editors: Amy Donovan, Bettie Loux Donley
Picture Research: Patricia Upchurch, Janis Knudsen
    Wheat, David Bridge
Assistants: June Armstrong, Francine Atwell

Design: Michael David Brown, Inc., Art Direction by
    Michael David Brown, assisted by Jeanne C. Kelly

Business Manager: Thomas A. Hoffman
Assistant: Christine Nonnenmacher

Separations and Engravings: Lanman Lithoplate, Inc.
Typography: Carver Photocomposition, Inc.
Printing: Rand McNally and Company

Marketing Consultant: William H. Kelty

Photography by Steve Altman, Ross Chapple, Henry
    Eastwood, Charles H. Phillips, and Smithsonian photog-
    raphers Kim Nielsen and Dane Penland

Illustrations by: Jan Adkins, John Huehnergarth,
    Pierre Mion, David Good, Peter Stone

Grateful acknowledgment is given to Derek de Solla
Price of Yale University and to the curators and staffs
of Smithsonian bureaus lending assistance to this volume: Office of American Studies, Anacostia Neighborhood Museum, Cooper-Hewitt Museum of Decorative Arts and Design, Freer Gallery of Art, Hirsh-
horn Museum and Sculpture Garden, National Air
and Space Museum, National Collection of Fine Arts,
National Gallery of Art, National Museum of History
and Technology, National Museum of Natural History, National Portrait Gallery, National Zoological
Park, Division of Performing Arts, Radiation Biology
Laboratory, Renwick Gallery, Smithsonian As-
trophysical Observatory, Smithsonian Institution
Traveling Exhibition Service.

Introduction

When President Ulysses S. Grant addressed the Centennial Exhibition, he remarked that the American machinery displayed there demonstrated that the United States rivaled the world, including the "older and more advanced nations." The Smithsonian Institution more or less inherited the Centennial—having transferred many specimens to the new Arts and Industries Building next to the Castle—and, along with the inheritance, a certain nationalistic pride in the inventions in its collections.

The editors of Smithsonian Exposition Books share that pride in the Smithsonian's role in advancing as well as chronicling inventive technology. Thus, when asked to create a book on the process of invention, they set out to compose a multichambered structure, with many Smithsonian artifacts under the lights and a host of American flags flying aloft.

But while the book was in its planning stage, a scholar with a pronounced British accent blew into the nation's capital and declared firmly that a book on invention from the Smithsonian should *not* be focused solely on the American experience. After all, he advised, the Smithsonian is an international cultural institution. It's all very well to consider that the inventions in the Smithsonian's vast collections are chiefly American, but remember, he urged, that this very Institution was founded by a bequest from a foreigner—an Englishman named James Smithson. What American institution should therefore be more mindful of the fact that many nations have provided the shoulders upon which mankind rests? For as the record uncompromisingly reveals, Americans did not invent everything wonderful and terrifying. As a matter of fact, Americans didn't invent their most noticeable technological product, the automobile. But, as explained in the introductory section, "The Yankee Perspective," Americans did invent the way to *sell* automobiles, lots of them.

They also invented the airplane—but not the parachute. As noted in the next section, "Origins of Invention," the parachute was produced by an Italian 300 years before anyone really needed one, and 500 years after the Chinese invented, for ceremonial purposes, a mechanical compass analogous in some respects to modern inertial guidance systems.

Tools. That's what this book is essentially about—tools, one of the chief distinguishing features of the human species. Tools: the Anglo-Saxon word for technology, the necessary handmaiden of international science. Tools: the essence of industry, of products both mundane and exotic. Therefore, the three central sections of the book, devoted respectively to technology, science, and industry, describe certain tools and systems as evolutions of parallel species.

In fact, our entire mechanistic world sometimes seems but a well-tooled invention—give or take a few unplanned tornados. We hypothesize, we invent, we engineer, and our innovations change our lives. Thus the final two sections of the book deal with the impact of invention on society and the opportunities for inventive minds in the future.

Yet, for all its sections and its divisions into text essays and picture stories, the editors recognize that this book is not exactly organized. Invention seems too protean, indeed too Promethean, to be locked into chambers of the same size or character. And just as our British consultant pointed out that the book should not be excessively American, so have curators within the Institution warned against making it monolithic in opinion. Are inventions good, after all? Should we pursue high technology with ever greater expectations or should we find alternative paths? The reader will encounter varying views, differing interpretations of where civilization has come from and where it's going, as he wanders through the book.

This book attempts to analyze invention—its process, its impact—and by no means pretends to mention all of the important inventions, nor to avoid some silly ones. It has come into being thanks to the inexhaustible good will of Smithsonian scholars and others to whom the editors can only bow in grateful humility. Inevitably it raises more questions about our most uniquely human impulse than it answers. But aren't questions, after all, the wellspring of invention?

The Editors

The Yankee Perspective

Like a brash new steam engine bursting onto the world scene, the United States—powered by a vital energy called Yankee ingenuity—startled the 19th-century world with its political, technological, and social innovations. The notion of the new, the fascination with inventive devices, the ability to bang together a marketable gadget, all seemed integral parts of the buoyant, expectant, American character.

Change at ever faster rates has marked the generations. Considering the old and new inventions of his times, a writer in the next few pages recalls iceboxes cooled by real ice, corrugated washboards, telephones with cranks, and motors that functioned only with much loving care.

U.S. invention has been a process that has made for heroes—Edison, Ford, Bell, and the rest. It is also a process that makes for questions: who are the real inventors, those who conceive of great innovations, or those who make them work? Or is invention usually the sum of both brilliant conceptualization and practical realization?

The Smithsonian's museums have wondrous collections of artifacts for display and study—everything from Stone Age axes to the famous Wright *Flyer,* as well as a host of things (like a magnificent laminated wood bicycle) that don't quite work for all their inventiveness. These start the mind ticking—what kind of human or national compulsion do they truly represent? They also cause some smiles and raised eyebrows. The Yankee tinkerer may be eccentric (like the aeronautical engineer in Peter Arno's "Back to the Drawing Board" cartoon), but he also gives that dynamic spring to American life.

Through a Victorian Glass

My office is in the old Arts and Industries Building of the Smithsonian Institution. This ornate Victorian structure contains many administrative departments, including the editorial workings of *Smithsonian* magazine, where I do my stuff. The building also houses a fascinating exhibit called "1876." It is an evocation of the display of human accomplishments which opened in Philadelphia in that Centennial year, and it is through these very tangible examples of invention that I make my way each morning.

I am overwhelmed with the past from the first moment when I park my car in the lot outside the Smithsonian Castle. Here once stood various outbuildings of the Institution, including stables. Staff members of a century ago would presumably clop to work in their carriages and have their horses taken care of right here. Another of these vanished buildings was Secretary Samuel P. Langley's South Shed where he did much of the work on his Aerodrome—the flying machine that didn't quite work and lost out to the Wright Brothers' *Flyer.*

I walk from the parking lot through a formal Victorian garden designed to recapture an attitude of the past—leisurely, gracious, roomy. By the time I enter the west door of my building, I am in the mood to nod a greeting to the great steam engines that bob and hiss and gesture, their weighty flywheels decorated, as was the way, with wreaths and flowers. I pass cases filled with gleaming tools, with heavy kitchen equipment, with prints and ladies' hats and dentists' instruments and brass telegraph sets. I say good morning to fire engines and firearms, to heating stoves and cooling fans, to sewing machines and screw lathes. There is so much invention on view that I doubt if I can ever see it all, no matter how long I keep my job.

Every day, then, I am reminded of the past and I find much of it familiar. I am old enough now to remember life more than half a century ago. And the tangibles that I see every day on the way to my office date from only about half a century before that. Much of what I saw as a child had not changed a great deal since 1876 and thereabouts—the time this exhibit represents.

When I was eight or nine I was big enough to help my father and older brothers get the ice in. We had a summer home in New Hampshire with no ice deliveries as there were down in Boston. There a horse-drawn cart would creak through the alley behind the house, and if the iceman saw your card in the kitchen window—a pale blue card with ICE in large letters—he'd stop and bring in a block. He lifted it with tongs and carried it on his shoulder where he wore a rubber cape, glistening with ice melt. He was always a big man with muscular arms.

In the country we got it ourselves. We drove Katy, a Model T pick-up, down to the village and backed her up at the ice dealer's platform. He'd snake a country-sized cake of ice out from the sawdust that insulated it, hoist it up on his scales, hose it clean, and weigh it.

"Hundred and fifty," he'd sing out.

"Fine," my Dad would reply, and the ice would be lowered into Katy, who would groan and list perceptibly. We'd cover it and hold it in place with bits of cargo and children and drive it home as it grad-

Katy

ually puddled under the August sun. Then we'd slide it across the kitchen linoleum and hoist it over the icebox, which Mother had emptied and cleaned. I remember helping to lower the big wet monster onto the corrugated zinc bottom and finagling the tongs out and chipping it to make it fit . . . and then, when everything was over, sitting on the lid of the icebox, drumming my bare heels on oak sides and being given a glass of milk and a Fig Newton.

The milk, incidentally, came in a glass bottle from the farm half a mile away. It was Guernsey milk, yellow-white, with a distinct band of deeper yellow extending down four and half inches from the top. This was light cream—"top of the bottle"—and was fine for breakfast cereal. But when you drank milk, you shook the bottle first so that the colors blended.

At the farm the milk went through a hand-cranked separator. I've seen its near double here at the Smithsonian—in the agricultural exhibit at the National Museum of History and Technology. This machine separated the real cream, which came to us in pint bottles. We used it for coffee and desserts, and it was so thick it had to be spooned out.

Nothing was pasteurized, nor was the herd tuberculin-tested back then. Years later I met an employee of the American Guernsey Cattle Club and told him all of this, a little wistfully, and he pointed out that I was damn lucky to be alive.

Bringing in the ice was exciting for a small boy, but the grownups must never have regretted switching to a refrigerator—no emptying the drainage basin, no swabbing the floor. The refrigerator just stood there quietly, refrigerating. A friend of mine who is a refrigeration engineer once pointed out how beautifully successful mechanical cooling is. "How often," he asked, "have you had a repairman in to fix your refrigerator?" And I admitted that all the ones I've ever known kept on running until I was sick of them or needed a bigger one.

Today's refrigerators often include an ice-maker. I love it. It's simple and quiet and obedient. Sometimes as you pass by your refrigerator you hear a muffled rumble from its innards, as though it had eaten too much chili, and that's your ice-maker faithfully chunking out another load of cubes up there in the dark. Marvelous.

I remember watching ice cutters at work on a local pond one Christmas vacation. They drove a team of horses with caulked shoes out on the ice to tug out the great blocks after they had been sawed free. Then the cakes would be coasted to the ice house where an endless chain, powered by a steam engine, carried them, rattling and clanking, up into the building. There they were stacked and buried in sawdust, forming a great damp hill in the darkness; wonderfully cool to play in on a hot summer day.

Refrigeration is really better. It doesn't ruin the skating on the pond and it theoretically frees that crew of husky young countrymen to do something more meaningful with their lives. It only takes a little electricity and water for the ice-maker. When I think of impending shortages of both of these things, I see the prospect in terms of my ice-maker and then I feel worried. It's my favorite invention, the icebox (as we used to call it).

We didn't get our refrigerator in the country until the place had been electrified. As a little boy, I was read aloud to at night by kerosene lamp. The wicks had to be trimmed, a nasty job, but later we got a mantle lamp that was easier to maintain and gave a better light, bright and white. To reach my bedroom in the dark, I lit a candle in a saucer-shaped candle holder—and learned just how fast I could move without its going out.

Our wood stove was converted to oil and we used kerosene in that, too. We had no radio, and our phonograph, always known as a "Victrola," had to be wound up—that was my job—to play "You Gotta See Mamma Every Night or You Can't See Mamma At All," while my siblings were grinding away on the ice-cream freezer. Ice cream has done nothing but suffer from technical improvements. Licking the paddles after we'd done a batch of ice cream— cream, sugar, fresh cut-up peaches or strawberries—was a treat we carefully shared as reward for endlessly turning that crank. No kind of ice cream has come along since that tastes so good. It's interesting that today the old-fashioned ice-cream-makers are back in demand.

Our water came from a well quite a distance off and was fed to us by air pressure. This was supplied by a splendid old one-cylinder gasoline engine with twin flywheels which we had to crank up every afternoon. I can still hear it. It would start with a series of explosions, then would settle into regular breathing interspersed by occasional good solid bangs: "BAM, BAM, huh-huh-huh-huh-huh-huh BAM, BAM, BAM," and so on. It only fired when the speed slowed. I pass engines almost exactly like it every morning in my building.

The pump engine, incidentally, required a sort of Rube Goldberg ingenuity that was not unusual 50 years ago. My father wanted to make sure it was still going after he had started it up, so in order to hear it he ran the exhaust pipe out of the pump house, a meadow away. That's simple enough. But how to make the thing shut itself off? Dad rigged a sort of bucket that would catch the drip from the pump's safety valve when it opened at a certain pressure. The bucket was hung from a light line that went around a couple of pulleys and then to the ignition connection on the pump engine. When enough water collected in the bucket its weight would snatch open the ignition breaker, stopping the engine. And,

of course, the bucket had to have a hole in it so it would drain and be ready for next time. My father was a resourceful man, quite able to devise ways of making life easier. He was fortunate to have some power tools of the day—a foot-treadle buzz saw, for example, which is almost exactly duplicated in the "1876" exhibit.

One of the uses to which my father put water was in shaving. He had seven straight razors in a leather case, each in a pocket labeled with a day of the week. Thus he would remove Tuesday's razor, strop it, and deftly attack his lathered face. The skill, the dry, sandpapery sound fascinated me, and I would watch him faithfully. It is curious that he went from straight razor directly to electric without stopping over to investigate safety razors. I learned to shave on a safety razor, dutifully moved on to an electric when one was given me, and then returned to the safeties for good when the double-track blades appeared on the market. For me, at least, that's a good invention.

We did have a telephone. Later, I worked in a very tiny New Hampshire village that still had the country phones. You turned the crank to get the operator. I loved it because the operator knew everyone, and if you called Bill Peters, she'd simply tell you that he'd just walked past the phone office on the way to the barber shop. That bit of small-town life has now been improved out of existence.

The small town that furnished me a clear

glimpse of the 19th century was a remote village in Massachusetts where two great-aunts lived. They had a large New England house, the kind with sheds attached so you could get out to the horses and the woodpile without plunging through snow. I would be taken there to visit, and they would kiss me wetly, brushing their spinsterly mustaches across my obediently upturned little face.

I would be driven there by car because I was too young to walk from the railroad depot, about three miles away. My older siblings walked it routinely, lugging their suitcases because it was unusual even to see a car on those forgotten roads.

The aunts' property involved a meadow, mostly garden, that stretched to the shores of a pond. They kept chickens, and I learned to gather real eggs and replace them with china ones which would inspire reluctant hens. *There's* an invention that must go back aways.

Such memories make me realize that the aunts bequeathed me one of those rare chances to touch base with the past. What a glorious reach of generations to contemplate—myself, now dodging dotage in the late 1970s, recalling two old ladies whose lives stretched back to the 1840s and '50s. The Mexican War; General Scott at Vera Cruz; Frémont exploring California; the Gold Rush; Daniel Webster; Henry Clay and John Calhoun. Wow!

I was too young to ask the questions I should have asked—did they remember, for example, what *their* ancient relatives had told them about the Revolution? — but they did show me, unwittingly, an old and authentic way of doing things. They pumped water with a hand pump in the kitchen and sometimes let me do it while they held a pitcher under the spout. The water tasted a little funny, metallic, maybe. But then, our water would probably taste a little funny to them.

They had an outhouse, situated in the passageway out to the sheds. No heat reached it. I confess that my memories of it are tinged with horror. I hated it—icy cold and incredibly aromatic. I was always happy to get back home to our own nice warm bathrooms with the water closets made of wood—at least that's what you saw—working with a simple pull of the chain. Admittedly, they went off with the thunder of a spring freshet, shaking the very house, but they were clean and simple and effective.

The Smithsonian's Museum of History and Technology has an illustrated description of these devices at the entrance to the Gentlemen on the Constitution Avenue level of the building. I do not know if the Ladies contains the same information, not being qualified to find out. However, the news from the Gentlemen is that the facility I remember as a boy seems to have sprung from a design by the J. L. Mott Ironworks in 1888.

The great improvement in this field lies in noise abatement. Those nicely shaped little tanks that are now activated by turning a handle deliver their contents in almost complete silence—at most a discreet gurgle. This decided improvement has been attained

The process of squeezing oranges against the old ribbed cone is messy and slow. I remember a hand squeezer that crushed the orange halves by pressing a lever downward. This rotated a geared shaft which interlocked with the cogs on the base of the crusher. Out came the juice, deliciously, into a reservoir. Incredibly, I found such a device recently and still use it. Someone suggested that we should get an electric juicer with that same ribbed cone. We don't see why. We have the best invention. No further improvements need to be made.

Clothes washing has seen many innovations, however, which have really improved the process. The basic requirements are simple: get clothes clean. But trying to do it simply is full of pitfalls. Once on a camping trip that included our youngest child—then a baby—my wife resolved to take the cleaning process back to the days of the Bible. She washed diapers in a creek, rubbing them against a flat rock. It polluted the creek and wore holes in the diapers.

My wife, an Australian, remembers laundry done in the 1940s in a huge round copper boiler heated by a wood fire. The clothes were brought to a boil, along with soap, then were banged around with a stick. It got them some kind of clean, but it wasn't easy on synthetics. The old washboard of my youth was supposed to accomplish the same thing. In both cases, the rinsed laundry was put through a wringer and hung on a line to dry in the sun. Clean shirts smelled wonderful, but of course today's washing machines and dryers are a vast improvement.

After World War II, I returned to New England to find an old friend, recently married, learning how to use one particular wedding present—the only dishwasher in town. He and his bride fussed with it and found that the only way it worked properly was when the dishes were washed the old way before being loaded in. "What it does," my friend explained, "is sort of sterilize them." "Also, it's a handy way to store them," put in his wife, a little dubiously. I thought of the hours, mainly happy, that I had spent as a family dishwashing team member and I wondered if this invention hadn't taken away more than it gave.

On the other hand, the first garbage disposal on the block was fascinating to me because in the country the job of burying the garbage always fell to the youngest child who was big enough to handle the wheelbarrow with the noxious can teetering aboard it. Since I was the youngest in my family, I stayed with the task far longer than my siblings and developed a special dislike for garbage. Seeing it get ground to gravy and sluiced away has always delighted me emotionally, even though I suppose it just pollutes its eventual resting place all the more.

without changing the essential details that have been in use for so long. The plug is still lifted mechanically, the water rushes out, the stopper falls back into the drain and the water then fills the tank until the float rises sufficiently to shut off the supply. It's a perfect example of what technology students call a feedback mechanism, and no fuel or electricity is required except normal house heating to take off the chill that my great-aunts lived with.

Their Massachusetts home was heated by a coal furnace which allowed warm air to rise through registers in the floor. It percolated least into the bedrooms on the second floor, and I remember how cold I was when I went to bed, and how incredibly comfortable the featherbed was. Say what you will about that mattress crawling with germs, it was warm, and so soft that you felt suspended in air when you slept in it. Today's orthopedic mattresses are doubtless much better for you, but nothing is so comfortable as a mattress full of feathers.

Cooking was done on a wood-burning iron stove. It was delightfully warm (especially after a visit to that damn outhouse) and cooked well. One of the things it cooked was pickles. The aunts had a pickle pantry lined with various kinds, each cunningly devised to go with certain meals. They cannot be found in today's supermarkets.

Food preparation reveals other inventions and developments that seem to have gone too far. I rediscovered fresh orange juice recently. It is, of course, much better than the frozen orange juice because the concentrated kind must be diluted with water, and water is now a solution of chlorine and other life-saving chemicals and tastes like it. Few of us are lucky enough to know how things that are mixed with water are supposed to taste. Frozen orange juice suffers because of this. So do tea and coffee and whiskey.

My aunts made mash out of their meager garbage and fed it to the chickens. Maybe all garbage disposal should have stopped right there.

The aunts' house was not really jumping with entertainment, but there were books and there was always a jigsaw puzzle. A stereoscope offered three-dimensional views of scenes from the Spanish-American War and great natural tragedies and the slaughter of revolutionaries in the Balkans and other subjects capable of entrancing a small boy. There was a kaleidoscope with a little crank to turn the barrel and tumble the bits of colored glass into endlessly varied patterns. Both of these appear in the "1876" exhibit, more familiar items to make me feel old.

Yet, perversely, when I leave my office for a weekend in good weather, my mind is on sailing, for that is what lies before me. And of all modern activities sailing must be one of the very oldest. Never mind fiber glass hulls and aluminum masts and Dacron sails and racing rigs, the act of making a vessel move by the action of the wind goes back to the beginning of history.

One Saturday evening, after sailing at length out in the Chesapeake Bay, we headed into a little creek where fields ran down to the water and trees rose from it and birds sang. There was just enough breeze to keep us moving, so without turning on the diesel auxiliary, we just sailed very gently up that creek. We didn't make a sound. We barely stirred the water as we passed, and we realized that we were traveling the way people traveled 5,000 years ago. It seems at such times that distant ancestors look down upon us and understand, knowing that in spite of our wonderful machines and new ways, we still have to cope with wet socks, stale news, and high garbage. Our ancestors see that the inventor will always have those verities to work on (along with greater tasks), though perhaps the best has already been done. ☐

Edwards Park

The American Genius

Robert C. Post

At 10:30 on a Monday evening in November 1936, NBC's Red Network aired a special program from the Grand Ballroom of the Mayflower Hotel in Washington, D.C. After an opening by announcer Floyd Mack, the audience heard another voice, the Voice of Progress. This voice belonged to a well-known radio personality, Gordon Hittenmark, aloft in a DC-3. The Voice of Progress told listeners what was in store—a salute to "America's immortal inventors from the clouds high above the Capital City of our Nation"—then turned the program back to Mack and to the "great conclave of America's men of science, invention, and industry gathered . . . to pay their lasting tribute to American inventive genius."

Mack introduced the Commissioner of Patents, who introduced the Secretary of Commerce, who finally introduced Dr. Charles F. ("Boss") Kettering, head of research at General Motors and Chairman of

Joseph Henry, physicist and first Smithsonian Secretary, leans on the column at center in an imaginary gathering of great American inventors. On the column's other side the artist added John Ericsson after his Monitor *fought the* Merrimac *in 1862.*

the National Committee on the Centennial Celebration of the American Patent System. Kettering explained that his committee had been charged with making a list of names, a very select list of inventors. "I have standing back of me four drummers of the United States Army Band," he said. "As they sound the drum rolls, the Voice of Progress, speaking from the Eastern Air Lines transport plane high above Washington, will reveal the names of those to whom this meeting and our Nation in recognition of their services to the American people do most signal honor."

With due pomp the Voice of Progress spoke the names: Alexander Graham Bell, Thomas Edison, Charles Goodyear, Charles Martin Hall, Elias Howe, Cyrus McCormick, Samuel F. B. Morse, George Westinghouse, the Wright brothers, Eli Whitney, Robert Fulton, and Ottmar Mergenthaler. Kettering then concluded with a declaration that "human courage, with human faith, and the proper degree of humility knows no end and the boundless future is the territory in which we may work." Sustained applause followed what had been—for all the campy flavor it has in retrospect—a dramatic event.

Even though an organization called the National Inventors Hall of Fame presently pursues an induction program, we may still consider this ceremony more than 40 years ago as consecration for the upper echelons of the True Pantheon of America's Great Men of Invention. With the two Wright brothers, there was a baker's dozen. Most of the names, one ventures to guess, are names that remain familiar to most Americans. While some would stumble over Hall (aluminum) and Mergenthaler (the Linotype), and many would erroneously credit Goodyear with the balloon tire and Westinghouse with the electric range, as pantheons go it is not bad. People need heroes, and Americans, more than any other people, have made heroes out of inventors—especially these inventors.

Still, historians who study invention fret over lists such as Boss Kettering's. Sometimes they worry about canonizing the unworthy. It has become apparent in recent years that, whatever may be said about the cotton gin, the concept of interchangeable parts for muskets was Eli Whitney's neither first nor foremost. Robert Fulton didn't invent the steamboat. Mythology has often been taken too literally.

Because a certain amount of dubious hagiography does cling to Whitney, to Fulton, and to some of the rest, historians of invention occasionally call for banishing them from the Pantheon and for substituting others—names such as Evans, Blanchard,

Robert C. Post is an historian in the National Museum of History and Technology. He organized the Museum's exhibit, American Maritime Enterprise.

Shreve, Deere, Colt, Yale, Otis, Ericsson, Hoe, Corliss, Stilson, Glidden, Sprague, Eastman, or Bendix. Yet, given the peculiar potentialities and constraints of American history, these names stand at a disadvantage. Mythmakers have been potent determinants of the historical record, and it is often futile if not actually misguided to try to divorce what people *believe* to have been so from what in some "objective" sense *was* so. If, now and then, other names may elicit a clear image (of elevators, say, or padlocks, steel plows, snag boats, six-shooters, screw propellers, stationary steam engines, or monkey wrenches), as a rule they are considerably less likely to draw a glimmer of recognition.

Make no mistake, objectively some of these men were nearly as important as the occupants of the Pantheon, if not indeed equal to them. But there are more perplexing problems with which to contend. Beyond the intrinsic utility of pantheons (mnemonic, inspirational, or what have you), is it really useful to study the phenomena of Yankee Ingenuity through a dozen—or a hundred, or a thousand—inventors responsible for something that hindsight shows to have been a "breakthrough" or a "turning point"? Melville R. Bissell invented the carpet sweeper, Walter Hunt the safety pin, Lewis E. Waterman the fountain pen. Wallace H. Carothers synthesized a polymer marketed as nylon. Clarence C. Birdseye devised a method of preserving foods by quick-freezing. It is conceivable that these novelties affected more lives more immediately than did the steamboat or vulcanized rubber. (This may even be true of Dr. Kettering's self-starter for automobiles.)

Yet, if analyzing inventiveness demands something more subtle than ranking inventors or counting inventions, how does one go about it? Beyond question there is such a thing as Yankee Ingenuity, and it has been a powerful determinant of our national destiny. An observation often recited in the late 19th century, usually attributed to a foreign observer at the Centennial Exhibition of 1876, states: "The American invents as the Italian paints and the Greek sculpted. It is genius." Unburdened by conservative traditions typical of many other peoples, Americans have indeed shown a unique penchant for innovation. This remains as true today as it ever was, even though many regard the 19th century as the Ingenious Yankee's heyday.

In fact, the Americans' innovative impulses did not start coming to the fore until after independence, and even then they emerged slowly. Oliver Evans sought a practical high-pressure steam engine and the mechanization of both textile manufacture and flour milling. John Fitch staked a credible claim to the first successful steamboat. Benjamin Franklin

Better tools for technology: awls, bits, and spokeshaves gleam in a Smithsonian re-creation of a Centennial exhibit.

less, the seeds of a fruitful innovative impulse had been planted by 1800, and they began to flower when Americans were forced to rely on their own resources as trade was disrupted during the Napoleonic Wars.

If that flowering had scarcely begun until the early 1800s, in no sense did it show signs of wilting at the end of the century. Indeed, the inventions of our own century have been far more numerous and conceptually far more brilliant than those of the 1800s. Historians should never drop their guard against "presentism"—the fallacy of judging past events by current standards—yet the fact remains that there is a truly substantial difference in the intellectual power required, say, to figure out how to make a cotton gin or to vulcanize rubber as opposed to what it took to devise the gyropilot or the laser. Yet the 20th century's inventors have been relatively faceless. How many people could correctly identify Robert Goddard or Peter Goldmark or William Shockley as the inventors or co-inventors of, respectively, the liquid propellant rocket, color television, and the transistor?

Or, having mentioned the gyropilot, consider Elmer Sperry. Sperry was fond of remarking that he preferred very difficult challenges, for by concentrating on these he was freed from vulgar competition. (Edison is the only one of Kettering's dozen who was conceivably Sperry's match as an authentic genius.) Technologically, his gyroscopic devices embody a sophistication unmatched by anything until the space age. But one could get dozens of people on the street to respond "telephone" and "light bulb" to the names Bell and Edison before the name Sperry would elicit anything but a vacant stare.

Yet, not only did Sperry create some of the most ingenious inventions ever, his bequest also included some profound philosophical insights. In 1930, the year he died, an essay he had written appeared in a book titled *Toward Civilization*. It was called "The Spirit of Invention in an Industrial Society" and the thesis was that modern civilization could not hope to advance solely through the application of logic, mathematics, and the laws of physics. Far more decisive was "the imagination, courage, and brooding meditation of the inventive faculty." "Brooding meditation"—a haunting phrase, but not overly melodramatic, for this trait comes as close as any to being a universal among inventors. Indeed, it comes much closer to helping us frame useful questions as to what the inventive process is all about than the phrase "a flash of genius," because a protracted siege of brooding ordinarily preceded the "Ah! Ha!" and frequently inventors are unable to pinpoint any perceptible flash at all.

We are left with the question of why inventors

is a top seed in each of several pantheons. But, aside from Whitney, Jacob Perkins, and one or two others, that about exhausts the roll of significant American inventors prior to the 19th century.

Because a handiness with tools and knack for trouble-shooting ultimately became storied Yankee traits, people have tended to assume a presence from the creation. Not so. The few true Ingenious Yankees in the early years of the Republic continually bemoaned "the low state of the mechanick arts." When Americans were forced to mechanize textile production they did so by swiping sketches of British machinery. When Fulton built the *Clermont* he ordered the engine from James Watt, an Englishman. Evans fought pigheaded prejudice by millers. Charles Newbold's cast-iron plow of 1797 excited fears that it would "poison the soil." Neverthe-

invent. There are numerous other theories, but most can be placed under one of two broad umbrellas. The first may be called "supply"—inventors invent simply because they can—because the current state of knowledge makes something appear technically feasible. The other may be called "demand"—inventors invent because they deliberately assess social needs and then sally forth to advance technology in a direction that satisfies those needs. At first glance it may appear that nearly all inventions must result from some rational assessment of social needs—that "demand" is the predominant motivation. This does indeed seem to have been so, given the perspective of 20-20 hindsight. But it may not be the case at all.

First, we tend to focus on inventions that historians have considered, most of which have changed society (usually under the rubric of "progress") and therefore must have been "needed." To be sure, we know of inventions that seem absurd—automatic hat tippers, "life-preserving coffins in doubtful cases of actual death." But even here the absurdity is often more apparent than real. In an age when hat tipping remained a strong social convention yet might be quite a discomfort in winter, why not automate the process? In an age when vital signs could easily be misread and getting "buried alive" was a common-

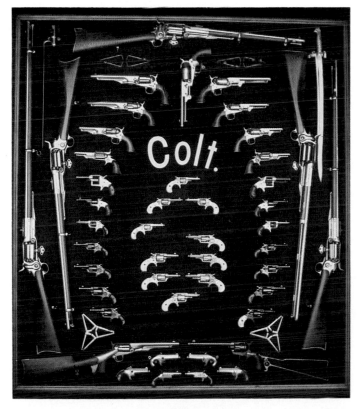

Six-shooters for the frontier: manufactured with interchangeable parts, Colt's revolving-cylinder rifles and pistols, and single-shot derringers, made a bold Centennial display.

place nightmare, why not a coffin that protected against such a ghastly fate? Still—even if many inventions that now appear silly were actually conceived in response to a clearly articulated "demand" —when one simply begins reading patent specifications at random, a great many seem to have been irrelevant to perceptible social utility.

Furthermore, even with inventions that became part of the fabric of American life, one must ask how often the demand *followed* rather than preceded their appearance. Did American society really "need" telephones and electric lights in the 1870s? Did it really need airplanes? That issue took a rather long time to decide—no commercial passenger service prior to World War II could have survived without government subsidies. The history of transportation technology is full of inventions motivated by "supply" rather than "demand." In some instances a "demand" subsequently was cultivated. People eventually did start traveling by airplane. Municipalities such as Morgantown, West Virginia, have actually installed "personal rapid transit" systems which blend all the miseries peculiar to private autos with all those of conventional rapid transit. In other instances no demand ever materialized, or else the demand resulted from an artificial buoyancy provided by overt or covert injections of Uncle Sam's money.

In any event, it is a fact that many inventors invent simply because they *can*—not out of altruistic or even greedy motives. Invention, much more than is commonly realized, can be an existential phenomenon—something pursued "just because." Even some of Kettering's dozen did this—the Wright boys definitely so. And, if George Westinghouse's air brake was an indisputable boon from the moment of its conception, one wonders about Charles Martin Hall's new material, aluminum.

Here was something with all sorts of interesting properties, yet nobody knew what ought to be *made* out of it. The most famous early application—a cap for the Washington Monument—was strictly an oddity and could just as well have been made of copper. No significant "demand" for aluminum developed until far into the air age, when engineers began thinking about planes that could fly fast, high, and far (again, not something for which it was easy to demonstrate an *a priori* need), and then turned to aluminum components whose light weight could help facilitate this. In a similar vein, nobody quite knew what to make of the first plastic, Celluloid—which was developed at roughly the same time as aluminum—except odds and ends such as collars and billiard balls.

Now, one should not dwell on existential motivations too long, simply because (to repeat) most American inventions treated as "historic"—improved

weapons, faster methods of transportation and communication, better farm implements, ways to save labor in factories—*were* regarded as necessities by a people irreverent of tradition who lived in a country characterized by unfriendly natives, widely scattered settlements, lots of good cheap land, and a shortage of individuals willing to earn their living working for someone else. The earliest American inventions, actually representing adaptations of things initially developed overseas, such as the long rifle, the flatboat, and the Conestoga wagon, all met clearly perceived needs. Oliver Evans of Philadelphia, our first unmistakably indigenous inventor, concentrated on labor-saving devices.

"Demand" likewise was the primary motivation for those inventors who rendered the steamboat practical—Fitch, Rumsey, Stevens, Fulton, and the rest; for those concerned with agricultural processes, such as Whitney, McCormick, and Deere; for those who designed more efficient weapons and produced them more efficiently, such as Colt; for those who sought to mechanize production, such as Blanchard; for those who speeded up communication, such as Morse and Hoe; and for those who aimed to make more efficient use of power, such as Corliss and Francis.

As one moves on into the latter half of the 19th century, however, especially as electrical and chemical sciences attain new levels, the pre-existing social need for many inventions now regarded as significant becomes less obvious. (That "research" as an organized cooperative activity began with electricity and chemistry is not something accidental.) Questions may be raised about a variety of inventions, ranging from do-it-yourself photography to all the electrical gadgetry that was being marketed as early as 1890. In the realm of consumer goods there are several classic inventions which provide endless grist for debates about the roots of invention. Take the typewriter: was it a cause of the liberation of women from the home, or was its acceptance merely an effect of a social transformation already well under way? Did it help revolutionize society, or was it only a ramification of something far more profound which would have been precipitated with or without the typewriter's assistance?

Whatever the answer, these questions are worth asking, for it is with such devices that the "genius" in Yankee Ingenuity starts to become something *promotional* as well as technological. If one wanted to pinpoint a specific invention, it would be the sewing machine. What would today be called the basic patent was Elias Howe's of September 10, 1846; yet the name of

Isaac Singer, left, lost a patent infringement suit to the sewing machine's inventor, Elias Howe, but went on to become the czar of a sewing machine sales empire.

Isaac M. Singer—a man whose technical contributions were relatively unimportant—soon became more closely associated with the sewing machine than Howe's. Howe may have had the technical savvy, but the promotional instincts of Singer were far more acute. Singer's company went after a consumer market, not clothing manufacturers, thus pioneering novel retailing techniques such as time payments. While the Singer firm manufactured and sold millions of sewing machines, the company Howe had founded sputtered out of business.

Singer and Howe symbolize two facets of Yankee Ingenuity—promotional and technological—with the middle of the 19th century as a watershed. There also was an event laden with symbolism in 1853. It was called the New York Exhibition of the Industry of All Nations—the first American world's fair, inspired by the London Crystal Palace Exposition of 1851. The grand resonance of its name notwithstanding, New York's own Crystal Palace was scarcely representative of the technological capabilities of "all nations." Most of what the Europeans bothered to send was unimpressive. Americans, on the other hand, took liberal advantage of the opportunity to show off. New York's Crystal Palace heralded the moment in our nation's history when technology modulated from a minor to a major key—and when it first became clear that promotional ingenuity was as important in its own right as unadorned technological virtuosity.

Prior to 1853, the entrepreneurial efforts of inventors had been confined almost exclusively to local "mechanic's fairs" and to tiny ads in the daily newspapers or in a handful of national weeklies, principally *Scientific American.* By 1893, at the World's Columbian Exposition in Chicago, trade-cards flew like confetti, advertising chromos were everywhere, and, in the words of Charles A. Beard, "huckstering shock troops . . . with a technique and verbiage all their own, concentrated on ogling, stimulating, and inveigling the public into purchases." In 1853, "mass production" was a reality for only a few select manufacturers of such items as guns, locks, and clocks. By 1893 the Ingenious Yankee had figured out how to mass produce and mass market (the relationship of course was symbiotic) almost everything. The United States had become the world's major producer of manufactured goods, a quantitative amplification just becoming perceptible at the Crystal Palace. Nothing comparable could have been marshaled 10 or even five years earlier.

American exhibits suggested an overwhelming concern with transportation and communication; with civil engineering, hydraulics, and mining; with timing and measuring and weighing; and with mechanizing the fabrication of building components and the whole

Dwarfing visitors, the Corliss steam engine powered all of the machines at the Centennial. William Dean Howells wrote that "in these things of iron and steel the national genius speaks."

range of operations relating to farming, food processing, textile production, and clothing manufacture. A check against the reports of the Patent Office and the observations made by foreign visitors confirm that these were precisely the areas of most intensive inventive activity in America just past mid-century.

The conclusion follows, then, that the Exhibition reflected the contemporary thrust of American technology quite accurately—this notwithstanding the perceptible distortions: some leading innovators in machine-tool design were absent, and some rising industries were unrepresented, locomotive builders for one. Granted, there was no dramatic debut of whole new worlds of invention. There was nothing comparable to the acres of precision metalworking tools at the Centennial Exhibition, nor to the myriad electrical appliances unveiled at the Columbian Exposition. Granted, too, the significance of some of the things displayed in 1853 had long been common knowledge. The cotton gin that Eli Whitney's son exhibited was a device already ensconced in the annals of American folklore. Samuel Colt had sold thousands of his six-

shooters. It had been almost a decade since Morse had inaugurated his commercial telegraph, and his company alone had more than 13,000 miles of line in operation. Litigation involving Elias Howe and his competitors had been in the news for years. Goodyear had discovered vulcanization of rubber in 1839.

And so one might continue. But that would be pointless, simply because even if much of what was shown at the Palace might have been familiar to a mechanic or millwright, it was decidedly novel to most every other kind of visitor. The very idea of speeding up all sorts of operations from sewing to shooting was novel—as was that of speeding up their mode of manufacture. Relatively few visitors had ever before seen an elaborate system of overhead line-shafting, much less a system driving an enormous variety of specialized production machinery. Many who toured the Palace no doubt had seen some of what was exhibited. None could have been acquainted with all of it.

For one thing, there were a number of inventions of very recent vintage—such as the typewriter ("typographer") capable of printing words "with scarcely less dispatch than they could be written." Like the electric motor on display, this was an innovation prematurely born. Yet there were many other novelties whose significance was immediately clear.

Previously, an American who sought to observe such a behemoth as the 60-horsepower Corliss steam engine at work would have had to visit some workaday plant, not a fancy exhibition hall. But George H. Corliss understood the value of showing off before a mass audience, something he later exploited to the utmost when he built the "Centennial Engine" for the Philadelphia Exhibition of 1876—the machine that became the symbol for an age.

Both the Crystal Palace engine and the Centennial engine were clean and unadorned. In striking contrast was the single large machine at the Crystal Palace that had been manufactured in the South, the *Southern Belle,* a steam engine from the Winter Iron Works in Montgomery, Alabama. The journalist Horace Greeley, who covered the exhibition in detail, scoffed at the *Belle* as "very showy, and (at present) very useless." The castings were flawless, the detailing exquisite, yet the awards jury committed an obvious gaffe by voting it a medal while ignoring the Corliss engine. Greeley thought that the key to success lay not merely in having something that was useful, nor just in promotional ingenuity, but in having something useful *and* in promoting it. He was right, though he apparently could not foresee the enormous potential for promoting things of marginal utility or for positing "needs" hitherto unperceived.

One might wonder, incidentally, why George Corliss, who attained towering status as an inventor-entrepreneur in the 19th century, was absent from Kettering's Pantheon. The answer is simple: unlike the others, his machines—reciprocating steam engines—were ultimately doomed to obsolescence by steam turbines and electricity. Half the residents of the Pantheon *were* represented at the Crystal Palace; three of the others, Edison, Bell, and Westinghouse, were only six or seven years old, while Hall, Mergenthaler, and the Wright brothers were not yet born. Even so, and even though technological innovations as such in 1853 had nothing like the popular impact that they would have at subsequent exhibitions, the displays at the Crystal Palace were full of intimations of a giant awakening. One senses that Americans had discovered their own inventiveness, that they knew—and now *knew* they knew—how to make very clever things, how to make lots of them alike, and how to mechanize just about anything "assigned in the old world to manual skill." And, all at once, they could perceive the incredible multiformity of innovations to develop, to patent, to publicize, and to profit from.

Besides the realization that they had something to trumpet about, the most important lesson American inventors or aspiring inventors learned from the Crystal Palace was that trumpeting definitely paid off. If, for instance, Horace Greeley was persuaded that "Dodge's Patent Premium Suction and Force Pump" constituted "a very happy invention" (as he told his readers), it meant that the Dodge brothers of Newburgh were going to sell more pumps. In two ways, then, was the Crystal Palace a turning point. The pace of inventive activity commenced a dramatic acceleration, and concurrently—in a relationship for which cause and effect cannot be separated—promotion and advertising started to assume tremendous importance. The American Genius soon revealed another facet—a genius for salesmanship.

Naturally, nearly any innovation stands to gain from promotion. Nothing—not in the realm of consumer goods, anyway—can succeed commercially except insofar as people can be convinced that it reinforces common social values. For reasons far too complex to analyze briefly, Americans have always put a premium on speed; Fulton thus succeeded because he made it possible to get around rapidly; Colt and Gatling because they made it possible to shoot enemies quickly; Morse and Hoe because they greatly sped up communications; all the inventors of specialized factory machinery because they facilitated rapid production.

One might multiply examples endlessly, but suffice it here to emphasize two points. Inventions that need promotion least are those whose social utility seems obvious from the outset—McCormick sold thousands of reapers before he ever spent a cent on advertising. In contrast, inventions that need promotion most are those whose pre-existing demand is either weak or problematic. Much contemporary household gadgetry falls into this category. The nabobs of the "Personal Computer Industry" talk confidently of there being a computer in every home within a decade or two. That will take a spectacular job of salesmanship, yet would not most of us have been skeptical of someone asserting in 1920 that every family would have an auto or in 1940 that every home would have a television? Or, to quote a bit of Henry Allen's evidence for invention being the mother of necessity, "Did college kids slouch all surly around college campuses on spring days, waiting for the Wham-O company to bring them frisbees?"

Inventing a frisbee (or an electric toothbrush or what have you) and then convincing people they need it is as American as apple pie. One can decry the wastefulness of "consumerism," but there is no denying that this is a key to something called the "American Way of Life," which is irresistibly attractive to peoples all over the world. There is, however, a different species of technological innovation for which a demand must be cultivated—the extraordinarily expensive hardware whose attributes include either an explicit or potential military utility. As usual, the demand is postulated on the basis of meeting a common social need, in this case the need to maintain superiority vis-à-vis our potential enemies. Rationalizations often are not very convincing, and the conclusion is hard to escape that here is invention based simply on supply in its most sinister manifestation.

It is possible, for instance, to devise ever more sophisticated and expensive missiles and weapons control systems, but it is quite doubtful that we "need" these. They do present a great technical challenge to engineers and scientists who cannot be blamed for pursuing exciting projects for which politicians provide the money. Somehow, though, it becomes easy to miss the analogy between the man who seeks to pursue an Aircraft Nuclear Propulsion Program (remember that?) simply for the challenge, and the man who seeks to talk through wires (or, to remind us of the original metaphor, to climb some mountain) for that same reason.

Indeed, it is curious that the inventor who acts not as *Homo economicus* but just for the sheer adventure of testing his own mettle and pushing beyond the limits of existing knowledge is now commonly regarded with suspicion. 'Twas not always so. Americans loved the Wright brothers when they showed that man could fly; nobody was concerned about the likelihood that very few people would ever want to fly. Or, take one of the most brilliant inventions in history—the annual automobile model change. Who needed that? Maybe no-

Illuminating city skies, colorful neon signs blink out persistent messages of American salesmanship. This display from the *Smithsonian's "Nation of Nations" exhibit glows with well-promoted ethnic delicacies for a consumer society.*

body did, yet the people who invented planned obsolescence remained (at least until quite recently) heroes rather than villains.

As for the inventor whose challenge was not the market but the invention itself, he once was regarded as a heroic figure, or at least a benign zany. But that was before it became evident how easy it would be to enlist Uncle Sam by talking strategic advantage (or, in the case of something such as the SST, "national honor"), and then to plunge into rarified technologies with monies from the public purse.

Are we then left with no heroes? Are the only inventors remaining either calculating hucksters shamelessly hyping the latest piece of wasteful gadgetry, or tarnished conspirators with the lords of the military-industrial complex, seeking to pursue their private enthusiasms at *our* expense? Well, hardly. The traditional sorts of heroes are still with us. Few actually pay *no* attention to potential commercialization. Nevertheless, for many of them the inventive act is close to an end in itself, and the main challenge is technological, not promotional. Most of these inventors ultimately would agree with Jacob Rabinow that "inventing is a hell of a lot of fun if you don't have to make a living at it."

Some contemporary counterparts to the old-fashioned Ingenious Yankee seek intensely practical ends. Others seek only to contend with some personally defined challenge. Prime examples of both types may be found among adherents to the "car culture," such as the "hot rodders" who first showed up in California in the 1930s and subsequently established a thriving subculture throughout the nation. They are unlike any of the residents of the Pantheon, for, first of all, none is famous. Some have come up with things we now consider "necessary", others could care less about that, especially those who place the ultimate premium on speed. Yet these people are merely probing an extreme of one of the most pervasive American social values. Moreover, in sheer ingenuity, in the capacity to define the dimensions of a problem and to seek solutions through a sort of transcendental empiricism, the best of them needs yield nothing to the best among the more traditional sort of Ingenious Yankee.

In his 1950 classic, *The Lonely Crowd,* David Reismann included an astute analysis of what hot rodding means to its enthusiasts: ". . . a wide range of standards of technique and design gives room to both the green amateurs and semi-professional car racers, while all the hobbyists have the comfort of working within the old American tradition of high-level tinkering. . . . Here, astonishingly enough, the top commercial product of the country, the Detroit car, far from driving out amateur performance, has only stimulated, perhaps even provoked it." A key word to remember here is "amateur." There is something about the American Genius that is peculiarly intertwined with amateurism, both as the term is popularly defined (Fulton and Morse were artists, Bell a teacher, and so on) and in its more precise dictionary definition: a person who engages in an activity primarily as an end in itself.

But now, as Yankee Ingenuity faces it greatest challenge, the end is something of utmost social need. Much of the history of American technology, until recently, was contingent upon the reality that our nation enjoyed a most bounteous resource endowment. Inventions, particularly in the realm of transportation and manufacturing processes, tended to wastefulness. The first kind of production machinery for which Americans became famous—highly specialized woodworking tools—enabled mass production of furniture, carriages, and railroad cars. But this machinery also turned enormous quantities of wood into shavings and sawdust, an affordable luxury in a day when farmers regarded forests as a nuisance and cleared them by burning. It is affordable no longer, but an optimist can foresee Americans adapting their production processes and proving as spectacularly parsimonious as they once were profligate.

Although one should avoid assuming that a simple counting of inventions indicates the general vitality of the American Genius, there is a compelling statistic: patent number 1,000,000 was issued in 1911; number 2,000,000 in 1935; number 3,000,000 in 1961; and number 4,000,000 has now come and gone. That translates into a pretty steep upward curve. Are any of these patents going to present-day Edisons and Bells? Perhaps, as personified in someone such as Gordon Gould. Who is Gordon Gould, you ask? Well, Gould recently won a 20-year fight to establish his rights to an invention underlying a billion-dollar industry, a device that amplifies light by stimulated emission of radiation—better known as a laser.

Although Gould has been elected "Inventor of the Year," his name hardly elicits that automatic response, Edison/light bulb, Bell/telephone. Nevertheless, he sounds like he may be an important national resource. While in no sense oblivious to commercial considerations, by the same token he is now pursuing something about whose genuine social utility there can be no doubt. "I have ideas that will lead to cost-competitive ways of generating electric power from solar energy," he says. "I'd spend most of my money so that I can do what I want to do instead of what the Department of Defense thinks it needs."

The American Genius is not something that has

An ultimate in the hot rodder's ingenuity—supercharged aluminum replica of mid-1950s Chrysler engine yields nearly 2,000 hp, can propel 1,400-lb. dragster from standstill to 250 mph in less than six seconds.

invariably presented such a clean face. Sometimes it has appeared as a genius for conceiving and promoting inventions that are frivolous, dangerous—anything but true and good. Still, there has always been the brave assumption that whatever needs to be done can be done. If we now need to face the hard facts of scarcity, what is needed (to quote a few words of Boss Kettering's again) is "human courage, with human faith, and the proper degree of humility." Kettering, recall, once confronted the problem of starting an automobile, something frustrating and even risky, and which thus foretold a limited future for that invention. Nobody thought it possible to design an electric motor powerful enough to crank an internal combustion engine yet compact enough to install under the hood of a car. Kettering proved them wrong by designing a motor strictly to deliver short bursts of power. If Charles Kettering—an Ingenious Yankee who was born the year Bell patented the telephone and who died the year Explorer I was put in orbit—could solve that electrical problem, who is to say that Gordon Gould cannot solve the stubborn electrical problem which concerns him?

The American Genius first manifested itself in the realm of inventions for "overcoming" the environment; let us trust that it can now manifest itself in ways that facilitate a harmonious accommodation. By the time of the Bicentennial Celebration of the American Patent System—who knows?—maybe the Pantheon will have a new set of residents. □

A Repository of Innovation

Fine old things have power—somewhat like lenses—to focus human energy and expectation. They have power to help us to know the past and to peer into the future. And that's one reason why people call collections of fine old things by the name "museum." They set us a-musing.

Now, with this collection selected from several museums of the Smithsonian Institution, begin an odyssey through our repository of invention.

We start with a stone tool, for that's where invention began. One tried and perhaps true scenario starts out when the first rudely fashioned man fashioned the first rude stone ax. Ever since that day of technical destiny, people have shaped tools, and those tools have gone on to help shape, and to define, mankind.

Just a word to help define our terms: "tool" and "invention" mean almost the same thing, but not quite. Scientists often refer to tools as simple inventions and to inventions as complicated tools. Such an insight may have prompted Benjamin Franklin to christen mankind the "toolmaking animal."

Some of our most interesting tools/inventions are not mechanical at all—language, math equations, religious faiths, constitutions, and madly racing traces of electricity zipping through printed circuits hardly larger than the period at the end of this sentence. And there's an even more complex kind of printed circuit—the alphabetical squiggles and pothooks which in different combinations can express nearly everything a person can see, experience, and think.

Ben Franklin, printer and inventor, might well agree and even go us one better. He knew how inventions can change a man's life. For instance, in the 1720s young Ben went to London to learn his trade. Supposedly in the 1760s he returned to the shop and its same old press. After a few pensive moments he cheered up and exclaimed, "Come my friends, we will drink together. It is now 40 years since I worked like you at this press as a journeyman printer."

At the Smithsonian's National Museum of History and Technology you can see the very same press that Franklin knew so well. Because of its association with American history, the old press was brought across the Atlantic in 1842. This example helps point out the international character of invention. Neither boundaries of space nor of time can stop it. Both the sharp flint flake chipped a million years ago and the laser ray used as a surgical tool are joined by a common bond of ceaseless human innovation.

Certainly, don't take our little repository as the last word. For in the world around you there'll be candidates for your own treasured repository. Momma's old sewing machine in the attic may transport you to the past. Or perhaps it's Poppa's straight razor or Colt pistol in the locked chest. Don't be afraid to remember, and collect, and to dream—that's the way the people we call inventors over countless generations have transformed the past into the future.

Stone-bladed, bone-hafted tool from a site in Switzerland helped prehistoric hunters scrape animal hides.

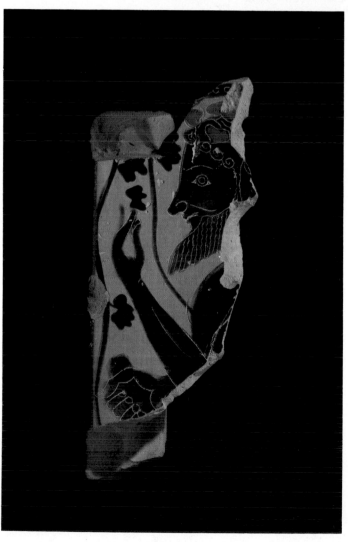

The clasp, top, was one of many spring fasteners made by the Romans. For easier production we sacrifice art in favor of the safety pin. Above, a bronze casting that crowned a standard-pole of ancient Persia's Lur tribesmen. Technologically difficult tan and black artwork survives on a Greek sherd, left. Colored glazes grew common as ancient artisans mastered fired pottery.

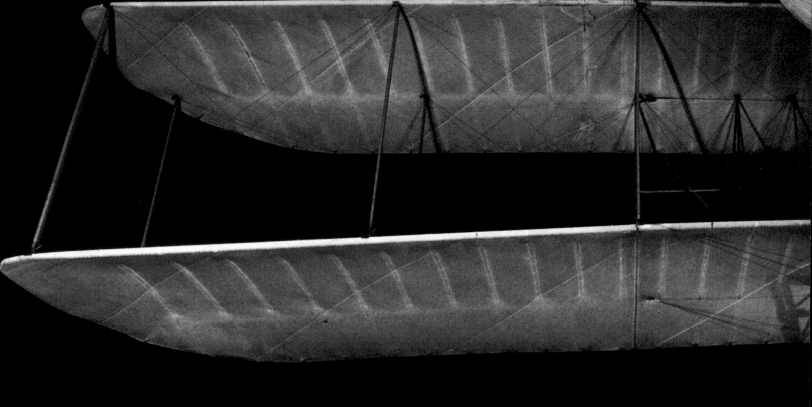

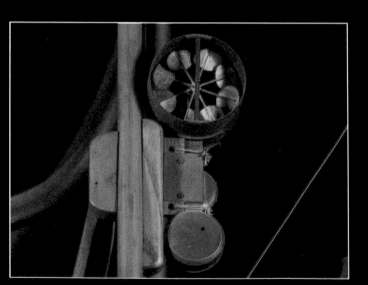

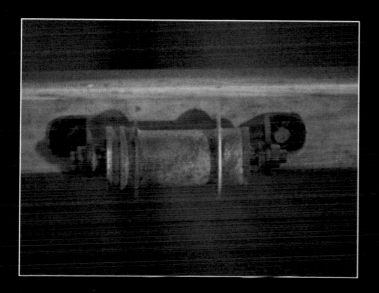

THE FIRST POWER-DRIVEN HEAVIER-THAN-AIR MACHINE
IN WHICH MAN MADE FREE, CONTROLLED, AND SUSTAINED
FLIGHT . . . These words appeared on the Smithsonian's
first exhibit label for the 1903 Flyer. They only hint at
the inventive magnificence of the Wright brothers' aerial
triumph at Kitty Hawk, North Carolina. The airframe,
built of spruce and covered with unbleached muslin, was
the product of extensive kite and glider experience, while
the 12-horsepower engine was also built by the Wrights.
Incidentally, Orville and Wilbur were accomplished
glider pilots. The vital wing or airfoil design grew out of
experiments made in Dayton, Ohio, with a wind tunnel
of original design. Propeller sprocket-and-chain drives,
detail, center, were modified bicycle parts. Front runner,
near left, was a bicycle-wheel hub which kept the Flyer on
a wooden rail until liftoff. A revolution counter on the
anemometer, far left, was used with a stopwatch to calculate air speed after each flight.

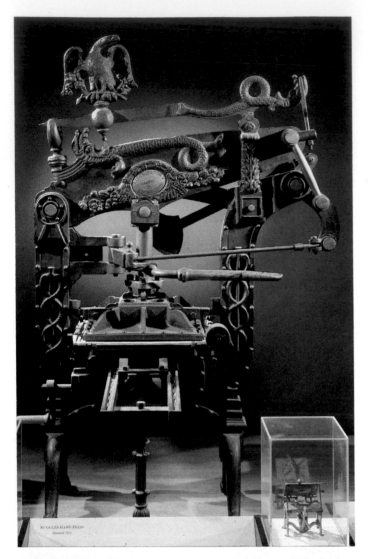

Designed in America but cast in Scotland, the Columbian Press, top, introduced a simple lever action. It saved time and labor over older screw-operated presses. "John Bull" of 1831, made in England but operated in America, is our oldest surviving complete locomotive. Opposite, the Model A replaced the Model T flivver. Ford produced five million Model A's between 1927 and 1931.

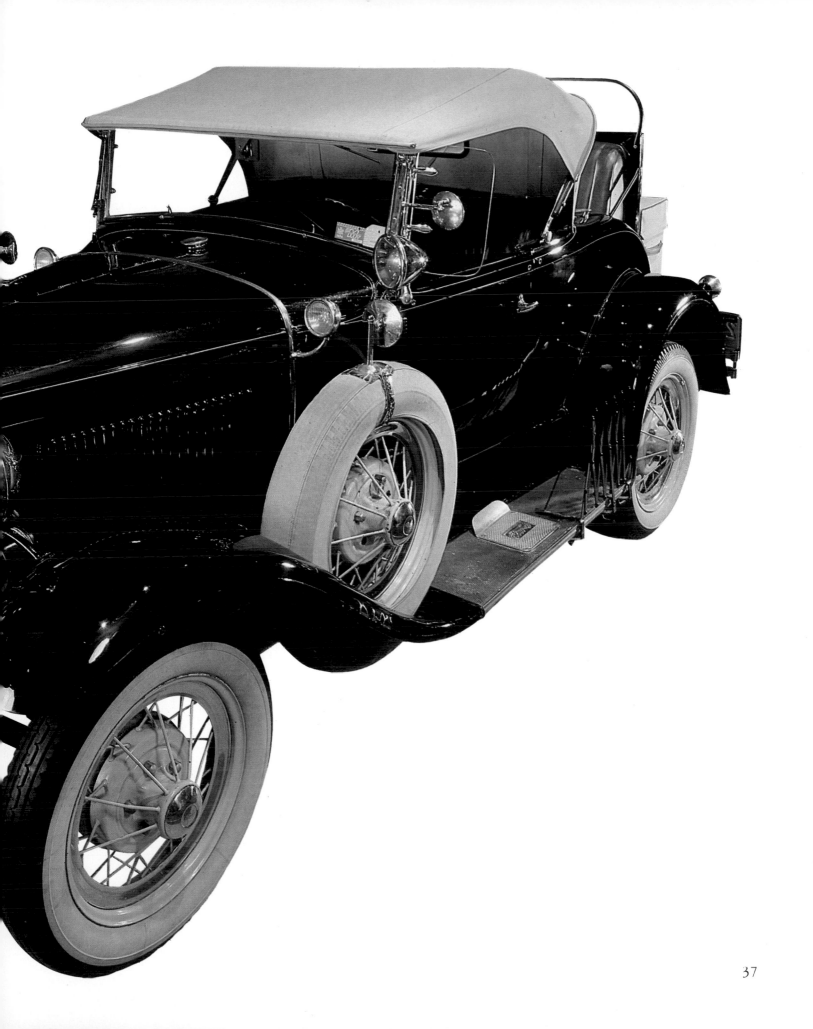

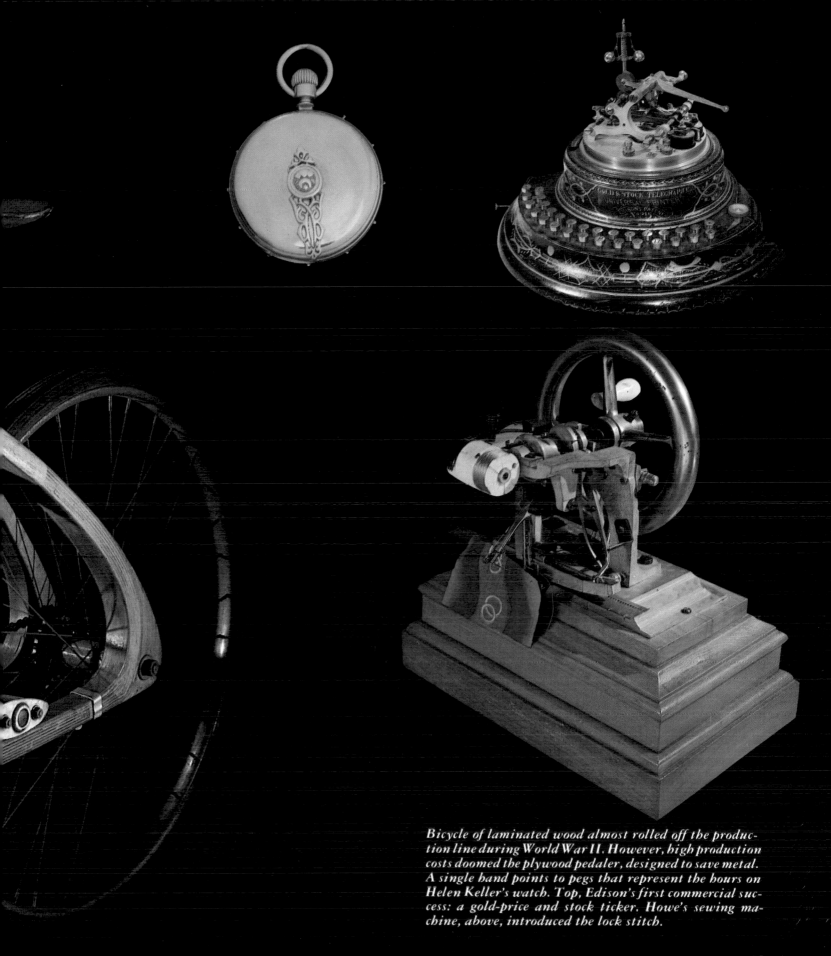

Bicycle of laminated wood almost rolled off the production line during World War II. However, high production costs doomed the plywood pedaler, designed to save metal. A single hand points to pegs that represent the hours on Helen Keller's watch. Top, Edison's first commercial success: a gold-price and stock ticker. Howe's sewing machine, above, introduced the lock stitch.

Trailblazers

The only reward I ever expected was the consciousness of advancing science, the pleasure of discovering new truths and the scientific reputation to which these labors would entitle me.—Joseph Henry

The Smithsonian's best known inventors were trailblazers of science. Example: Joseph Henry, the Institution's founding executive, developed a rudimentary system of electric telegraphy a decade before Samuel F. B. Morse. And whereas such men as Morse and Alexander Graham Bell applied basic electromagnetic theory, Henry developed the theory and built the first large, efficient electromagnet.

Yet Henry chose not to reap the inventor's reward; instead, he concentrated his acumen and insights on the Smithsonian as a nurturing force for science.

The Institution's third secretary, Samuel Pierpont Langley, successfully launched his model Aerodrome #5 in 1896. The prototype flew three-quarters of a mile powered by a steam engine. A man-carrying aerodrome failed on launch in early December 1903, only days before two brothers from Dayton, Ohio, succeeded in manned, controlled, and powered flight at Kitty Hawk, North Carolina.

Both Henry and Langley received what was perhaps science's ultimate accolade. International standards—the henry and the langley—were named for them. Thus they joined the company of such immortals as Volta, Watt, Ampère, Ohm, Roentgen, Gauss, and Faraday.

In the 1930s, Charles G. Abbot, the Smithsonian's fifth secretary, carried on the tradition of solar research which Langley pioneered. At the age of 100 he still came into the office, designing solar machines that a later generation might rediscover.

Robert H. Goddard never worked at the Smithsonian, but a timely research grant from the Institution assisted him as he developed the first liquid-propellant rocket—a historic breakthrough if ever there was one. Yet the limelight of rocket research fame fell on Wernher von Braun, whose development teams in Germany paralleled much of Goddard's brilliant, yet unsung, theory and application.

Such reports of trailblazing, basic research, and unselfish work for science tell little of the Smithsonian's broad-based encouragement of invention for more than a century. Even today, hundreds of inventors in government and business have been helped by technical consultation, research grants, publications, museum displays—and by continuing inspiration from the example of the Institution's founding fathers. □

Joe Goodwin

ROBERT H. GODDARD

U.S. AIR MAIL   8C

Joseph Henry—a founding father of the Smithsonian—designed and built a carefully insulated electromagnet with parallel windings, above. Other inventors put Henry's practical and theoretical work to use in such devices as the telegraph, telephone, and electric motor. Robert H. Goddard, left, used a Smithsonian grant to invent the first liquid-propellant rocket. A flier of 1896, below, was the steam-powered model Aerodome #5 of Samuel P. Langley, a Smithsonian Secretary who pioneered in the investigation of flight and longed to invent the airplane. His hopes were dashed. Only nine days before the Wright brothers went aloft, a large Langley craft crashed on takeoff. Charles G. Abbot, far right, records readings from a silver-disk pyroheliometer, an instrument to measure the sun's radiation. Secretary Abbot invented numerous solar devices, including the sun-tracker at top right. A cheap clock mechanism moved a dish which caught and focused sunlight to power a small steam engine. Abbot brewed his morning cup of tea with the help of a sun-heated samovar, and designed a solar oven. His well publicized efforts contributed to an era of ambitious solar and windpower experimentation in the 1930s, brought to a close by World War II.

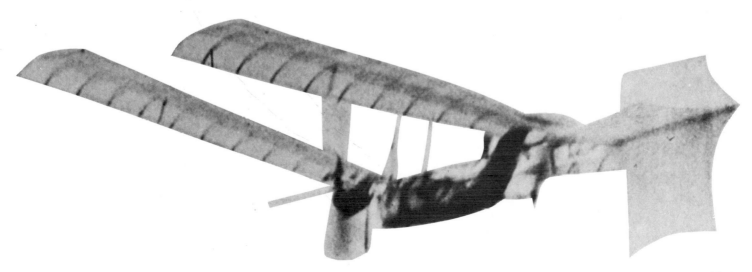

In the Public Eye

Because Americans have never quite known how to regard the inventor—whether to fear or to revere him—they have often made him a figure of fun. In the escapist fiction of the funny papers, the radio soap operas, science fiction, or magazine cartoons, the inventor appears as a crazy, frizzle-haired character or a wild-eyed adventurer, intriguing to all classes and ages of Americans. In the 1930s, E. C. Segar's Sunday strip "Sappo" entertained millions with the wild schemes of Professor O. G. Wotasnozzle and his admiring sidekick Sappo. A delightful egomaniac who boasted, "I accomplish things that other inventors wouldn't even dare dream about," Wotasnozzle engaged in a running feud with Professor Finklesnop over who was the smarter inventor. Although Wotasnozzle created such risible inventions as a life-reversing ray to make you grow backward and one to make you invisible, he was almost undone by Finklesnop's mechanical look-alike men who drove Wotasnozzle, in his own words, "coo Koo."

"The Inventions of Professor Lucifer G. Butts, A.K." announced the appearance of another wacky inventor, immortalized in cartoons by Rube Goldberg. The fecundity of the Professor's creative power was phenomenal. When not choking on a prune pit and coughing up an idea for an automatic typewriter eraser, he was making a parachute jump, forgetting to pull the string, and waking up three weeks later with the idea for a device to keep screen doors closed.

Two funny radio shows, departures from the melodramatic soaps of the '30s and '40s, highlighted inventors and inventiveness. Frank and Anne Hummert's "Lorenzo Jones" helped you "smile a while" with the "lovable, impractical" Lorenzo, who yearned after supper to "go out to the workshop and experiment until the wee hours." "Vic and Sade," a soap written by Paul Rhymer, was a fantasy of quirky characters with fanciful names. Godfrey Dimlok once invented a bicycle that could say "Mama." Uncle Fletcher's birthday gift to his landlady was a four-foot length of railway track weighing 400 pounds. "A wonderful doorstop," ruminated Fletcher.

Invention in the pages of science fiction owes much to the mind of Hugo Gernsback. An inventor himself, he designed the first home radio set. Pulp fiction writing and editing were other skills he practiced throughout his life. He laid claim to beginning the science fiction genre in the United States in 1908 with his first magazine, *Modern Electrics,* devoted to radio. His science fiction novel, *Ralph 124C41 +—Romance of the Year 2660,* began in 1911 in serial form in *Modern Electrics.* Studded with inventions, the book prophesied the future: night baseball, vending machines, metal foil, radar, and television.

Another prolific contributor to pulp fiction who fired the imagination of countless boys with the thrill of invention was Luis Philip Senarens. Frequently using the pseudonym "Noname," he wrote 1,500 novels, creating Frank Reade, "the most noted inventor of the known world." Nothing fazed Frank. From his teeming brain poured magnetic gun carriages, bicycle cars, electric sea engines, and steam men. A few pennies gave readers 50,000 words of pure adventure spanning the globe.

No matter in what guise he appears—laughable buffoon, glowing super-hero, or evil genius—the inventor has become over the years a kind of American folk-hero. He represents the typically American urge to tinker with gadgets, and he symbolizes the American dream to control the uncontrollable, to create the perfect invention and the universal solution. Americans have ever thrilled to the derring-do of inventors in pulps such as *Amazing* and *Astounding;* they have laughed over the whimsical inventions of zany professors in the funnies. And now in the movies and on TV they see an escalation from such shudderingly funny grotesques as Boris Karloff in Dr. Frankenstein's laboratory to Dr. Strangelove plotting the destruction of the world. Perhaps the inventor isn't all that funny anymore; but, for a time, his droll characterizations helped us to cope with the confusions of a too rapidly changing world. □

Jane M. Ross

With an enlarged head, Wotasnozzle plans to eradicate "that sap, Finklesnop." E. C. Segar also created "Thimble Theatre" with a cast of characters to rival Dickens: Popeye, J. Wellington Wimpy, the Sea Hag, Alice the Goon, and Olive Oyl.

Rube Goldberg considered Professor Butts "a subconscious off-spring" of his student days in analytic mechanics at the University of California's College of Mining. Other creatures from his teeming brain ran in a Sunday-only strip pitting Boob McNutt against "the fiendish Doctor Zano." Also included were Boob's girl, Pearl, and Bertha, the Siberian Cheesehound.

June

25 Cents
Canada 30¢

HUGO GERNSBACK Editor

Science WONDER Stories

A GERNSBACK PUBLICATION

NEW
SCIENCE NEWS
OF THE MONTH

Science Stories by
H. G. WELLS
Dr. D. H. KELLER
STANTON A. COBLENTZ

L. P. Senarens, above, was a prolific 19th-century science fiction inventor. The Frank Reade Weekly Magazine, right, featured such vehicles as the "New Electric Car" and the "Engine of the Clouds" that hovered over the ancient city of Jerusalem, exciting "... the wonder of the entire population ... who ... looked upon the Pegasus as something supernatural."

Artist Frank R. Paul's "Warriors of Space," left, decorates the first cover of Hugo Gernsback's Science Wonder Stories. Ralph and Alice, above, in Gernsback's prophetic novel Ralph 124C41+, meet via the telephot, or picture-phone, the first of many inventions aiding the couple's romance.

"Next."

"Death ray, fiddlesticks! Why, it doesn't even slow them up."

EUREKA! I HAVE INVENTED THE CAN OPENER!

TERRIFIC! WHAT'S A CAN?

"Hey! Come back here with my lazy Susan!"

As a figure of fun, the inventor continues to attract the barbs of modern cartoonists. Whether he existed in the Stone Age or in contemporary life, he was a disquieting spirit to his society. One of his unfortunate characteristics, in the cartoonist's eye, has been his passion for death-dealing inventions (which don't always work). But at least he has the insouciance to try again, as depicted in Peter Arno's cartoon, opposite.

"*Well, back to the old drawing board.*"

Drawing by Peter Arno; © 1941, 1969 The New Yorker Magazine, Inc.

Origins of Invention

The primal elements of the ancients—earth, air, fire, and water—bred life and eventually mankind. And after hundreds of thousands of years, men and women began, tentatively, to till the earth, bringing about in a span of a few centuries what we call civilization.

Civilization flourished with astounding brilliance in the Orient, and with it invention, the creative spirit that in turn profoundly affected the West and powered its rise to civilization. For it wasn't until medieval times that the interest in the mechanical arts, so characteristic of Western civilization, began to flower, when the water-driven mill, the windmill, and the horse-collar relieved men of much labor; when the parachute was thought of before it was needed, and that greatest of medieval inventions, the mechanical clock, began to order civilization in a new way.

Yet a case can be made that the chief architects of our technological world have been artists who, beginning in ancient times, sought new materials and new techniques for purely aesthetic purposes. Then, finding them, these artisans laid the groundwork for much of today's innovative science and industry.

How did the accumulated wisdom of Europe and the Orient find its way to American shores? Partially, at least, through such Enlightenment men as Thomas Jefferson and Benjamin Franklin, who filtered and transmitted science and technology from Old World to New, even as they molded the future of the new republic. Inventors in their own right, as well as statesmen and diplomats, such men tried to set an enlightened course for the country as it entered the Industrial Age.

The Beginnings of Agriculture

Edward S. Ayensu

In the saga of human history there has been one major preoccupation—man's quest to feed himself. For more than a million years small bands of evolving mankind accomplished this by gathering fruits, seeds, vegetables, and roots, and by hunting game animals in their immediate surroundings. But as these local resources became less plentiful and population pressures slowly mounted, men began to give up their somewhat sedentary existence and became nomads, pursuing migratory animals for hundreds, even thousands, of miles and gathering plants along the way. From generation to generation, as the millennia ticked slowly by, the change in human life-style must have been imperceptible.

By 30,000 years ago, man had made a major adaptation—one that presaged one of his greatest innovations—the domestication of food. In response to a climate turned bitterly cold, he learned to use fire and to build shelters. He gave consideration to clothing and body ornamentation, and began in earnest to develop ceremonial rites. All of these new activities involved further uses of plants and animals. Until this time man had done very little to control his environment, but all along he must have acquired a vast store of empirical knowledge about the nature of plants and animals in his surroundings—their seasons, their behavior, their useful properties. The plants and animals that he came to rely on had been evolving and hybridizing naturally; the wild ancestors of wheat, barley, corn, and other grasses had adapted to the increasing areas of savannah, developing seeds that could sprout quickly in disturbed soils. Then, by 10 thousand years ago, the ice sheets had withdrawn northward, leaving behind a gentler climate and new kinds of vegetation that ultimately enabled mankind radically to change his way of life.

One can only guess how the domestication of plants began. Perhaps seeds of wild, hybridized grasses such as wheat and barley were inadvertently spilled

Edward S. Ayensu, Director of the Endangered Species Program at the Smithsonian, has recently published Medicinal Plants of West Africa.

along regular trails and around areas of human habitation. As these seeds grew to be adult plants, people would have noticed the effects of seed broadcasting and thus, possibly, agriculture as we know it today was born or "invented." Whatever the process, we know that it occurred many times and in many places.

What is certain is that man knew about seed broadcasting long before agriculture as such came into being. Tools such as the digging stick, the mortar and pestle, and sickle-like blades existed as long ago as 10,000 B.C. Most likely, hunting and gathering families began at some point to create small, temporary gardens in areas that had been cleared to attract game—gardens that would have provided a small fraction of their diet. But as populations grew and game resources dwindled, these gardens and the knowledge of plants that had been of only marginal use to a hunting group, would have provided a needed stopgap.

People began to settle down, and as they did so, the birthrate increased, exerting even further pressure to develop reliable sources of food. By 9000 B.C. people in the Near East and elsewhere had begun cultivating plants in earnest, and by 6000 B.C. full-fledged farming villages dotted the Near East, with domesticated foods the primary source of nutrition.

Until recently, most scholars assumed a single cradle of agriculture in the vicinity of southern Europe, North Africa, and the Near East. Then about 30 years ago, N. I. Vavilov, the world-renowned Russian geneticist, published *The Origin, Variation, Immunity and Breeding of Cultivated Plants.* While serving as director of the All-Union Institute of Plant Industry in Leningrad he identified eight major centers of plant origin—six in the Old World and two in the New World. But extensive studies prompted by his publication among paleobotanists, paleontologists, and archeologists have since identified many other centers of origin. Numerous crops may have had more than one center of origin.

Consider the origin of wheat, for example, unquestionably the most intensively cultivated crop in the world today, with annual yields over 360 million metric tons. Most scholars now believe that man originally domesticated three basic kinds of wheat from wild varieties. Perhaps the oldest of these is *Triticum monococcum,* commonly called einkorn, a one-seeded wheat with seven pairs of chromosomes. Jack Harlan of the University of Illinois has suggested that einkorn was probably domesticated in southeastern Turkey and from there spread to western Europe, never quite reaching Egypt. It is still grown in limited quantities in the hilly regions of some parts of southern Europe and the Middle East. Dark bread is sometimes made from it, but because the unpalatable bracts remain tightly clasped around the grain and are difficult to remove, the whole ears are fed to cattle and horses.

The second group of wheat is commonly known as emmer. Wild emmer, *Triticum dicoccoides,* still grows in the Middle East; true emmer, *T. dicoccum,* is known only from cultivation. Considered the most successful of all the wheats in ancient times, it may have originated in either Palestine or southeastern Turkey. In Egypt, emmer was the most important wheat until it was replaced by the common bread wheat, *Triticum aestivum,* when Alexander the Great conquered Egypt in the fourth century B.C.

The genetics of emmer seems to indicate that it may have been naturally derived from the crossing of einkorn with a wild grass of the genus *Aegilops.* The crossing of einkorn with *Aegilops,* which both have seven pairs of chromosomes, provides a fertile, plump hybrid with 14 pairs of chromosomes. Emmer is still a crop in Ethiopia, Yugoslavia, and southern India. Open-eared, the seeds of this wheat will scatter in the winds when the ear breaks up; thus it is self-seeding, like wild wheat.

The third group of wheat, *Triticum timopheevii,* has 21 pairs of chromosomes, probably the result of a further hybridization of emmer with yet another wild grass. It seems to have originated in Transcaucasian Georgia, USSR. Not only is it plumper than emmer but the ears are also tighter and tend to break up easily. As the philosopher Jacob Bronowski remarked about the occurrence of this wheat, "Suddenly man and plant have come together, man has a wheat that he lives by,

About eight inches long, this stalk of wheat was made from gold in northern Greece about 2,000 years ago. Such items were often used as funerary objects, which suggests the significance wheat had gained in the lives of these people.

Sustained in part by grain harvests, hunters build the earliest villages as at Ali Kosh, reconstructed at right in the Museum of Natural History. Finds includes flints, grindstone, pots, and beads, top. Animal statuette, also from Iran, may depict a humped bull. Above, king with clay, from nearby Mesopotamia, symbolically affirms his peoples' debt to the soil.

but the wheat also thinks that man was made for him because only so can it be propagated."

Why men began to plant wheat in the Near East remains unknown: at the time the area supported an abundance of wild wheat and other grasses such as barley and oats. Harlan calculated that a person could gather a year's supply of wild wheat in about three weeks. But perhaps population pressures drove people into marginal regions where they were forced to plant seeds they had brought along with them. At any rate, one finds evidence of domesticated cereals as far back as 9000 B.C. By 7000 B.C. in the Near East there were remarkably sophisticated villages, housing as many as 200 people, where cultivated peas and lentils had become dietary staples. A thousand years later, only 30 generations, many Near Eastern settlements like Jericho were fed almost entirely by cultivated food resources.

On the other hand, Carl O. Sauer and others have postulated that the cradle of the earliest agriculture may have been southeastern Asia, rather than the Near East. Theoretically, Southeast Asia had most of the physical and organic diversity that could lend itself to early agricultural practices by man. The climate was, as it is now, generally mild with alternating abundant rainfall and dry periods. Recently, archeologists in Thailand have found domesticated plant materials, including what seem to be peas and beans, dating from 7000 B.C. If the finds and the dates are confirmed, it can be concluded that agriculture was practiced in this part of the world as early as it was in the Near East. Furthermore, Dr. Sauer suggested, asexual or vegetative reproduction of plants may have been the common method of cultivation in this area. For example, a piece of stem, tuber, or root is placed in the ground and allowed to grow into an adult plant. In this way the cultivator obtains plants that are identical to the parent instead of the possibly variant progeny that may result from planting seeds. Two root crops, the yam and taro, are thought to have been cultivated in the humid parts of southern Asia between 13,000 and 9000 B.C. If

Ancient agricultural practices are seen in "Field of the Blest," a painting of a frieze from the tomb of Jennudjem of the 19th-20th Dynasty in Thebes, dating from about 1200 B.C.

these findings prove true, they will add another dimension to the creative genius of prehistoric man.

Agriculture in tropical Africa today closely resembles that of Southeast Asia, but few records of prehistoric African domestication exist, for two reasons: little authenticated information points to the where and when of agriculture's beginnings; and climatic conditions in tropical Africa are not as conducive to the preservation of artifacts as they are in the arid Near East. But it remains certain that Africa saw the domestication of the Guinea yam as well as sorghum, which we know occurred first somewhere in East Africa and was later distributed in North Africa, the Near East, India, and China.

The New World is something of a special case; relatively speaking, man is a newcomer to the Americas. It is generally accepted that man arrived here via the Bering Strait—most likely in small bands on foot accompanied by the dog, his only domestic animal. This wave of migration, resulting in the spread of man southward and eastward throughout the Americas, occurred over long periods of time, probably beginning some 30,000 years ago. It seems certain that man was never more than a hunter during this migration, so we can presume that agriculture evolved separately in the New World.

Fruits such as avocados and tomatoes, edible seeds such as amaranth and groundnuts (peanuts), tuberous vegetables such as potatoes and manioc, several kinds of squash, pumpkins, chili peppers, cotton, tobacco, and, of course, corn—all of these and many more came under cultivation in various parts of the New World, beginning about 5000 B.C., and spread throughout the two continents.

Four distinct areas of domestication emerged. The chief centers, Mexico and Peru, produced a remarkably large array of cultivated plants. Certain food plants, like manioc, the sweet potato, groundnut, and pineapple, were first cultivated in lowland jungles and later spread to Mexico and the Andes. Early Indians of eastern North America may also have independently begun domesticating crops. Remains of what seem to be cultivated sunflowers have been discovered there, dating before maize, which, as it spread out from Mexico, became the main crop of southwestern and

eventually eastern North American Indians.

The rise of New World agriculture, and with it, civilization, is best documented through the excavations of archeologist Richard S. MacNeish in the arid highlands near Tehuacán in south-central Mexico. Here MacNeish found wild corn dating from 80,000 years ago. A small-eared popcorn with the kernels encased in pods and the ear growing out from between two leaves, this self-seeding plant is generally believed to be the original source of the more than 200 races of maize that ultimately became the dietary staple.

From 10,000 to 7000 B.C. the valley near Tehuacán was inhabited by a few families, predominantly hunters, who used a few simple implements of flaked stone. In the next 2,000 years, the people became predominantly plant collectors, gathering wild beans, amaranth, and chili peppers. They brought squash under cultivation and used new tools—pestles, choppers, and grinding stones. In the next 2,500 years domesticated plants—corn, gourds, squash, amaranth, beans, and chili peppers—came to supply about 10 percent of the diet.

By 3400 B.C., domesticated food supplied 30 percent of the diet. The people established fixed settlements with pit-house villages and were joined by the dog. By 2300 B.C., there were many more hybridized species of corn, and pottery was in use. By 200 B.C. irrigation was practiced, and the turkey, tomatoes, peanuts, and guavas had been added to the array of food sources. Substantial hilltop ceremonial centers were surrounded by fixed villages. By A.D. 700 agriculture supplied 85 percent of the diet, and the hilltop ceremonial centers had given way to true cities with the trappings of civilization—complex religion, extensive trade, crafts such as pottery, and standing armies.

This 12,000-year evolution, so uniquely documented at Tehuacán, no doubt occurred many times throughout Mesoamerica and in the Andes as hunter-gatherers learned the techniques of agriculture and settled down.

The origin of agriculture cannot be defined strictly as an "invention." Rather, it was a great innovation or, as we have seen, a series of innovations—combinations of evolution, natural hybridizations, and, over countless decades in numberless locations, inter-

ventions in a dimly understood process by shrewd observers of nature. Man is thought of as uniquely a tool-user, and it can be said that agriculture was the major catalyst to man's inventive genius, the driving force behind his evolution thenceforth. Hunting and gathering had called forth the digging stick, the blade, the grinding stone, and fire. But the cultivation of crops cried out for more tools and, in the relatively brief intervals between the earliest domestication of plants and the origins of writing, man had developed a panoply of tools, materials, and accessories that remain in use today, essentially unchanged through time: pots, shovels, nails, knots, buttons, saws, ovens, wine presses . . . the plow. But the plow—and the wheel—were not invented in the New World. As Bronowski pointed out, these two primary technological developments called for draft animals, which were not used in the New World until the arrival of the Europeans. (Wheeled devices were used in pre-Columbian Mexico as toys for children, but wheels were never tools in that remarkable civilization.)

Hand in hand with the domestication of plants, the use of animals played a critical role in the evolution of agricultural man. Indeed, animal husbandry seems to have preceded human control of plants. The origin of animal domestication is as full of uncertainties as the cultivation of plants. Probably the first animal to become associated with man was the dog. Archeologists have discovered the teeth and jaws of dogs in a human settlement in Iraq that dates back to 12,000 B.C. Similar remains occur in Idaho, dating to about 11,000 B.C. However, recent paleontological analysis suggests that the domestic dog traces its origins to an Asian wolf—somewhat smaller with a shorter snout than other wolves—in turn suggesting that the dog is an Asian innovation. Just why man and dog joined forces is unknown. Perhaps the dog ancestor showed promise as an assistant in the pursuit of herds of game. One can imagine, at any rate, that the impulse came in part from the dog, just as plants had become preadapted for human manipulation.

By 20,000 years ago and probably earlier, man had become a highly efficient, cooperative hunter, stampeding herds of animals into ambush. He learned to run wild herds over cliffs or, more effective, into

Near the ancient Egyptian city of Memphis, farmers continue using age-old technology. Turned by a draft animal, the Persian wheel, top, raises buckets of irrigation water. Above, the same task is done by an Archimedian screw.

natural corrals, killing what was necessary and letting the rest go—a step between straightforward hunting and domestication. This kind of manipulation was well under way in 16,000 B.C. on the coast of present-day Israel, where gazelle herds were "managed." But by 10,000 B.C. the coastal plains had vanished under the water released by the receding glaciers, and the pressure to manage animals shifted to other species—sheep, goats, pigs. The first signs of this appear in about 9000 B.C., just as plant domestication was becoming a serious enterprise. Archeological excavations in Iraq by Ralph S. Solecki of Columbia University indicate that goat and sheep populations lived near man at that time. The Ali Kosh site in Iran has yielded information on hornless, or domesticated, sheep and goats dated at 7500 B.C., and bone remains of sheep, pigs, dogs, and goats from 7000 B.C. have been found in the farming village of Cayonii in Turkey. This was all part of the now rapid process of settling down.

At Çatal Hüyük in Turkey, excavations by James Mellaart of the United Kingdom have revealed more than 50 shrines embellished with bulls' heads and horns dating to about 6500 B.C. Other animals closely identified with man's earliest agricultural pursuits include the donkey, known in domestication in Egypt by

3000 B.C., and the water buffalo, which has been a domesticated animal in India since about 2500 B.C. The horse may have been domesticated, or at least tamed, in central Asia or southern Russia around 3000 B.C. The domestication of animals clearly illustrates man's drive to conquer his surroundings. The animals selected for domestication were certainly not the most docile species, for had this been the case, man could have easily tamed such creatures as the antelope, the gazelle, and the deer. Rather, for obscure reasons, he chose to domesticate the elusive, often dangerous wild ancestors of such animals as the horse, mountain goats and sheep, cattle, and the buffalo.

The goat was very likely the first of a series of herd animals domesticated by man. Extremely well distributed throughout Europe, Asia, and Africa, its main line of descent seems to be from the Asiatic bezoar goat (*Capra aegarus*), a mountain goat ranging from the west of the Indus to the Caucasus. The sheep's domestication seems to have followed the general pattern of the goat, *Ovis vignei* being the main breed from whence all varieties stem. Cattle originated from a wild stock (*Bos primigenius*) ranging from Europe into western Asia, with *Bos namadicus* being of Indian origin. These wild cattle are considered the most savage of game animals. However, domestic cattle, useful as draft animals and providers of meat and dairy products, appear to have been tamed during the height of agricultural activities in upper Mesopotamia. The domesticated buffalo in Asia must have originated from *Bos arni* of the jungles of Assam, and the domesticated Jaffarbadi buffalo of India resembles the wild Cape buffalo of Africa (*Bos caffer*).

The pig most likely originated in Asia. Its remains have been found in the Far East from as early as 7000 B.C., and in the highlands of New Guinea it certainly dates back to 6000 B.C., when farming is thought to have begun there. It may even have been in New Guinea as early as 10,000 B.C., giving it a very much earlier origin than on the Asian mainland.

The familiar domestic fowl (chicken) is a descendant of the jungle fowl of India, or possibly of China, but there are several other breeds that are indigenous to many parts of the world, particularly the tropics. From the beginning, fowl and domestic ducks have been treated as scavenger birds, reclaiming nutrients that would otherwise be lost.

As with plants, animal domestication in the New World is a special case. While the Old World produced relatively few domestic plants but many domestic animals for meat, milk, wool, and animal power, the situation is reversed in the New World. Except for the dog, which came across the Bering Strait with man, the people of the Americas domesticated little else but the guinea pig and the turkey, partly taming the llama, the

alpaca, and the vicuna as well. The dog was an important part of the Mexican diet in 7000 B.C.; for the rest of their meat protein, the Americans had to rely on the skills of hunters taking what they could from a relatively small number of game species.

The examples presented in this essay comprise a small proportion of the plants and animals that man must have seen and used during the pre-agricultural period. They illustrate that from the very beginning man began a selective process of screening, reducing the number of managed species, which resulted in the few major sources of plants and animals that form the basis of our diet today. For example, of the well over 3,000 potentially economic food plant species in the world, we now depend on about 30. Similarly, out of the countless number of animals available, we have pinned our hopes on about seven.

Jack Harlan warns, "The trend for more and more people to be nourished by fewer and fewer plant and animal food sources has reached a point today where most of the World's population is absolutely dependent on a handful of species. . . . As the trend intensifies, man becomes ever more vulnerable. His food supply now depends on the success of a small number of species, and the failure of one of them may mean automatic starvation for millions of people." If this trend, the legacy from our early ancestors, is not reversed by intensive exploitation of the many plants and animals with culinary and economic promise, man will certainly face untold difficulties should disaster strike the select food sources that dominate his diet.

A honeybee tops Greek coin, above. Below, design—generally believed to be pomegranates—denotes fertility. It and a chalice appear on Jewish shekel. A.D. 68-69.

The slow and no doubt painful process by which man gained control of his food sources thousands of years ago left a more immediate legacy, but one we also still live with. It made it possible, indeed necessary, for people to settle down in discrete communities. It brought about an explosion of inventiveness—tools, art forms, elaborate religious practices, and buildings. One can suggest that as agricultural settlements grew they fostered the "haves," while nomadic peoples became the "have nots." Thus what we think of as organized warfare must have begun as nomads ranged out of the mountains to attack the farmers and plunder their rich food supplies, and the farmers built walls and fortifications in defense. What remains unquestionably clear is that the transformation from random food gathering to the art of plant and animal domestication was the foundation for the highly combative civilizations which soon flourished and evolved over only a few thousand years into our present-day technological societies. □

Genius in the East

From ancient Ur of the Chaldees to modern Tokyo of the Ginza, Eastern peoples have bequeathed a vast legacy of invention. Millenniums ago they invented agriculture, architecture, and the alphabet. By controlling fire they pioneered ceramics, metallurgy, and chemistry.

Early on, Easterners wrought that invention of inventions—civilization itself. The archetypal city arose, with its storehouses, schools, palaces, shrines, a ready work force, and fortifications against attack.

Powerful empires spread through great river valleys. Their ruins now lie beside the Nile, the Tigris-Euphrates, and China's Yangtze and Yellow Rivers.

Lesser streams, too, nourished dynamic and inventive cultures. Afghans beside the Helmand originated the windmill. Lydians of Turkey's Meander River coined money—and, incidentally, coined a word for all wandering rivers. Caravans from Oxus River lands helped spread inventions across Asia.

The seeds of genius grew even in Asia's arid lands. Harsh desert experience shaped Jewish law and tradition. Thence sprang Christianity, spiritual light of the West. Multiply such Asian roots a hundredfold, and today nearly everybody on Earth cherishes some spiritual or material possession from the East. Consider china, for instance—the porcelain, not the country. By A.D. 1000, Chinese royalty had built the world's first great industrial complex, mass producing ceramics for the court. An extensive supply network fed the kiln city of Ching-te Chen with vast quantities of purified kaolin clay and chemicals from which the first true translucent porcelain was made.

A story from China's pottery lore sums up the patient trial-and-error process by which Eastern artisans invented. The potter Lang-yau, it seems, had very bad luck with the fire in his kiln one day. Greasy smoke poured out of every cranny and peephole. All of the pots were ruined except one, and that last glorious vase shone with a new kind of lavender-ruby glaze: the first piece of *sang de boeuf,* or sacrificial red pottery.

The emperor praised the pot and wanted more. But for the life of him, Lang-yau couldn't turn the trick again. Finally, in terror of imperial wrath, he threw himself into the glowing kiln—and behold, every pot came out red. More moderate potters smoked up the kilns with dead donkeys, and eventually with wet straw. Historically, the tale may be a myth. Chemically it is true. To create sacrificial red, the kiln must contain an oxygen-poor atmosphere, as is produced by burning soggy vegetable matter—or flesh.

Through just such empirical methods, Asians worked wonders. With scholarship, artistic insight, and imperial power, Easterners time and again nearly made the breakthrough from art into science. Culturally resurgent Europeans ultimately achieved it, with the increasingly refined technologies that attended their dynamic society. The East, however, supplied much of the technological base from which Europeans made their quantum leap into the future.

Complex working model of star motion, the astrolabe—shown in a very rare English version—first appeared in the ancient East and reached Europe through Moslem scholars. Japanese ceramic rabbit (three inches high) once held incense.

Caravans

When Charlemagne led the Franks, Haroun al Raschid of the *Thousand and One Nights* ruled the Baghdad caliphate. Around 800, Haroun sent Charlemagne an elephant—dramatic evidence of how one culture can impart something new to another. More important, the caliph sent his dhows along fabled Sinbad's water route, following Asia's southern rim. Arabs traded with Japanese and Chinese.

The same exchange had occurred on land a millennium before Sinbad. Silks and other Oriental luxuries reached the Greeks and Romans via the 7,000-mile Silk Road. It sprang up in the wake of Alexander the Great, who conquered yet inspired Asians from Turkey to Central Asia to India, where remnants of Greek culture survive and villagers speak of "Iskander" as a friend who passed their way just yesterday.

That yesterday is more than 2,000 years gone by. Caravans drifted westward from China to Turkey and back again. The cargo included not only silk but also jade, lapis lazuli, and turquoise; roses and attar of roses; goldfish; the world's first gunpowder; paper money; tea, and the china cups to drink it from; medicines; campfire tales by the millions. By the dawn of the Italian Renaissance, members of the Polo banking family traveled between Venice and Peking. From their time to ours the Orient has poured out uncountable treasures—the products of innovation.

Yet how ironic: the East's magnificent creative momentum seemed to lessen just at the time that the Europeans began to exult in their own Age of Discovery. Gunpowder exemplifies this process. Its inventors, the Chinese, preferred to use the miraculous chemical tool in fireworks and in mostly ineffectual war rockets. But when Europeans got wind of black powder they soon combined it with bell-casting technology to make overwhelming cannons. Westerners never hesitated to use their superior cannon, often mounted in superior ships, in their relentless drive to change the world, East and West.

Asian artisans over thousands of years elevated ceramics, metalwork, textiles, and other arts to levels seldom reached in the West. From a 14th-century Turkish tile, near right, artwork includes: gold medallion of 11th-century Iran, showing a mounted ruler. Equestrian skills probably originated in nearby Central Asia and spread westward, bringing ideals of gallantry that influenced European chivalric tradition. Next, a recent miniature portrait of a Persian princess, Qajar Dynasty. A brightly colored bowl from Nishapur was turned in the 900s. Chinese bulb pot of the 1500s reveals rich overlays of color. Symbols on the map indicate Eastern innovations.

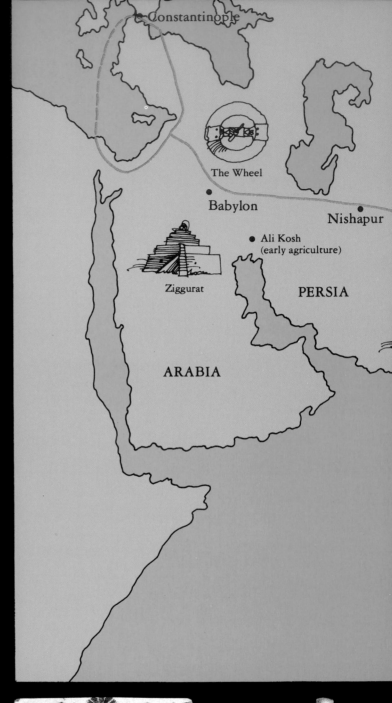

Constantinople

The Wheel

Babylon

Nishapur

Ali Kosh
(early agriculture)

Ziggurat

PERSIA

ARABIA

CENTRAL ASIA

Great Wall

JAPAN

Camel Caravans

Peking

Nara

CHINA

THE GREAT SILK ROUTE

Ching-te Chen

ndmill

Kite

Sericulture

Stern Rudder

Elephant
Domestication

INDIA

Oriental Travelers

Few people cared more about directions than the old Chinese. Their concern sprang from geomancy, a religious practice which dealt with the movements of evil spirits. Such an interest inspired the Chinese to devise two kinds of compasses—the familiar magnetic needle compass, and the intriguing, though conjectural, "south pointing chariot," opposite.

Gears and shafts linked the chariot's wheels to a wooden goddess. The parts worked together so that no matter which way the cart headed, the figure always pointed toward the direction in which it originally had been set. The Chinese chariot resembles the modern mechanism that holds a battle tank's cannon on target while the tank maneuvers on its caterpillar treads.

Strangely, the wooden lady stayed home while the magnetic compass spread around the world. But the Chinese jade lady at right has traveled far. Known as Kwan Yin, the Goddess of Mercy, she resides in the Smithsonian's Hall of Minerals. Oriental artists shaped her with a wide range of traditional lapidary tools and materials, including several sizes of abrasive grit.

Gem cutting, like woodworking, is a straightforward craft. Not so with metallurgy. "Most people don't realize," explains W. T. Chase of the Freer Gallery of Art, who tracks down old metal-working techniques, "that in China money really did grow on trees." They were part of a mass-production technique. Workers pressed clay into stone dies to make coin molds. Tubes in the mold connected the coin-mold spaces. Molten metal ran into the tubes and filled the molds. When hardened, bronze coins bristled on bronze branches like leaves on a tree. Coins were broken off for use and the branches remelted.

One such mass-produced coin, the *cash*, supplied English with its word for any ready money. Furthermore, the Chinese invented tree-pulp paper and on it printed not only books but also the first paper money. One might say that in Old China two kinds of money grew on trees, bronze coins and leaves of the splendid folding green. Curiously, though we use the Chinese kind of paper, we gain our word for it from a rather different writing material, papyrus sheets of laminated fiber from a water reed in ancient Egypt.

It all goes to prove that from the Nile to Japan's far shores, showers of inventive blessings have poured on the West. So, oh brash and uncultured Occidental, one day soon incline yourself toward the Orient and whisper a heartfelt word of thanks. □

Joe Goodwin

Pegged gears turn shafts to keep the arm of a wooden goddess pointed south as the entire cart turns in different directions. Part compass, part differentially-geared turntable, such a gear system may have been used in China by the first century A.D. Carved and polished jade radiates an aura of peacefulness and permanence in the Chinese Kwan-Yin figure above. The artifact blends Buddhist ideals from India with China's dedication to feudal and scholarly conservatism.

PART

2

The Flowering of Medieval Invention

Lynn White, jr.

In the mid-15th century, as the Byzantine Empire neared exhaustion in its long struggle with the encroaching Turks, a Greek cleric named John Bessarion went to Italy to enlist Western help against the infidel enemy. Amazed at the spectacle of water wheels operating both sawmills and the bellows of blast furnaces, Bessarion wrote from Italy in 1444 urging the Byzantines to send young men to the West to learn the mechanical skills, especially the making of superior weapons and ships.

Though Byzantines and Westerners were not ig-norant of each other, the Byzantines had taken little interest in Western technological accomplishments. Despite Bessarion's pleas, Constantinople and the Byzantine Empire fell to the Turks in 1453.

The moral of this is not necessarily that the inventive spirit of the West might have saved Byzantium; it is merely that different groups of human beings have exhibited the most varied attitudes toward technological innovation. A medieval Islamic proverb makes the point: "Allah created three marvels: the hand of the Chinese, the brain of the Byzantine, and the tongue of

From the late 13th-century English "Windmill Psalter," this is the first depiction of a horizontal-shaft windmill. Wind-turned blades transmitted power through gears to a vertical-axis flour

mill beneath. Such small "post-mills" were centrally pivoted; the miller turned the entire structure to face the breeze. Horizontal-shaft windmills soon spread all over Europe.

the Arab." Indeed, it appears that from roughly the time of Christ until about 1350, when Europe began to surpass it, China showed the world's highest level of inventiveness. In contrast, the detailed and ample bas-reliefs of the Buddhist temple at Borobudur in Java, built about A.D. 800, indicate a gentle, in some ways sophisticated, art-focused society living at a quite simple technological level. The only items demanding much engineering skill are the great bronze bells used in Buddhist worship and the ships that connected Java with both India and China. Moreover, Borobudur itself, while wonderfully beautiful, is structurally as rudimentary as Egypt's pyramids. Clearly, the eighth-century Javanese directed their innovative urges toward activities other than the technological.

The same held true for the Byzantines. In 673 a Syrian Greek-speaking engineer in Constantinople, named Kallinikos, invented Greek fire, a petroleum-based incendiary very useful for burning enemy ships and siege machinery. Thereafter not a single technical invention emerged from medieval Greece. Yet for centuries Constantinople remained one of the world's wonders: in theological speculation and in all the arts except sculpture-in-the-round it was magnificently creative, until the Turks seized it.

To our 20th-century Western minds, which consider the high significance of technology—for better or worse—to be axiomatic, Byzantium's indifference toward technology is incomprehensible. But the history of paper making illustrates the medieval Greek attitude. Paper originated in China and reached Islam in A.D. 751 when a Muslim army captured some Chinese paper makers near Samarkand. Its manufacture spread quickly in the caliphate—but, curiously, the Byzantines never made paper. They held no prejudice against it; indeed, by 1050 they were using it not merely for books but also at times for imperial documents. They simply chose to buy it from Islamic merchants rather than produce their own or improve it for their own purposes.

Significantly, the first clearly documented paper making in the West took place in 1276 at Fabriano in Italy's Central Apennines, and the pulping of the rags there was done by a watermill. We have no firm evidence that Muslim paper making ever was mechanized. Presumably waterpower reduced labor costs and enabled Italians to undersell Muslims. At any rate, Italian paper shortly drove Islamic paper out of the Byzantine market. Why didn't the Greeks produce the paper they used? Why didn't the Muslims apply power machinery to paper making? Neither group lacked in-

Lynn White, jr., former president of the American Historical Association, is a professor emeritus of history at the University of California, Los Angeles.

Marshaling the power of technology, forces of good sharpen swords with a rotary grindstone, right, while older whetstones suffice for evil. From the ninth-century Utrecht Psalter.

ventiveness in other activities. They simply were interested in different sorts of things at that pivotal time.

In the Americas and Europe today, educated people normally think of the path of our Western culture as starting with the ancient Greeks and Hebrews, then running through the Romans and the Latin Middle Ages to ourselves. In literature, philosophy, religion, and the visual arts, this interpretation has some merit. In economics, social structures, and technology, it is less useful. Specifically, in technology, while nothing useful of ancient Greek or Roman engineering perished along the road, the attitudes, motivations, and most of the basic skills of modern technology before the electronics revolution originated not in Mediterranean Antiquity but during the Middle Ages.

Periclean Athens, like eighth-century Java, was an aesthetic miracle built on a technologically primitive foundation. Despite their geometry, the Greeks of that period could not put together a good beamed roof for the Parthenon; the solution of such problems had to wait for Roman engineers. Alexander the Great's conquests were aided by the invention of ingenious new sorts of stone-throwing engines. After his death, machine design developed swiftly, especially at Syracuse and Alexandria, involving such innovations as pulleys, cogwheels, and screws. The new machines, however, with rare exceptions were not intended for production of goods, but rather for increasing the magnificence of rulers, the mystery of temples, or the accuracy of astrological predictions.

The greatest Roman contribution to engineering was in structural design. The dome of the Pantheon, an overwhelming achievement, is likewise overwhelming in its extravagance. Having looted the Mediterranean world, the Romans disregarded cost-accounting. The great defect of Roman engineering was failure to see that economy of means can often add elegance. So many Roman structures have survived the centuries in part because the mass of their masonry is out of all proportion to function. For example, Roman architects often incorporated segmental arches into solid walls to reduce the vertical pressure on lintels. However, in building bridges, aqueducts, and the like, they clung to the semi-circular arch, overlooking the fact that considerable masonry could be saved by using broader arches of less than 180 degrees. Our modern sense of the importance of economy of means had to wait for the Middle Ages. Both the 14th-century Ponte Vecchio and the famous bridge at Avignon exemplify the innovative segmental arches.

The emergence of Gothic architecture clearly shows this new sensibility. When Christianity became the official religion of the Roman Empire, it naturally built its Western churches in the late-Roman manner, with wooden ceilings and beamed roofs. During the early Middle Ages, liturgies grew steadily more elabo-

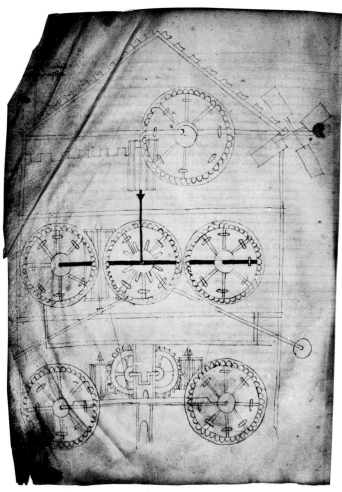

In this plan for a self-moving vehicle by Guido da Vigevano, power is carried from blades on the conical cap through gears and crankshaft to axles. As perspective was not yet understood, the lowest gears were depicted vertically instead of horizontally.

rate, and apses were increasingly filled with carved wooden choir stalls and textile hangings. For great celebrations altars were flooded with light from masses of lamps and candles, especially in Northern Europe with its long dark winters. Occasionally, a catastrophic fire resulted, reaching the timber ceiling and roof and destroying the entire edifice. By the 10th century, architects were beginning to provide fire protection both by increasing the height of churches and by replacing the combustible ceiling with a thin shell of masonry vaulting to shield the beams of the roof from sparks. Both arches and vaulting, however, continued to be semicircular, which meant that as nave and choir grew more lofty the lateral thrust of the weight of the vaults required ever more massive walls and buttresses. All stone was quarried by hand, and the transport of heavy material was costly. By the late 11th century it must have seemed to many that the limits of financial feasibility had been reached, especially in relation to the church's charitable obligations.

Then a new idea came out of South Asia. Some 900 years earlier Buddhist monks in India, for purely decorative purposes, had invented both the horseshoe arch and the pointed arch. Both gradually worked their way westward. The former, which structurally had no advantage over the semicircular arch, became popular in Moorish Spain. By the 10th century the ogival arch was dominant in Egypt and much of North Africa. Thence it moved on to Amalfi, a city with close Egyptian trade relations. In 1071 the church of the Benedictine motherhouse of Monte Cassino was rebuilt with an entrance porch of pointed arches and vaults. Their intention seems to have been simply ornamental. (To find an Islamic element in the new church at this famous cradle of Western monasticism should cause no surprise at that moment. Monte Cassino was Europe's chief center for translation of Arabic medical works into Latin.) Nine years later the abbot of Cluny in Burgundy, already planning what was to become the greatest monastic church of Europe, visited Monte Cassino. This was the moment of truth. Either he or his engineers saw that such pointed structures as those on the porch would shift the lateral thrust of arches and vaults at an angle downward and thus permit use of lighter walls and buttresses.

In 1088 work on Cluny III commenced, and when in 1120 it was effectively finished, it had nearly 200 ogival arches and many pointed vaults. Meanwhile, the Benedictine abbey-cathedral at Durham, begun in 1093, also incorporated the new structural forms, and with each successive edifice the technical possibilities were advanced. In 1144 the great Abbot Suger completed the rebuilding of the abbey church of Saint-Denis near Paris, generally regarded as the first fully realized Gothic church.

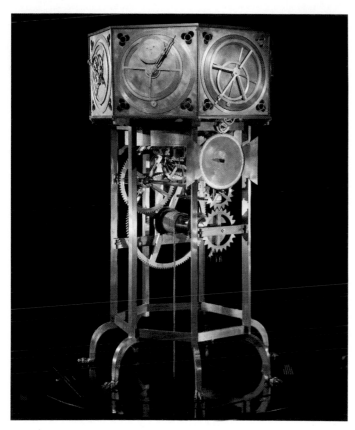

Faces of this reconstruction of a lost 14th-century dé Dondi clock at the Museum of History and Technology reflect the Ptolemaic conception of planetary motion.

The emergence of proto-Gothic construction in the 11th and 12th centuries symbolizes the difference between Greco-Roman technology and medieval-modern technology. More than cost-saving was involved: obviously the adventurous architects of Cluny III had no intention of erecting a cheap eyesore. Yet problems of cost were clearly considered, and we today share that concern. The Romans, however, did not. Their famous roads were built primarily for marching legions and were too steep in places for wheeled traffic. The massive road surfaces of stone slabs cemented to a rubble foundation did not allow for contraction or expansion with temperature changes. Water seeped under the slabs and in freezing weather they became loose and cracked. Maintenance remained a great and perpetual expense. Even in the relatively stable Eastern Mediterranean region the successor regimes made little or no effort to perpetuate the Roman roads; they were not worth it.

The greatest technological concern of the post-Roman West has been the reduction of human and animal labor. The watermill appears in the Mediterranean world in the first century B.C., and the Greek poet who gives us our second bit of evidence for it is sensitive to its beneficence: he urges the slave women, who formerly rose early to grind the day's flour, to sleep late because the water spirits have assumed their task. Note that these were, in his mind, real nymphs, not just poetic conceits. Yet watermills did not become common in Roman times, and there is no firm evidence that the Romans applied waterpower to any process other than milling grain. Perhaps the ancients were a bit fearful of harnessing sprites.

The major spread of the watermill in Europe occurred after the West Roman Empire had disintegrated and the population was generally Christianized. The first clearly documented evidence of waterpower used for any industrial process other than milling cereals comes in the 840s in the schematized plan of the abbey of St. Gall in Switzerland. Here mills were built with powerful stamps mechanically designed to make the mash for beer. By the 11th century every village had at least one flour mill, and other industrial applications were increasing rapidly. From about the middle of the 12th century we have two independently written, enthusiastic monkish descriptions of how, at St. Bernard's abbey of Clairvaux, mills fulled cloth, tanned leather, worked forge hammers, automatically sifted the flour that they had ground, attended to the laundry, and generally made themselves available for whatever needed to be done. One of the writers ends by thanking God for such wonderful machines to lighten the labors of both man and beast.

This exhilaration over new productive devices, the conviction that they were profoundly good in human terms, the clear sense that further inventions would follow: these emotions and beliefs, so different from those generally held in Antiquity, show the Middle Ages beginning to breathe the technological atmosphere that we still largely share.

New developments, in fact, came rapidly. For example, in the early 1180s the horizontal-axle windmill was invented, probably in eastern England, on the analogy of the horizontal-axle watermill. It proved very useful in flat regions where the sluggish flow of streams rendered watermills ineffective unless one built a dam, which often flooded agricultural land. By 1192 European-style windmills were being built in Syria by German crusaders. Indeed, toward the end of the 12th century, windmills were spreading as rapidly as the cinema did in the early 20th century. Within little more than a decade of their appearance, the pope was trying to tax them.

By the second half of the 13th century no small number of western Europeans were beginning to envisage invention as a unified human undertaking. People of that period, of course, entertained no notion that scientific findings could solve technological problems; that idea seems first to have been formulated in 1450 by the intellectual German-born Cardinal

The fall of the hypothetical parachutist above, sketched by a late 15th-century Sienese engineer, would have been little hindered by his plumes of cloth. The conical model below, by the same engineer, lacks only a hole at its apex to approximate the modern airman's lifesaver. Later, about 1500, Leonardo da Vinci suggested that "a tent made of linen" might provide safe descents; his pyramidal parachute would "enable man to throw himself down from any great height." Thus did Renaissance ingenuity produce a device for which there would be no need for almost 300 years.

Nicholas of Cusa, but it did not become widely effective until about 1850. Nonetheless, Western society was metaphorically ready to try its wings.

Shortly after A.D. 1000 a monk of Malmesbury Abbey in England built a glider, flew some 600 feet, and then crashed because, as he said, he forgot "to put a tail on the rear end." His was an isolated experiment. About 1260, however, Friar Roger Bacon was writing not only about "flying machines . . . in which a man . . . may beat the air with wings like a bird" but also, in the same sentence, about technological needs in the whole area of transportation—machines "by which the largest ships . . . will move faster than if they were filled with rowers; wagons may be built which will move with incredible speed and without the aid of beasts; . . . machines will make it possible to go to the bottom of seas and rivers." Bacon indicates that inventors are in fact working to perfect just such ideas.

In 1335, learned Italian physician Guido da Vigevano, who also was interested in machine design, presented to the King of France a volume containing drawings of new engines, including the first known likeness of an automobile, a vehicle powered by men working the first known crankshafts. Another of his sketches showed a submarine with paddlewheels operated from inside by man-powered crankshafts. A third sketch depicted a siege-tower powered, like the automobile, by internal crankshafts, man-powered and supplemented, in case of a good breeze, by a windmill that fed additional power into the gears—the first instance of a two-motored machine. Guido's novel ideas would seem to have been carried forward at first in theatrical machinery at the courts of France and Burgundy. In the 15th century they became part of general European engineering literature.

That Europeans were becoming aware of invention and its ever-burgeoning importance is shown by a vernacular Italian sermon preached in 1306 in Florence. "Not all the arts," said the preacher, "have been found; we shall never see an end of finding them. . . . indeed, they are being found all the time. It is not twenty years since the art of making eyeglasses was discovered . . . I myself met the man who invented and made them, and I talked with him."

Astronomers and physicians who had to cast astrological horoscopes of their patients felt a need for a timekeeper more accurate than the waterclock. In 1269 an unworkable magnetic clock was proposed. In 1270 a chronicler named Robert the Englishman pointed out that the solution was a weight-driven clock. For decades technicians labored over the problem, until at last, around 1330, an anonymous genius devised the foliot escapement, and the mechanical clock emerged. Elegant solutions to the problems of the mechanical clock demonstrate a vast advance in machine design and instrument-making skills. The new clocks spread explosively all over Europe, and in 1338 some Venetian merchants sold one to the Sultan of Delhi in India.

The gestation of most inventions remains hidden from us. The Chinese formula for gunpowder was known in Europe by about 1260 and was used for rockets and firecrackers. The cannon appears to be a European invention; it turns up suddenly in the account books of the Signoria of Florence in 1326, and in 1327 we find an English picture of one. The first Chinese cannon known to us is dated 1332. Since many Italians were in China at precisely that time, presumably they took the idea along with them. The cannon reached Islam, India, and Japan not from China, but from Europe.

One of the most interesting aspects of medieval inventiveness is seen in Europe's ability to take germinal ideas, like gunpowder, from alien and distant cultures, and to develop them in novel ways.

In musical technology, for example, the fiddle-bow was invented in Java about the time Borobudur was built. The Javanese themselves paid little attention to it; their music is still percussive. The bow was diffused throughout Islam and reached Christian Spain about 980, shaped at that time like the weapon from which it took its name. This meant that as the bow-string was drawn over the strings of the instrument, the tension varied and the tone wobbled. By the 12th century the French were flattening the bow's back to secure an even tension in the bowstring, and also were developing the "nut" or "frog" at the bow's lower end to help tighten the string. Their efforts produced an increasingly smooth tone. By the late Middle Ages bowed instruments were vastly popular not only in worldly orchestras but also—to judge by pictures—in the celestial ensembles of angels.

The British Library holds a manuscript sketch-book from the late 1470s and early 1480s of an engineer who probably lived in Siena. One of its pages shows a man jumping from a considerable height, his descent braked only by two large, fluttering, cloth streamers attached to his belt. A sponge between his teeth protects his jaws from the shock of landing. He looks frightened. He should be. The next pages of this manuscript are filled with hoists for careening ships, military machines, a variety of items. But clearly our engineer-sketcher remains worried about the man; something better must be devised for him. So, after 21 pages, the same jumper reappears, now in a more confident mood. The sponge in his teeth is strapped around his head so that if he cries out in terror he will not lose it. More important, the streamers have been replaced by a conical parachute, the world's first.

Slightly later, Leonardo da Vinci sketched a pyr-amidal parachute: the idea, if not the thing, had taken form. The true parachute reached publication in 1615-1616 in the *New Machines* of Faustus Verantius, a Hungarian bishop. After that, every engineer knew of its possibility; the trouble was that there were no specific situations in which one was needed. Only after the Montgolfier brothers developed the hot-air balloon did the parachute find a function. The first actual jump was made in 1797. Our anonymous Sienese engineer had created a concept which lay dormant, although known, for 300 years before it was applied. Medieval technologists showed great skill in elaborating ideas borrowed from other cultures, as well as in opening up novel and useful engineering concepts. But also, at times, they planted seeds that sprouted only much more recently.

How can we account for the range and dynamism of medieval inventiveness, of which our modern technological thrust is the direct prolongation? Nothing so historically important happens for a single reason, but rather for various interconnected reasons. To articulate those reasons:

(1) Deep in pre-history, the Near Eastern style of agriculture was introduced to all of Europe. Its chief tool, the scratch plow, was drawn by two oxen. Since it did not turn over the sod, cross-plowing was necessary to pulverize the soil and, in the arid Near East, to reduce evaporation. The resulting field shapes were squarish, and usually walled or hedged. In most of Mediterranean Europe, which shared light soils and a semi-arid climate with the Near East, production by these simple means was fairly satisfactory. In Europe north of the Loire and the Alps, however, the richest soils were sticky clays and the climate was so wet that field drainage, rather than conservation of sub-soil moisture, was essential. Scratch plow agriculture could not cope well with this environment; the result was that cereal production was low, and the Celts and Germans depended for food more on their herds than on their fields. When the Romans conquered Gaul, southern Germany, and Britain, they experimented occasionally with new agricultural methods but never solved the problem. The resilience of the Near East was related to the fact that time-honored farming techniques worked there; the fragility of the northwestern part of Rome's empire under barbarian pressures was related to the inappropriateness of the same agrarian practices in that very different ecology.

One can detect the beginning of the greatest agricultural change in the history of Northern Europe among the still pagan Slavs. It happened no later than the early sixth century. A new basic tool was invented: a heavy wheeled plow with a knife to cut the line of a furrow, a share to slice under the sod, and a moldboard to turn over the ribbon of loosened earth. Two oxen could not pull such a machine; eight were normally used. Arable land was now plowed in strips, and all the community's strips were included in large open fields fenced as a unit.

We can reasonably estimate that the shift from the two- to the three-field system, and from ox to speedier horse as the primary work animal, under ideal conditions increased productivity per peasant by some 200 percent. In a society in which over 90 percent of the people were living directly on the land, the social consequences were seismic. Surplus rural population moved to the rapidly expanding cities. Improved peasant purchasing power stimulated industry, general commerce, and inventiveness. By the end of the 11th century, burghers and feudal powers were already contending for dominance on a new economic base.

The agricultural revolution also had a profound psychological impact. In the era of the scratch plow drawn by two oxen, land was held by peasants in units designed to support a single family; the assumption was subsistence farming. When the new heavy plow was adopted, no single peasant could afford the eight oxen to pull it: a group of peasants pooled their draft animals and distributed the plowed strips in proportion to their contributions. Formerly, man had been part of nature. Now man was drawing income in terms of the labor and capital that he invested in exploiting nature. Man and nature became two different things, and man felt himself to be dominant.

(2) In Greco-Roman Antiquity, pagans believed in a hierarchy of spirits, from the quarreling gods of Olympus to the spirits of rocks, trees, springs, and the like. Anyone interfering with nature ran the risk of offending some spirit, and keeping these unpredictable entities placated was a perpetual task. Christianity, following its mother religion, Judaism, eliminated spirits from the objects of nature. Demons and angels, of course, remained, but they were not localized: if a Christian cut down a great tree, he felt no need to make a propitiatory offering to the spirit of the tree. Of course, animism long survived in some isolated populations. In general, however, the victory of Christianity liberated Europeans to manipulate nature without qualms and according to their wishes. God, the Latin church taught, had created the visible world for mankind's use and instruction, and for no other purpose. The plow and the new religion gave the same message to men of the early Middle Ages, developing an atmosphere cordial to technological innovation.

(3) From about the sixth century before Christ, the upper classes of the ancient world had been pervaded by contempt for anyone—slave or free—who worked with his hands. The exception to this attitude was found among the Jews. The rabbis taught that Yahweh had commanded his people to work six days

and to rest on the seventh: the duty to work was considered as important as the duty to rest. Indeed, the rabbis themselves often worked as craftsmen.

In the late third century after Christ, in the Near East, pagans were pouring into the Church so rapidly that they could not be properly indoctrinated. Christian rigorists felt that to battle corrupting influences they must return to the ways of the primitive Church—that is, to the pattern of life when Christianity was still essentially Jewish. The result was monasticism, with its rabbinical insistence that work is worship. In the sixth century, St. Benedict codified the basic Western form of monasticism, with a strong insistence on the necessity of manual labor as part of the spiritual life.

Because of the great prestige of the working monks—and we have already noted evidences of monastic enthusiasm for technological advance—the early Middle Ages in the West were often called "the Benedictine Age." In the 13th century both Franciscans and Dominicans developed adjunct "tertiary" orders of devout laymen who tried to live holy lives not in convents but rather in their families, communities, and jobs. The potential sanctity of lay life began to be realized, including the work ethic. Unless labor, especially manual labor, is to some extent respected in a society, technology will not thrive. The sequence of the ancient Jewish rabbis, of the Benedictines, of the Tertiaries, and of the post-medieval Puritans helps to explain the vitality of inventiveness in Western culture from the early Middle Ages until today.

(4) The famous Utrecht Psalter, illuminated near Reims about 830, contains a picture showing preparation for battle between the forces of good and evil. At the left—the *sinister* side—is assembled a considerable troop of the Ungodly. At the right—the *dexter* side—stands an alarmingly small cluster of the Righteous led by the Psalmist, King David. God's hand blesses David from a cloud, while a protective angel hovers nervously over him. The picture focuses on the sharpening of two large swords, one in each camp. The Ungodly are using an old-fashioned flat whetstone. The Righteous are using the first firmly datable rotary whetstone, and it is being twirled by the first crank found outside China. The monk who made that remarkable drawing was saying emphatically that technological advance is part of God's moral expectation of mankind. This conviction has continued almost to our own time.

In trying to explain medieval European—and modern—technological inventiveness, one must not oversimplify by exaggerating religious motivations. Clearly, the first agricultural mutations of the early Middle Ages originated among northern pagan groups. Clearly, as China and the Hellenistic age re-

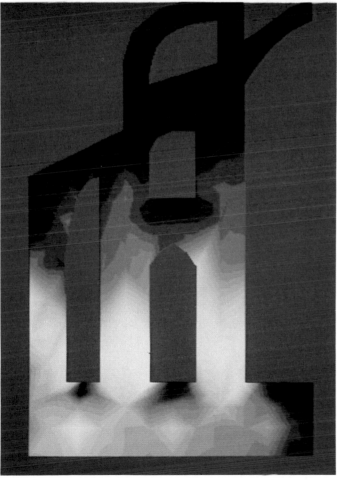

Scientists at Cornell University used computer graphics to analyze structural characteristics of the 13th-century Chartres Cathedral. Top projection shows how flying buttresses transfer the vault's thrust outward to flanking piers; bottom, green and white areas reveal stress concentrations in walls and piers.

veal, invention can prosper without benefit of the Gospel. Clearly again, Eastern Orthodox Christians, far from sharing Latin Christian technological enthusiasm, were often suspicious of machines. The most complex engine of the early Middle Ages, the pipe organ, was considered a secular instrument in the East and thus was never permitted in churches. Beginning in the ninth century, the organ was vastly elaborated in the West and became central to religious music. When, in the 1330s, the even more complex mechanical and astronomical clock was invented in the West, it spread quickly in and on Latin churches as a visual sermon on the orderliness and magnificence of God's creation. In sharp contrast, the Greek Church prohibited clocks of any sort in churches; to have admitted them would have been to contaminate eternity with time. The Christian East felt physically uncomfortable with intricate mechanisms, whereas the Christian West not only enjoyed such machines but concluded that technological advance was part of the divine will for mankind.

Historians of religion have long recognized that the pieties of the Christian Orient and the Christian Occident have two very different flavors, and that this difference produces contrasting cultural results. In the East, sin implies error in thought, to be remedied by illumination. In the West, sin involves wrongdoing, to be remedied by mending one's ways. Greek saints appear generally contemplative; Latin saints tend to be activists. Technology thrives best in a society that values productivity. The ninth-century Benedictine who made the Utrecht Psalter, the Cistercians of the 12th century who rejoiced in the waterpowered industries at Clairvaux, the artists of the 15th century who placed Temperantia's feet on a windmill and decked her head with a clock, Elihu Thomson at the dawn of our own country—all expressed the same fact: that in our Western world, since the end of antiquity, engineering advance has been more closely and explicitly connected with the spiritual values of the dominant religion than has been the case in any other major culture. That is the chief reason why the medieval and modern West has poured such devotion, intelligence, and capital into technological inventiveness. ☐

From the Artisan's Hand

Jon B. Eklund

If necessity were indeed the mother of invention, then ancient technological innovation would regularly appear first in objects of utilitarian intent. Yet it doesn't happen that way. Cyril Stanley Smith of M.I.T., the distinguished metallurgist and historian of technology, realized some years ago that many of the primary sources he had selected for study were objects found in art museums.

The message grew increasingly clear: time and time again it was the artist and the artisan who through close observation and experience discovered and exploited not only basic, but even very subtle, properties of matter.

The debate sparked by Professor Smith's ideas is, in fact, a valid measure of the importance of his

Josiah Wedgwood's 1780 pyrometer—a device for measuring high kiln temperatures—and his famed Portland Vase of 1795 appear together, opposite, to symbolize the union of art and science pioneered by such men as Wedgwood. Glassmaking art joins science at the RCA Laboratories to create a new solar cell, below, intended to draw cheap electricity from sunlight.

theories; little ideas provoke little comment. And his ideas are especially important because the written record is so scant for early periods of civilization.

Over the centuries, as Dr. Smith points out, the attitudes, needs, and achievements of artists have provided a continuing stimulus to technological discovery. They even have served to bring to the reluctant attention of scientists many aspects of the complex structure and nature of matter that science, in its dedication to simplification, would have liked to ignore. The role of sensory experience has been downgraded since the Greek philosophers turned toward the universe of ideals, yet such major achievements as the voyages to the moon depend on men making metals as well as on men making computations based on the theories of Newton and Einstein.

These historical ideas are best demonstrated in the forms and surfaces of artifacts such as those shown here. Most have utility but are hardly utilitarian. In all of them the aesthetic motivation has been substantial and often dominant. Perhaps the only exception is our single example from the present day: the amorphous semiconductor solar cell at lower left. But even this bears the undeniable imprint of the designer, and might well be found in a modern art museum on the basis of its combination of function with form.

A product of a very sophisticated science, the cell serves to remind us first that even solid-state physics incorporates the activities of the artist as part of its prehistory, and second that the great distance to the frontier of modern materials science now keeps the jeweler, the painter, or the potter from being as active in the invention and exploitation of new materials as they were in the past.

Josiah Wedgwood's exquisite Portland Vase and his famous pyrometer for measuring very high tem-

Jon B. Eklund, a curator of chemistry at the National Museum of History and Technology, specializes in 18th-century chemistry and the history of materials.

Photographs by Ross Chapple

74

peratures take us back to the time when the artisan led the scientist in the field of high temperature research. Although Wedgwood was in some ways the epitome of the "hard-headed businessman," he was also a lover of classical art and a contributor to the science of his time.

Wedgwood tried to apply the science of the 18th century to his industrial problems, but usually found himself ahead of contemporary developments and had to play the role of innovator. Through intuition, tireless experimentation, and a highly systematic approach, he solved his problems before they could be handled by the mainstream of science.

The pyrometer he developed, the first to measure temperatures above the boiling point of mercury, is a good example of this pattern. The small white test cylinders of standard dimension and material were exposed to the temperatures he wanted to measure. The resulting shrinkage in the clay was taken as a measure of the degree of heat, determined by reading the dimensions of the cylinder in the ceramic gauge. Wedgwood's perceptions of the properties of his material, gained both from observation of and interaction with clays and other mineral substances, allowed him to invent both new ceramics and a technical device to measure the conditions for firing them.

A somewhat different group of aesthetic needs and practices led ultimately to a deeper knowledge of the structure of metals. For several millennia, artists used corrosive substances to remove selectively portions of materials that did not yield readily to mechanical manipulation. The path from the etched beads produced by the Harappan cultures of Chanhadaro, India, some 4,000 years ago, to etchings by great masters like Dürer or Rembrandt, leads through countless chemical attacks on pieces of stone, shell, and steel.

The legendary swords of the Middle Ages gained in the estimation of both friend and foe when etching brought out patterns produced in the forging processes. The light and dark areas strongly suggest that the material has an internal structure.

In the early 19th century, etching was applied to the very special steel that made up iron-nickel meteorites (which, curiously enough, had long been thought to give special significance to edged weapons). The specimen pictured is of the same type as the famous Elbogen meteorite, the first to be studied in this way. The microcrystalline patterns brought out by the etching are known as Widmannstatten patterns after Alois Widmannstatten, the scientist responsible for metallographic investigation of the Elbogen meteorite.

The visible texture of many crystalline solids in nature is quite suggestive of strong internal regularity even without the mediation of etching. To anyone with an eye for structure, it is impossible to ignore the dramatic external forms of such striking minerals as

Artisans across the ages have marveled at nature's own precise handiwork—crystals of nickel-iron in a meteorite, opposite, and crystals of stone, calcite, above. With new tools and techniques, especially those of atomic physics, scientists solve nature's longkept secrets and turn answers to the use of mankind.

the calcite crystal group shown above. The external regularity reflects the internal arrangement, and in fact mineralogists eventually developed our understanding of the internal arrangements of atoms and ions from the partly aesthetic study of external forms.

But it was a knowledge of aggregate properties rather than the detailed structure which the artist needed to produce the magnificent Chinese ceremonial bronze vessels. Among the earliest civilizations to work bronze, the Chinese displayed a genius for this art that outshone that of their Western counterparts.

Rarely have manipulative skills and artistic design been more closely allied. Although the detail of the surface designs would suggest to modern practitioners the use of the lost-wax method, vessels of this type were actually cast in a clay mold made up of separate sections. This technique gave the artist access to the inner surfaces of the mold which carried the decoration of the piece. Thus each surface design could be worked on separately before the sections were assembled into the final mold. The sectional mold process inevitably reflected the artist's knowledge of the properties of bronze at the temperatures which could be achieved at the time. His knowledge determined the size of channels for the molten metal, the internal sup-

Chinese founders created history's most celebrated bronzeware, cast ceremonial vessels like the type Fang-ting of about 1200 B.C. at left. Above: Chinese "oil-spot" glaze attests to the high excel-lence of Oriental potters. While China originated most of the arts practiced in Japan, the Japanese sometimes advanced technical skills far above levels reached in China.

ports for the mold pieces, and the placement of exhaust holes.

Certain design features also reflect the artisan's knowledge gained from experience with the way metal behaved in sectional molds. The sections of the mold were difficult to seal at the joints, tending to create unpleasant breaks in the surface decor or even "fins" where the metal had flowed into the joint and hardened. A brilliant solution to the problem was to make the breaks part of the design, and to exaggerate the fins into uniform protruding rectangles called flanges. Both thus became a design component instead of disrupting the surface decoration.

The beautiful patterned black surface of the famous "oil-spot" *temmoku* ware of Sung dynasty China illustrates the complex physical and chemical properties manipulated by the ceramic artist. The delicate silvery pattern comes from an interaction of light with two different kinds of crystalline matter at or near the vessel's surface. When the cooling rate was properly controlled, hematite crystals with a metallic luster could form, often after the iron oxide molecules migrated to the site from relatively long distances.

The aesthetic beauty of the surface arises from a complex combination of oxidation, diffusion, and nucleation processes which is only now beginning to be understood. The artist did not need to know the details of the chemistry and physics of these processes, but he did need to understand the processes in terms of his manipulations of the materials and the effects of his fiery furnace.

Although steel is all too often overlooked as an artistic medium, it may well offer the best example of the relationships between art, technology, and science. The technique of etching, developed by the artist for such socially crucial artifacts as the famous Damascus blade and the ornate German morion (beautiful examples of both appear in this article), led ultimately to our scientific and technical knowledge of ferrous metals through the science of metallography. In addition, the artisan's ability to produce iron and steel objects which had such a wide variety of structural properties posed a tremendous challenge for the scientist, as did the incredible miracle of smelting, in which metal came from mineral, malleability from brittleness, reflective lustre from dull earth. The answers began to come in the 18th century, and led to a great deal of research in chemistry and technology, and ultimately in the new disciplines of solid state physics and materials science.

The Japanese sword, however, provides the supreme example of art in steel, as shown by one of the products of the early 14th-century master, Suyemitzu, pictured on the following pages. Though it looks like a single piece of steel, it is actually complex. The core is soft, imparting flexibility. Welded around this is steel of the highest quality which forms the cutting edge and sides. The quality of steel, curiously enough, depends on the amount, nature, and distribution of impurities in the iron, and on the way it is treated thermally and mechanically. The Japanese smith transformed iron into steel through forging, folding, and reforging the hot iron. Each fold creates two layers, so 20 foldings and reforgings would give some two to the 20th power, or more than a million layers. In each layer, the temperature and the blows of the hammer were controlled in a way reflective of each smith's training and experience and beliefs about the material. The same held true for the final process in which the very edge was suddenly cooled, or quenched, while the rest of the blade was protected, leaving the edge intensely hard while the body remained tough.

The result was a welded whole which was at the same time a highly organized assembly, replete with subtle gradations in properties depending on variations in such intimate structural features as grain size and carbon content. The final blade was far more than a weapon: it was an expression of cultural ideas and philosophy as, in varying degrees, is any artifact carefully and skillfully wrought by the hand of man.

As Professor Cyril Smith himself delights in pointing out, "There are many aspects of nature that nature itself, for all its diversity, could not discover until man set up the conditions for it to do so. But the reasons that man did so at first was in order that he could enjoy the results." □

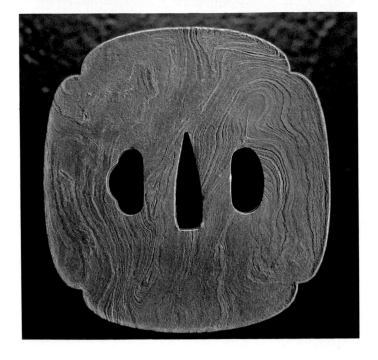

Applying acid, an artisan etched a German helmet of steel circa 1580. Smiths altered iron's crystalline grain by forging to create a Damascus steel blade, above, with detail and sword guard of Japan, bottom. Japanese smiths fashioned the best blades of all time; a 14th-century example is pictured on the following page.

Godfather of American Invention

Silvio A. Bedini

More than any other American public figure, Thomas Jefferson epitomizes the man of invention. Preoccupied throughout a lifetime with the conservation of time and energy, he authored several inventions and modified or adapted numerous existing devices for his own convenience and comfort. "One new idea leads to another," he once wrote to a correspondent, "that to a third, and so on through a course of time until someone, with whom no one of these is original, combines all together, and produces what is justly called a new invention."

Although a born aristocrat, Jefferson was by inclination and conviction a liberal. He had a thorough knowledge of the classics and kept abreast of scientific thought, maintaining a keen awareness of the advances being made in the arts and sciences on both sides of the Atlantic. In fact, he served as a sort of national information center, collecting news of achievements abroad and relaying them to his many correspondents in the new republic. His consuming interest in time and labor saving, with his passion for noting statistics on mundane activities, resulted in numerous devices, even during his career in public office.

Jefferson realized the potential of each new discovery and invention and the manner in which it might be adapted for the common good. Sophisticated in science and skilled in the practical application of mechanical principles, it was in technology that Jefferson distinguished himself as an inventor in his own right.

Jefferson held an obvious advantage over many others of his time in that he was an able draftsman, well equipped with both the skills and the tools required to render an idea into detailed visual form for the guidance of the craftsmen who would produce it. At Monticello, he owned more than 100 slaves, many of them trained with special skills in woodworking and other crafts, who could produce and experiment with the device the master designed. Although he always intended to use his own hands to fabricate these devices

Silvio A. Bedini is the Deputy Director of the Museum of History and Technology. His books include Thinkers and Tinkers: Early American Men of Science.

and prominently displayed an elaborate chest of tools, he never found time to do so.

Moreover, few of Jefferson's ingenious devices at Monticello or his summer residence at Poplar Forest constituted original inventions. The majority were adaptations of others he had noted on his travels. For example, the double dumbwaiter built into the dining room fireplace at Monticello for the provision of table wine from the wine cellar was almost certainly a modification of a similar arrangement in the Café Mécanique in the Nouveau Palais Royal in Paris.

Devices which were probably original with Jefferson include the three-stick folding campstool he used during attendance at church services and while observing the construction of the University of Virginia, the folding ladder for winding the great clock at Monticello, and the folding music stand for a quintet or quartet. The portable copying press, modified from the large stationary copying presses marketed by Boulton & Watt, was his own design adapted from his earlier modification of the portable writing desk. His revolving chair noted in accounts of the day may have also been an original concept.

One of his most important inventions, and one that was completely original with him, might have revolutionized diplomatic and military secret communication from the late 18th century to the present had Jefferson applied it. This was the "cipher wheel," a cryptographic device which employed concentric rings to scramble or unscramble letters in a message. Jefferson prepared detailed instructions for its production and use, and indeed probably did apply it to diplomatic correspondence when he served as Secretary of State. As with most of Jefferson's other inventions and modifications, the genesis of the cipher wheel is readily apparent, inspired by the word or cipher locks commonly used in that period for safeguarding diplomatic dispatch boxes. Interestingly, the cipher wheel was independently "re-invented" just prior to World War I and used from 1922 until recently by the U.S. Army and other military services in the form of Cipher Device M-94. Jefferson's early development of it was not discovered until after the device had been issued as standard Army equipment.

Equally important are Jefferson's inventions in agriculture and agricultural processing. Having concluded that flax was unproductive and injurious to the land, he directed his attention to hemp, which had the disadvantage of requiring considerable effort and time for breaking and beating. To overcome this problem, he devised an efficient hemp-break attachment for threshing machines. He also devised a new timesaving machine for the fulling of wool, and altered a purchased carding machine which resulted in "a less fatiguing composition of force and velocity." His threshing machine combined all parts of the thresher on a single portable frame carried from field to field on two axles of a wagon, thereby expediting the threshing process considerably.

Yet Jefferson's most commonly known invention is his plow, featuring a new moldboard which would "receive the sod after the share has cut under it, to

Thomas Jefferson proudly stands before his finest creation—one shared with other lawmakers—the Declaration of Independence. He is flanked by scientific instruments mentioned in his writings. Bottom right, Jefferson's plow.

raise it gradually, and to reverse it." Having studied the various types of plows in use in Europe and America, he applied scientific principles to the design of a new and more efficient moldboard which would be lighter, more easily made, and capable of plowing a deeper furrow than before with much less effort. Eventually he had the moldboard cast in iron and fitted to a light wooden plow pulled by two small horses, tilling a furrow nine inches wide and six inches deep. Jefferson's description of the plow with drawings was published in the Transactions of the American Philosophical Society, and the moldboard was displayed at the Philadelphia Society for the Promotion of Agriculture. His description was also published in the *Edinburgh Encyclopedia* and in the *Annales du Museum National d'Histoire Naturelle.* In 1807 the Société d'Agriculture de Paris awarded Jefferson a gold medal. Although the moldboard received wide acknowledgment, it did not achieve universal adoption because it was almost immediately supplanted by the all-iron plow developed during the same period.

Despite his concern for the improvement of the quality of life through invention and adaptation of existing conveniences, Jefferson's philosophical opposition to monopoly in any form led him to oppose the granting of patents. "Tho the interposition of government in matters of invention had its use," he wrote to a correspondent in France in 1787, "yet it is in practice so inseparable from abuse that they [the American government] think it better not to meddle with it. We are only to hope therefore that those governments who are in the habit of directing all the actions of their subjects by particular law, may be so far sensible of the duty they are under of cultivating useful discoveries, as to reward you amply for yours. . . ."

Jefferson was concerned that the new Constitution being proposed did not include a bill of rights, for such a bill should provide "clearly and without the aid of sophism . . . for the restriction of monopolies."

In time Jefferson found himself weakening in his position. In 1789 he wrote to James Madison that he approved the Bill of Rights as far as it went, but would like to see the addition of an article specifying that "Monopolies may be allowed to persons for their own productions in literature, and their own inventions in

Cipher device M-94, above, reveals the message Alexandria, Virginia, USA, *when its metal wheels are properly aligned. It was used in World War II. The 18th-century cipher lock opens when the word* ROME *appears. Jefferson probably adapted a cipher lock to make his cipher device, reproduced at top.*

ent system. First of all, the American system was modeled too closely, in his opinion, after that of the British, and he disliked anything that was British. Secondly, he was opposed in principle to the granting of monopolies which might withhold technological progress from individuals and the American public at large. Finally, he continued to quibble over the period for which patents were issued, a period which was also an adoption from the British system. Was the standard period of 14 years adequate in a country which was so large and so sparsely settled and in which he believed that ideas would spread much more slowly than in a densely populated nation like England?

Despite his prejudice against monopolies, Jefferson's experience on the patent board succeeded in persuading him that inventors should be rewarded with a limited monopoly if the arts and manufactures of the new nation were to progress. He later admitted that the patent law "has given a spring to invention beyond my conception." Many of the petitions received were trivial, but he agreed that some of them proved to be of importance when put into practice. Although the fire that destroyed the Patent Office in 1836 left few traces of the earliest patents issued, the record can be partially reconstructed and is revealing if not impressive. The first patent granted by the U.S. was awarded on July 31, 1790, to Samuel Hopkins for "Making Pot and Pearl Ashes." The second was issued on August 6 to Joseph S. Sampson for "Making Candles," and the third granted on December 18 to Oliver Evans for "Manufacturing Flour and Meal."

A new patent law was enacted on February 21, 1793, abolishing the patent board and incorporating some of Jefferson's objections to the original act. It provided for a registration system specifying certain formalities which were all that were required for the granting of patents. The new law was so liberal that it found wide support; in particular it benefited New England, and adoption was advocated by the Federalists and by General Washington. Jefferson continued to have numerous objections, however, expressing particular concern about redundant and "frivolous" patents and the problems they presented.

Jefferson undoubtedly had inventor Oliver Evans in mind when he voiced his reservations, for Evans exemplified a number of his concerns with the abuse of monopolies. Evans was an important late 18th-century American inventor and entrepreneur with many fields of interest and claimed inventions in most of them. He was particularly preoccupied with the movement of materials in manufacturing processes, the best example of which was the flour mill he had constructed in 1785. The mill featured a number of elevators, conveyors, and other equipment for the mechanical transfer of raw materials through the proc-

the arts, for a term not exceeding——[sic] years, but for no longer term and for no other purpose."

The first patent act, introduced during the first session of Congress in 1789, was enacted into law on April 10, 1790. It provided for the creation of a three-man board comprised of the Secretary of State (Jefferson), the Secretary of War, and the Attorney General, who were empowered to grant a patent in the name of the United States "if they shall deem the invention or discovery sufficiently useful and important." Indeed, the American patent system—the system that has both controlled and encouraged the development of American inventions for nearly 200 years—was shaped largely by Jefferson's efforts and by the standards which the first patent board initiated.

Jefferson took great pride in his role as a member of the patent board, but he was constantly aware of the heavy burden of the responsibility, particularly since he continued to doubt the constitutionality of the pat-

ess, including some conveyors that he had conceived and used for the first time, as well as other types already known in principle, but adapted to flour milling by Evans. He applied for and received patents for his flour-mill machinery from the states of Pennsylvania, Maryland, and New Hampshire between 1786 and 1789, and on December 18, 1790, as noted, he was granted the third U.S. patent for the same invention. This was a most important patent for it not only served to test the first patent system, but became the subject of prolonged legislation and political controversy.

Evans's flour mill patent expired in 1804 after having run the established period of 14 years, during which he had collected royalties on mills built by others which incorporated his patented principles. Naturally, he was loathe to surrender his monopoly, and he sought to have his patent renewed or extended.

Evans proved tenacious in his pursuit of what he claimed to be his rights, and his patent continued to be a source of concern and irritation to Jefferson. After the court had declared his patent to be invalid, he was successful in having Congress enact a special law "For the Relief of Oliver Evans," which was approved by President Jefferson (undoubtedly with reluctance!) on January 21, 1808. A new patent was granted Evans on the following day.

The new patent was not *ex post facto* and did not cover the period between the expiration of the first patent and the issuance of a new one. Nevertheless, even before the new patent became effective, Evans proceeded to collect damages and royalties from those who had constructed mills incorporating his principles. He was brash enough to send his collector to then-President Jefferson himself, since the latter's overseer at Monticello had, without Jefferson's knowledge, adopted Evans's improvements in a mill on the plantation. Years later Jefferson commented on the matter to Isaac McPherson: "It happened that I had myself a mill built in the interval between Mr. Evans's first and second patents." Jefferson informed McPher-

son, "I was living in Washington and left the construction to the mill-wright. I did not even know he had erected elevators, conveyors, and hopper-boys until I learned it by an application from Mr. Evans's agent for the patent price. Although I had no idea he had a right to it by law, (for no judicial decision had then been given,) yet I did not hesitate to remit to Mr. Evans the old and moderate patent price, which was what he then asked, from a wish to encourage even the useful revival of ancient inventions."

Jefferson's foreboding about redundant patents proved sound, the Patent Act of 1793 having created more problems than it resolved. The courts became filled with litigation to determine infringement suits and to resolve questions of originality. While patent acts had given considerable incentive to industry and manufacturers, that advantage was soon modified by the great volume of worthless and conflicting patents issued, instances of fraud, distortion, and excessive litigation. A bill thoroughly revising the Patent Act was finally passed on July 4, 1836. The new act provided for the establishment of a Patent Office as an independent bureau of government, headed by a Commissioner of Patents, staffed with its own complete organization, and requiring systematic examination of applications. It was hoped that this patent system could meet the needs of a nation entering its own spectacular industrial revolution.

Jefferson practiced as he preached; he never sought nor obtained patents for any of his own inventions or improvements of those of others, such as the moldboard, hemp-break, or other devices. On the other hand, he clearly stated that he did not wish others to have exclusive rights to them for their own profit. After describing his hemp-break to a correspondent, he added that "as soon as I can speak to its effect with certainty I shall probably describe it anonymously in the public papers, in order to forestall the prevention of its use by some interloping patentee."

Individualist, liberal, and aristocratic genius, Jefferson had labored long to mold his particular philosophy into the structure of the republic. Both devotion to the magnificence of the inventive act and his concern for the rights of the inventor were subordinated to his quest for an egalitarian state in which no one, not even legally buttressed patent holders, would jeopardize the popular welfare. Although he lived in another era with ideals suited to its less centralized, pre-industrial social state, nonetheless, as a man with a critical eye for the proper position of the inventor in the *res publica*, Jefferson remains peerless. □

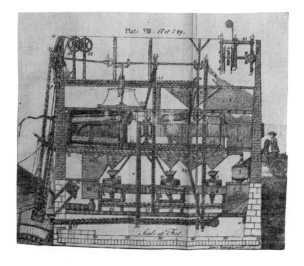

Jefferson tangled legally over patent rights for Oliver Evans's flour mill—perhaps the world's first automated factory—developed and operated in Philadelphia about 1800.

3
PART

Engines of Technology

Inventions, as we all know, sometimes lead to new technologies—new tools, new methods, new products. But what exactly is technology? In the broad, anthropological sense, technology encompasses a society's knowledge of the ways to make or do things. But in a narrower vein, technology is the application of the fruits of research to practical ends—usually industrial or commercial. Engineers are the practitioners of this kind of technology, and in America at least, we often think of them—unfairly, perhaps—in terms of the huge machines and structures they create. We see this tendency toward the very large manifested in the engineering of the landscape, which has rearranged the flow of nearly every American river with dams and provided us with the toothed skylines of our cities.

But there are also technologies of the small and the commonplace. The camera, for example, known in the 17th century, had to await the invention of usable film before it could become a tool for art, a cumbersome one to be sure. And it was not the urge to aggrandize but rather to miniaturize that in recent decades has placed a camera within the reach of virtually anyone.

Some inventions, however, create no new technology at all; alongside such marvelous but impossible devices as perpetual motion machines exist numberless other dead ends. Indeed, many seem mere flashes in the pan, usually well intended, sometimes downright fraudulent. Yet what a wealth of technological benefits invention has brought us, for all its peculiar nature.

Bigger, Better, Faster

Today, airplanes are the most highly visible form of high technology. Thousands of jet airliners carry hundreds of thousands of passengers daily—at the speed of a pistol bullet—with all the excitement of a city bus ride . . . and far less hazard.

Of course, it wasn't always so, although the pace of aircraft design has been astonishing even by the accelerated standards of the 19th and 20th centuries. There are still many alive today who can remember skies without airplanes. In the 1880s and '90s, when those people were young, there was intense interest in flight in Europe and America, and it was evident that technology and materials would soon enable someone to build a practical heavier-than-air machine.

In 1891, in Germany, Otto Lilienthal made the first of several thousand successful flights in gliders controlled, like hang-gliders today, by the shifting of the pilot's weight. American-born Sir Hiram Maxim, inventor of the machine gun and many other devices, tested a huge, overly heavy steam-powered flying machine at his English estate in 1894.

In late-Victorian America, experiments were being conducted with both gliders and powered machines by such notables as eminent bridge builder/engineer Octave Chanute and Secretary of the Smithsonian Samuel Pierpont Langley. Langley, interested in

powered flight, had perhaps the greatest resources available to any of the American experimenters. He conducted numerous sophisticated aerodynamic tests and successfully flew steam-powered models in 1896. Then came war with Spain, and in 1898, with an initial grant of $50,000 from the War Department, Langley began the development of a large, man-carrying flying machine. Beset by innumerable difficulties, not the least of which was the growing skepticism of the War Department, Langley at last felt that the machine was ready for a test flight. In October 1903, with his assistant Charles Manly at the controls, the machine was launched; failing to achieve even level flight, it nosed into the Potomac River. In a subsequent test in December, it collapsed, just nine days before the successful Wright brothers' flights at Kitty Hawk.

It was left to the relatively unknown Wright brothers to be first to fly a controllable, heavier-than-air, powered machine—their 1903 *Flyer*. The Wrights were anything but the "bicycle mechanics" that legend has made them. They owned a prosperous bicycle sales and repair concern in Dayton at a time when bicycling was perhaps the most popular sport in the Western world. Above all, they were careful men, first-rate engineers though not formally trained, so when they decided to fly, they went about it in a careful, organized way. They built box kites and then gliders to try out their theories of aerodynamics and control. After their second glider proved unsatisfactory, they built one of the earliest wind tunnels in America and conducted thousands of meticulously recorded tests of airfoils and control surfaces. Their third glider had much improved control devices.

When they returned to Kitty Hawk in the winter of 1903, they brought with them a powered machine (they had made the engine themselves) capable of sustained, controlled flight. They actually made four

Gleaming six-foot driving wheels, left, of the Museum of History and Technology's Southern Railway locomotive highlight the glorious power of the steam age. The Boeing 747's cavernous fuselage, right, can swallow over 350 people, then whisk them a quarter of the way around the world nonstop.

The Wrights—Orville (1871-1948), left, and Wilbur (1867-1912) with one of their later machines, by Albert Herter, ANA.

Duesenberg Js, thought by many to be America's greatest automobiles, were fast (120 mph), expensive ($8,500 for chassis alone), and rare (about 450 made). The 1930 dual-cowl phaeton seen here typifies the classics of the 1920s and '30s.

flights on December 17, 1903, Orville the first and Wilbur the last. The last was remarkable in that the machine flew over 800 feet and remained aloft for 59 seconds, a feat that no one else (except the Wrights) equaled for more than three years.

By the end of World War I in 1918, almost all of the elements of the modern airplane had been at least conceived, if not built. Jet propulsion, radio, all-metal construction, retractable landing gear, and the host of other features of the modern airplane were available as ideas or crude devices; but the techniques, the materials, and the impulse to put them together were lacking. Fifteen years of fits and starts would pass before the next breathtaking leap.

Oddly enough, it was in the depths of the Depression, 1932 to 1936, that all of the techniques and materials came together. There were at the time almost no passengers; but as technological progress made it possible to build a comfortable, safe, economical airliner, the impulse of the more far-sighted airlines was to order it and develop the market around it. The result was the birth of the modern airliner and the subsequent growth of air travel.

The first of these modern airliners was the Boeing 247, an all-metal, twin-engine monoplane carrying 10 passengers in addition to its two crewmen. The 247 entered service in 1933, but was swiftly outdated by the Douglas DC-2. Carrying 14 passengers, the DC-2 was larger, faster, and cheaper to operate than the Boeing 247. And on the heels of the DC-2 came the DC-3, carrying 21 passengers—even faster and more comfortable than any of its predecessors. It benefited from all the technological advances of recent years: wind tunnel testing, improved engines, variable-pitch propellers, wing flaps, improved fuels, immensely durable all-metal construction, more efficient operating procedures, and hundreds of others. Above all, the DC-3 was economical: its seat-mile operating costs were one-half to one-third lower than those of any other airliner of the time. In all, just under 12,000 civilian and military versions were built. Hundreds if not thousands are still flying today.

The Second World War prevented the successors of the DC-3 from following too closely upon it, but as soon as the war was over, a parade of bigger, faster, higher- and farther-flying types came into airline service. Radar became common and cabins were pressurized, permitting higher and faster flight. Operating costs actually rose toward the end of this period, as the technological limit was reached with these propeller-driven, piston-engined types.

Then, with a roar, in 1959 the big jets arrived. Boeing, using its experience gained while building advanced jet-engined bombers and transports for the Air Force, had first flown the 707 in 1954. The 707 and its

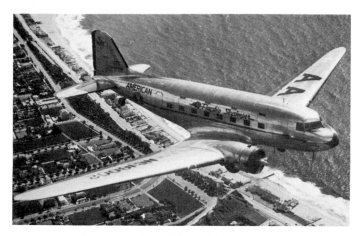

Once queen of the skies, the indefatigable DC-3 still serves many airlines and corporations. Some DC-3s have flown over 80,000 hours, a total of more than nine years in the air.

chief competitor, the Douglas DC-8, were nearly twice as fast as their immediate piston-engined ancestors and carried about twice as many passengers. Moreover, they were, again, much more reliable, safer, more comfortable, and cheaper to operate, per seat-mile, than the older generation.

The story since then is well known. Most of the commercial niches have now been filled by jet or propeller-driven gas-turbine aircraft of various sizes. Wide-body jets, taking advantage of the economy of scale, carry 350 or more passengers many times more efficiently than did the best piston-engined airliners of 25 years ago.

Just as the airliner has come to dominate long-distance mass transport in America, so has the automobile been this country's overwhelming choice as the vehicle of personal transportation. The automobile represents a single idea—individual motorized transport—carried to an extraordinary extreme in an attempt to reach every corner of a huge and diverse market. If every combination of color, model, and make offered by the four largest American auto makers today were counted, the possible choices would run into the thousands—but all would still be variations on the same theme.

Today's situation is very different from that which prevailed early in this century, when hundreds of small manufacturers offered highly idiosyncratic machines. Particularly after the introduction of the electric starter for gasoline engines in 1912, the short-range, low-speed electric automobile died, to be followed into limbo by the steamers (though one luxury steamer, the Doble, lasted well into the 1930s).

The roots of the gasoline-engined automobile are obscure, although it is generally accepted that Nikolaus Otto built the first commercial four-stroke-cycle gasoline engine (the progenitor of millions) in Ger-

many in 1877, and that Gottlieb Daimler and Karl Benz used similar engines in 1886 in, respectively, a four-wheeled vehicle and a tricycle.

In America, the genealogy is equally murky. However, it can be said with assurance that the Duryea twins, Charles and Frank, of Chicopee, Massachusetts, drove a phaeton carriage powered by a single-cylinder gasoline engine 200 feet on September 20, 1893.

During the early days, demand for automobiles, whether cheap or expensive, was mainly from urban areas. Rural roads and even most intercity roads were rutted, often muddy, and nearly impassable by automobile. As demand from the cities grew and automobiles began to be big business, the horseless carriage's quaintness and simplicity quickly disappeared. As in the case of airplanes, most of the features of the modern automobile were conceived very early on. Advanced engine designs, welded and stamped body panels, automatic transmissions, power steering and brakes, independent suspensions, and other now standard elements had all been tried in one automobile or another by the 1920s.

However, the automobile needed a wider market. Only if millions were sold would America's roads improve—and the many technological advances be incorporated into machines the average man could afford. Henry Ford built the car that both created and fitted the market.

The Model T was introduced in late 1908. By 1926, when production of the Model T ceased, more than 15,000,000 had been sold, some for as little as $290. The Model T's 20-horsepower four-cylinder engine was as straightforward and simple as anyone far from a service station could hope for. Its two-speed (and reverse), pedal-operated transmission was easy to operate. Its high ground clearance and supple suspension usually defeated those rutted, muddy rural roads, and its high-strength steel chassis made it nearly indestructible. All in all, it was the perfect car for a suddenly car-mad population.

Henry Ford is popularly credited with introducing the mass production line; of course, he did nothing of the sort. But he did introduce the moving assembly line, a manufacturing innovation that contributed immeasurably to the low cost of the Model T.

Then, during much of 1927, the great Ford factories were largely silent as they retooled for a new design—the Model A. But almost simultaneously, General Motors initiated the annual model change, which Henry Ford had always spurned, and with the model change came the revolution in automobile manufacturing and merchandising. In those terms, at least, the industry has never looked back.

However, the American automobile, like the airliner of the '40s and '50s, sat on a technical plateau for a long time. After the end of the Second World War, each year's new models tended to be bigger, faster, and more reliable, but less economical to run.

Now, as oil supplies dwindle and fuel prices rise, the trend is swinging toward smaller, more efficient machines like those developed so successfully by fuel-poor Europe and Japan. But there is much room for invention here. If we are to continue to enjoy our personal automobiles, they must be made even more efficient. To do so will require careful analysis of the benefits and drawbacks of the various alternate power plants and construction materials, for we cannot afford the time and expense to repeat the 80-odd-year-development of the conventional piston-engined automobile. Whatever the automobile of the future is made of or propelled by, it seems clear that small is going to be beautiful.

While the end of the 19th and beginning of the 20th centuries saw the railroad's prime, the automobile's childhood, and the airplane's birth, it also witnessed the decline of American maritime commerce. The sea has always made conservatives of shipbuilders as well as seamen, and ship design and shipbuilding technology evolved very slowly before the 19th century, at least by today's standards. But at about that time, in several countries, individuals with little, if any, connection with the sea turned their inventive energies toward adapting the steam engine to the boat. In America, beginning in 1786, John Fitch, James Rumsey, Griffen Green, John Stevens, Robert Fulton, and others designed or built river steamboats, though Fulton's *The North River Steamboat (Clermont)* of 1807-1808 was the first commercial success. By 1811, steamboats had reached the western rivers, where they rapidly evolved into their famous "wedding cake" appearance. The western rivers' seasonally low water and rapid currents forced the design of shallow-draft boats with large, high-pressure engines mounted on the main deck and other decks built in layers above.

Before railroads penetrated the heartland, steamboats flourished; 757 of them plied western rivers by 1855. But steam took much longer to become established at sea; early engines were inefficient and coaling ports few and far between. So while steam awaited its time, sail experienced a sudden last evolutionary spurt or two before becoming extinct. The beautiful, brutal clipper ships of the 1840s and '50s were perhaps the highest expression of wooden shipbuilding. Heavily sparred, sharp-built vessels from Boston and New York amazed the world with their speedy passages to California and China. But they were doomed by their very design. Driven like racing yachts, they were too lightly built to last, and were mankillers besides. Their fine lines reduced cargo capacity, while their immense sail area required large crews. Faced with economic depression at home and steamship competition at sea, they died before the Civil War.

The practical steamship, mostly a British development, appeared when powerful steam engines, screw-propulsion, and iron (later steel) construction made possible large, reliable vessels, able to steam long distances without refueling. While Great Britain, dependent on imports to feed its mighty industrial machine, vigorously built a great steam merchant fleet, the United States turned away from the sea after the Civil War and poured its energy and population into the development of the vast midcontinent.

The U.S. merchant fleet has remained relatively large, though a number of foreign fleets are larger, and foreign-flag vessels carry much of the freight and oil that enter this country today. Recent technological advances have made possible high-speed, container-carrrying freighters, giant tankers, and improved navigation systems. However, much remains to be done in design and control of shipping, as recent tanker disasters have shown.

For those who loved them, the passing of the great ocean liners, victims of air travel, has been a grievous loss. Like the clippers, the ocean liners were big, fast, and ultimately inefficient. Take, for example, the last American liner and the fastest of them all, the S.S. *United States,* designed by William F. Gibbs and in service in 1952. On her maiden voyage, she set a record that has yet to be equaled—traveling 2,949 nautical miles in three days, 10 hours, and 40 minutes. But her huge crew, prodigious thirst for oil, and low speed compared to an airplane, made her uncompetitive. She was laid up in 1969.

Ships, airplanes, automobiles, and locomotives, like most other products of technology, follow evolutionary patterns of growth, stasis, decline, then either extinction or rebirth in a new form. In America, at least, all have grown larger and larger, mostly in the name of efficiency. Yet recently, it has been determined that the most efficient means of transportation known is the bicycle. The bicycle requires less energy to move a person than a jumbo jet, an ocean liner, a railroad train, an economy car, a horse, or even that person walking on his own feet. How ironic that we've been working all these years toward the bigger, the better, the faster when, all the time, the ultimate form of transportation has been used principally to deliver newspapers. □

Alexis Doster III

Mighty screws turned by 240,000 horsepower once drove the S.S. United States's *53,350-ton hull 868 nautical miles in one 24-hour period, a feat never equaled by any other ship.*

Rails: from Old World to New

John H. White, Jr.

American railroad engineering practice illustrates several basic trends that seem characteristic of most United States technologies. These involve the adapting or refining of foreign inventions to our needs, cheapening the mechanism without impairing its effectiveness, and markedly increasing its capacity for greater productivity. We did not invent the railroad, but we did reshape it for our specific needs, devising ways to produce economical rolling stock, tracks, and structures to suit our small purse. And in time we greatly enlarged all elements of the railway on a scale rarely attempted elsewhere in the world.

There are factors involved in railroad engineering which can be found in other areas of the mechanical arts, factors so obvious that they tend to be overlooked in most histories of inventions. In art or science, invention can be done for its own sake. The individual's urge to create and explore is satisfied. The end can be an

John Hoxland White, Jr., Curator of the Division of Transportation in the National Museum of History and Technology, is also the Editor of Railroad History.

original theory, an imaginative formula, or simply a beautiful object. But in engineering, invention must have a practical end. It must not only work satisfactorily, it must work within a given cost range and yield a predictable profit.

It was this overriding concern with cost that forced American railway pioneers to modify radically England's greatest 19th-century invention, the steam railway. England possessed the technology and capital to do everything on a grand scale and so it is not surprising that her first public railways were engineering monuments. Imposing stone viaducts spanned valleys, and magnificent, temple-like stations were erected in major cities. Locomotives and cars were highly finished and lavishly trimmed. Rails were solid wrought-iron bars fastened to stone block sleepers. It was all splendidly and expensively done, but it was necessary to build a first-class system if the British railway were to compete with the already established canal and highway networks.

The situation in North America differed greatly with that continent's vast area, small population, and

Inspired by colorful British engines, the green and gold livery of the Southern Railway's Pacific-type locomotives gave a different look to usually funereal U.S. railroads of the 1920s. Built by the

American Locomotive Company, 92-foot-long Number 1401 now stands in the Smithsonian's Railroad Hall, retired in 1951 by less magnificent, but more efficient diesels.

few, widely scattered cities. Canals and roads were scarce, and no rivers connected the settled seacoast regions to the interior because of the mountain ranges stretching from Maine to Georgia. Thus the railway was viewed by some visionaries as the best way to solve our transportation difficulties.

Naturally, the first American railroad builders turned to England for their models. The Boston and Lowell line was a near-perfect replica of the Liverpool and Manchester, while the Baltimore and Ohio began bravely building great stone viaducts and laying track after the British style. But climate and economics soon forced the pragmatic Yankee engineers to find alternative ways to build a railway. They did not set out to produce a better railway than the British, but to fabricate a cheaper one, and the most direct way to lower costs was to lower standards. Level, direct lines involving excavations, fills, tunnels, and bridges were expensive, whereas meandering routes that followed rivers and ran around obstacles were, though less efficient, far cheaper to build. Scarce capital dictated the choice, and the lines could always be rebuilt later (as indeed they were, many times).

Americans proved masters of the art of building an inexpensive railway. Great forests offered excellent timber in seemingly inexhaustible abundance. Why build railways of stone and imported iron when so much wood was at hand? We turned quickly to the expediency of strap rail and wooden beam tracks, timber trestles, and wooden stations. Embankments and culverts were framed or cribbed with log retaining walls. Wood was used for locomotive fuel and car construction. While the British boasted of their Iron Roads, we could only apologize for our seedy, frequently unsafe, but inexpensive Wooden Roads.

These construction techniques enabled us to build a provisional system of railways rapidly. And no one laid down track faster than Americans. Despite wars and depressions we averaged 2,500 miles of track a year between 1830 and 1890. By the beginning of the 20th century more than one-half of the world's rail mileage crisscrossed this country.

Track construction assumed its modern form during this period, with Robert L. Stevens's introduction in the 1830s of T-section rails and wooden crossties. These replaced the older iron strap, wooden beam rails which, being weak, could support only light, slow locomotives and furthermore tended to peel up, causing numerous accidents. Stevens's T-section rail and wooden crossties are now a worldwide standard.

Early American engineers, then, reshaped the British railway and track structure. It should be noted that at the very time these developments were under way, other engineers modified and redesigned British locomotives and cars. Here again, the goal was to change only that which was necessary to adapt the mechanism to local needs. English inventors had developed the locomotive from the cumbersome steam carriage of 1804 to a fast and well proportioned unit of motive power by 1829. The general arrangement remained fixed from that date until the end of steam locomotion in 1960. The horizontal, multitubular boiler, separate firebox, power transmission by connecting rods (rather than gears), and blast-pipe exhaust remained fundamental. Of course, the locomotive grew dramatically in size, and many auxiliary appliances were added over the years, but the basic plan stayed the same.

From the tender, coal passed via stoker screw to the firebox, where it heated boiler water to provide steam at 210 pounds per square inch to a pair of 27 inch-in-diameter cylinders. Polished steel rods connected the cylinders' pistons to six-foot driving wheels. The four-wheel front, or pilot, truck guided the 280-ton locomotive and tender around the next bend.

The first locomotives used in this country were imported from England in 1829. While they could perform admirably on the level, straight British lines, they were ill-suited to our crooked, feeble tracks. They had trouble negotiating the sharp curves and tended to derail frequently. An English engine on the Mohawk and Hudson Railroad was said to give "audible complaint of hard service" when passing through a curve. The line's chief engineer, a gifted man named John B. Jervis, found the British locomotive to be as near perfection as possible for a steam engine, but sadly lacking in the agility required for the makeshift American tracks. Jervis solved this problem in 1832 by designing an engine with a four-wheel carriage, or truck, attached under the front of the locomotive by a center pin so that the truck was free to swivel as it followed the track, thus guiding the locomotive around curves.

British regulations called for smokeless locomotives, and the only sure way to accomplish this was to burn coke, a distillate of bituminous coal. At the time, America mined very little coal and produced almost no coke; however, wood was our common fuel, and so deep, narrow fireboxes became the hallmark of American locomotives. Because of the need for more power to overcome grades, American engineers began to increase boiler pressure which subsequently increased the danger of explosion—much to the horror of overseas rail officials.

Because our operations differed so from those of the British, our locomotives were soon loaded with appurtenances. Bells and steam whistles were added to warn pedestrians, cattle, and carriages to clear the tracks. Headlights were a necessity for night running, and the cowcatcher was introduced to cope with the foolhardy steer that would not yield the right-of-way to the train.

Climate, too, had its effect on locomotive design. Bitter winters, for example, necessitated shelters for the operating crews. The earliest engines provided a railing around the platform or the cab floor, and some enterprising engineers began to erect shelters as early as 1831. Gradually the cab became more common, particularly in New England, and by 1850 it was a standard fixture.

Less obvious than the addition of headlights, cabs, and cowcatchers was the substitution of materials used in American locomotive construction. Here is a fine example of innovative engineering at the shop level, one almost never reported in the histories of inventions that tend to dwell on inspired geniuses and great leaps forward, thus disregarding much of the real progress made by ordinary men in workaday situations. Our engineering ancestors discovered many ways to lower the cost of locomotives by using cheaper materials than those employed by European builders. Wrought iron was substituted for copper fireboxes with no loss of efficiency or safety, and we made wholesale use of cast-iron parts in place of iron forgings. Cast iron was often cheaper because iron castings required less machinery and skill than the manufacture of wrought-iron parts. Wheels, tires, and even such unlikely parts as crank axles were made of cast iron. In 1880 it was estimated that 33 percent of an American locomotive was cast iron.

Railroad car design also came to America from England, in the form of small, four-wheel cars with side doors, normally divided into three compartments like contemporary city omnibuses. This style proved unsatisfactory for American use, and so between 1831 and 1835, car builders invented a new style of railroad passenger car. The new body, a long, open, single compartment, held seats arranged on both sides of a center aisle. The entrance doors were positioned at the ends rather than on the sides of the body. Platforms at the end of the car permitted access to the doors. The car was carried by two wheel sets or trucks attached to the underframe by center pins, and so were free to swivel, permitting the car to traverse sharp curves. The American coach had several advantages over its European counterpart. The double-truck running gear did away with the galloping ride characteristic of four-wheel cars, while the elimination of multiple compartments made construction lighter, stronger, simpler, and less expensive. The basic soundness of this plan is demonstrated by its endurance. The most modern American rail cars, including the Metroliner, continue to be built on this old arrangement.

Inventiveness should not be thought of only as the discovery of a new device. It can also involve a new way of using existing tools. Straightline developments requiring no new machines often result in the greatest benefits to mankind. American railroads' efficiency and carrying capacity began to soar in the 1890s, not

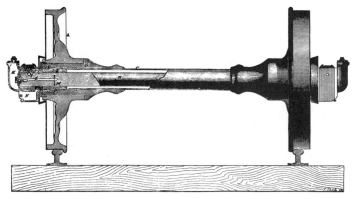

Patent Compound Car Axle: George W. Miltimore.

A feature common to all modern railways, the flanged wheel riding on an inverted T-shaped track can be seen in this otherwise unusual wheel-axle scheme submitted by a hopeful inventor.

Silver Palace Sleeping Car Number 76, top, exemplifies cars that sold railroading to Americans after the Civil War. Above, central aisles frequently had upper berths folding down from the wall. Seats converted into lower berths.

because of radical technical innovations but because of a growth in all elements of the physical plant. Bigness became the essence of American railroading. Twenty-five- and 30-ton locomotives gave way to 60- and 90-ton machines. And these were not just a few special monsters built for pusher service; they were commonplace engines built for standard use. Passenger cars, though still all wood, stretched out to 70 or even 80 feet in length. Freight cars grew from 10- to 30-ton capacity, and all-steel cars began to be produced commercially. Longer trains were being assembled and operated at higher and higher speeds. For many years 25 miles an hour was the best average one could expect, even aboard the fastest trains. In 1875, the New York Central's finest New York-to-Chicago train took 37

hours to make the trip. By 1938 the time was reduced to 16 hours.

Care must be taken not to ascribe these advances exclusively to better locomotives and cars. The whole railroad had to be upgraded. The steam locomotive, since the time of the *Rocket* (1829), had demonstrated its ability for fast running. But the tracks of the early period, as we have seen, were not built for such speeds. Only after traffic increased to provide larger earnings could the industry justify large-scale improvements in tracks and rolling stock. Greater traffic was, of course, directly tied to an increasing industrial output and population growth. As the American economy matured, so did the railroads. As tonnage and passenger mileage mounted, the railroads had no choice but to increase their capacity. At their peak in 1916 they were carrying 77 percent of the intercity freight traffic and 98 percent of the intercity passenger traffic. The nation at that time was more dependent on the railway than it is today on the highway.

What was true in 1916 is but a memory today. Passenger traffic has all but disappeared, and freight tonnage has slipped to less than 40 percent of the total goods moved in the U.S. The railroad has become essentially a bulk carrier, a new role which has generated new equipment and operating procedures. What is seen by some as a dying industry depends on the inventive process to stay alive. Since the Second World War, diesel-electric locomotives, introduced in 1924, have almost completely replaced steam locomotives, while freight cars have grown from 40 to 70 feet and have reached 100 tons in weight. A variety of special-purpose cars has emerged, such as the triple-deck automobile-carrying cars. The idea for these cars came from Europe but, typically, we greatly expanded the unit size and more fully capitalized on the carrying ability of such vehicles. As a result, the railroads are now carrying a major portion of the new automobiles shipped—a market they had almost entirely lost to motor trucks by 1960.

The American railroad has evolved remarkably in the past several decades. While mileage, employment, and the number of locomotives and cars have declined significantly, its carrying capacity, based on ton-miles, has nearly doubled. This seeming paradox will not surprise anyone who has studied American railroad history and understands the industry's ability to survive by subtly modifying its technology to meet new challenges. □

3
PART

Engineering the Landscape

"I think I could stop here myself and do miracles," exulted Walt Whitman in viewing the engineering challenges of the American land. He yearned to span the continent, to connect America with the world by the "strong light works of engineers." And when one considers the highways, bridges, dams, and towers that have sprung up since Whitman wrote—some of the highest, tallest, longest in the world—one can share his sense of excitement.

Though Whitman felt that Americans were divinely called to "hook and link" their riven land together, others have wondered whether our engineering tendencies have not been more of a curse than a blessing. The Austrian commentator Francis Grund, who traveled through America in the 1830s (a generation before Whitman), spoke of how, with our ceaseless constructions, we had barbarously treated nature as a conquered subject. American engineers, he wrote, had "burned the forests, dug up the bowels of the earth, diverted rivers from their courses . . . and annihilated the distances which separated the North from the South, and the East from the West."

Road building was indeed an initial need of a republic striving to organize as a nation. And in that tradition the present-day U.S. highway system, covering four million miles of our country with asphalt and concrete, is regarded by some as a monument to American engineering. Yet here, as with other aspects of the engineer's art, one may question how much mankind has actually won when nature has been defeated, or at any rate bulldozed.

While roads stimulate the economy, they have always been expensive. The first notable—and cost-excessive—American road was the National Road, which ran from the Potomac River at Cumberland, Maryland, over the Alleghenies to Wheeling, West Virginia. It was built in the early 1800s before the invention of a well drained macadam road surface had come to these shores. Actually, macadam owes as much to the French military engineer Tresaquet as to the Scotsman J. L. McAdam, for it was in France that the method of paving roads with broken stones pounded or rolled into a turtle-backed shield was first established. Built of loose stone, sand, and gravel, the National Road was expected to cost the people $6,000 a mile for each of its 112 miles, an expenditure that seemed justified as Ohio's rich farmland was being set-

Wrapping 2,150 iron wires in two thick cables slung over stone piers, John Augustus Roebling successfully suspended an aqueduct across the Delaware River, above, in 1850. He went on to build the famed Brooklyn Bridge, sire of today's Verrazano-Narrows Bridge, left. Following where Roman and English road designers led, American engineers create complex structures like the multilevel Georgia intersection, opposite.

tled. Yet on its completion in 1818, the road came in at about $13,000 a mile. An army engineer investigating the scandal reported that one factor contributing to the overrun was that the contractors tended to charge twice for the materials they supplied (and of course the government paid twice). The U.S. government withdrew from the road-building business immediately, leaving the paving of the nation to states and private companies. It wasn't until automobiles became numerous in the 1920s that the government set up the Public Roads Administration; the first cloverleaf bloomed in the early '30s, turnpikes spread, and the era of the superhighway was upon us.

Roads lead eventually to bridges, and it is in the special craft of bridge building that engineers have displayed some of their finest art. City pride, not national programs, has led to great bridges in the U.S. Such pioneering structures as James B. Eads's 1874

bridge across the Mississippi at St. Louis (the first American bridge to use steel in large quantities) and John Augustus Roebling's 1883 Brooklyn Bridge (at 1,600 feet between towers, the longest suspension bridge of its day) sprang forth because city fathers saw free-flowing transportation as the way to keep their ports thriving. It is a tribute to the engineering genius of Eads and Roebling that both bridges still stand— though recent underwater inspections of the Brooklyn Bridge have revealed that poor maintenance is threatening the stonework of the piers.

Roebling was both the technical wizard who developed the long-span suspension bridge (giving us, by inheritance, such modern wonders as the Verrazano-Narrows Bridge), and the philosopher who saw that an engineering event might be a geographical celebration: that nature might be enhanced rather than effaced by a massive structure. In the preface to his re-

After medical teams discovered sources of yellow fever and malaria, President Theodore Roosevelt's army engineers could

complete work on Panama Canal, including the massive Culebra Cut, below, and six double locks large enough for battleships.

38-X² Culebra Cut, Culebra, Looking north from Contractor's Hill, May 17, 1913.

port on the bridge, he stated, perhaps immodestly, "The contemplated work, when constructed in accordance with my designs, will not only be the greatest Bridge in existence, but it will be the greatest engineering work of this continent, and of the Age. Its most conspicuous features, the great towers, will serve as landmarks to the adjoining cities, and they will be entitled to be ranked as national monuments."

Like many engineers of his day, Roebling abandoned iron for steel when designing the Brooklyn Bridge. He invented a sheave some five feet in diameter that spun steel wires into cables as it whirled back and forth between the shores. Each wire (of which there are 21,184 gathered in the bridge's four cables) measures one-sixth of an inch in diameter, with a tensile strength of 160,000 pounds per square inch. Heavy wire ropes hanging from cables support the bridge's roadway; stays radiating from the towers lend

Photos, right and below, show boats going up- and downstream through fabled Erie Canal locks.

solidity, and trusswork stiffens the roadway. Roebling feared that winds or the eventual traffic might make the suspended bridge sway, but lack of vibration remains one of the bridge's most notable characteristics.

Just as certain bridges seem to fulfill Whitman's dream of bringing man and nature together, so do some canals, especially the older ones, convey a kind of harmony between man the engineer and the land on which he works. Looking at the locks of the 1825 Erie Canal at Lockport, New York, it is possible to admire both the ingenuity of the builders and the charm of the towns that grew along the canal.

The Erie took eight years to build—the sweating labors of Irish and German workers being quite as remarkable as the engineering accomplishments. Some anonymous inventor devised a stump puller on giant wheels that enabled a team of horses and seven men to lever out more than 30 stumps a day. Whereas hydraulic cement had to be imported at first from England (as was the very idea of canal building), an Erie engineer assisting Chief Benjamin Wright discovered in New York State the kind of limestone suitable for making cement. From then on work on the locks' foundations went forward using native materials.

To make the climb from the Hudson River to Lake Erie, the canal had to rise 420 feet in 363 miles, calling for some 83 locks. Their size (50 feet by 10 feet) determined the canal's destiny, as they could not accommodate the larger canal boats needed for the growing commercial traffic. The life of this most profitable of the many canal-building projects spawned in the first half of the 19th century—before railroads took over the scene—therefore ended with that century. The Erie was replaced by the New York State Barge Canal, which today permits large carriers to make the historic run from Albany to Buffalo.

Of course, not all American canals have made a pleasant peace with their landscapes. The staggering example to the contrary is the Panama Canal, which James Bryce once called "the greatest liberty man has ever taken with nature." This great canal rivals the Suez as the world's most important; 40 miles long, wide enough for a battleship, it was carved through the backbone of the Continental Divide to link the Pacific and Atlantic Oceans.

Thoughts of such liberties continue to haunt the imagination as one stands at the base of Hoover Dam or Glen Canyon Dam, both in Arizona and both on the list of the world's 20 highest dams. They're the tallest, broadest walls you've ever seen (700 feet from

river to rim), restraining virtual seas (Lakes Mead and Powell, respectively). In plan, they're both arches with the heads pointing upstream. Historians point out that, for all the ingenuity in building these curved and fragile-looking dams of the West, the basic form originated in the sixth century A.D., designed by the same Byzantine architects who gave us the ethereal but solid domes of Santa Sophia.

For their huge successes on the ground, American engineers have been best known for their works that penetrate the clouds . . . the skyscrapers. And although the tallest of them all, the 1,454-foot-high Sears tower, stands in Chicago, New York has ever been the skyscraper's home. Indeed, Manhattan Island, with its granite base and restricted area, seems naturally designed to host a battalion of towers marching from the Battery up to Columbia Heights.

Controversy rages as to who invented this characteristically American form. One strong argument is that Vermonter Elisha Otis should be regarded as the skyscraper's inventor because his passenger elevators

Conceiving works that span whole regions, engineers build huge harnesses for this country's resources. Seeming to glow with the power they carry, pylons march away from the Jim Bridger Steam Electric Project in Wyoming, opposite, transporting electricity to the Pacific Coast. Visible even from space, lakes backed up behind Hoover and Glen Canyon dams were spotted by astronauts as they circled Earth. At Glen Canyon, top and left, engineers blocked the Colorado with a 710-foot-high dam.

made them possible. A difficulty here is that Otis, having demonstrated that his lifts were perfectly safe at the Crystal Palace in New York City in 1854, died in 1861, aware only that they had been successfully installed in a couple of limited-purpose buildings. Another candidate is insurance company vice president Henry Baldwin Hyde, who combined an elevator with an office building so successfully in 1872 that other Manhattan real estate hustlers began to raise their mansard roofs and take eager tenants up to spaces previously shunned. Yet a third contender is William LeBaron Jenney, who introduced the load-bearing iron frame structure in Chicago in 1885, a system that reached New York by the end of that decade and enabled even loftier towers to be constructed. Whether inventor, realtor, or engineer, the practical dreamer who gave us the skyscraper can look with pride at such splendid towers as the famous 1902 Flatiron Building on Broadway, even while wondering about such latter-day examples as the twin monoliths of the World Trade Center in New York and the pyramidal Trans-America building in San Francisco.

Credit belongs to the inventive engineers who have given Americans these structures for having shaped a kind of Brobdingnagian nationscape. Everything is immense—as impressive as the power pylons that stride across the desert, or as dynamic as a Buckminster Fuller geodesic dome, or I. M. Pei's commanding new building for the National Gallery of Art. Everything works, but only in the way that *things* work, which—as power blackouts and dam failures witness—is neither constantly nor forever. One is reminded of that other challenge: to achieve a certain natural balance between our environment and our constructions.

Yet perhaps, with our entire culture under examination, it's unfair to expect the engineers alone to create a harmonious, earthly paradise. We may be best advised—as we in fact were advised by the philosophical John Augustus Roebling—to straighten ourselves out first. Admonished he: bring your own interior nature in union with the outer world, and harmony will be established. Meanwhile, we can assume that engineers will go ahead with the best they've got. □

Russell Bourne

Networks of engineering systems, modern skyscrapers such as San Francisco's TransAmerica pyramid, right, and New York's World Trade Center, under construction opposite, are but sophisticated sisters of the Flatiron Building, top, and other turn-of-the-century structures. For future needs, however, architectural engineers experiment with new forms and techniques, as witnessed by I.M. Pei's unparalleled, angular design for the East Building of the National Gallery of Art, overleaf.

Technology of the Portrait

William F. Stapp

In August 1839 a Frenchman named Daguerre perfected a chemical process that made "light produce permanent pictures." Incredible excitement seized scientific and artistic circles of Europe and America. The public eagerly awaited disclosure of the secrets of the process; the birth of photography was hailed as the most miraculous discovery of the age.

"Daguerreotypomania" spread literally as quickly as word could travel. By September 1839, traveling on the very first mail boat out of France, Daguerre's proc-

William F. Stapp, Curator of Photographs at the Smithsonian's National Portrait Gallery, is preparing a history of American portrait photography.

ess had crossed the Atlantic Ocean: the first American daguerreotypes were made on September 16, only three days after the first British ones, a remarkable fact considering the vast difference in the widths of the English Channel and the Atlantic, and one that accurately predicted the future of photography in America.

Indeed, nowhere else except in France was the daguerreotype adopted so quickly and so enthusiastically as in America, and nowhere else did it flourish so long or reach such a lofty state of technical perfection. It may have been the French invention, but it became the American medium.

Exactly what made photography (and especially the daguerreotype process) so fascinating to scientists, artists, and laymen alike? Man had finally invented a purely mechanical technique for making permanent, factually objective, visually accurate graphic records that far exceeded the capabilities of the finest

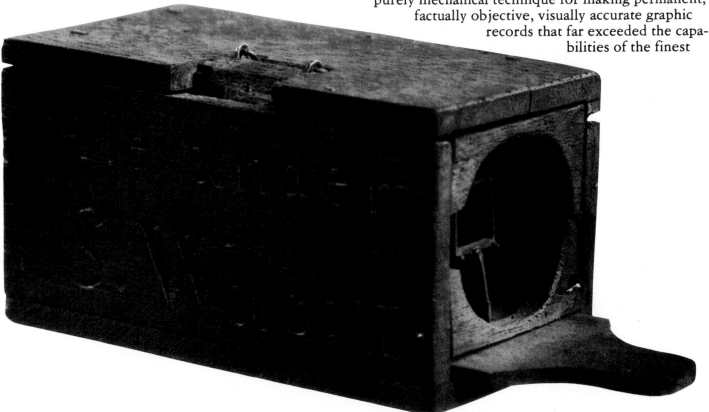

A small wooden box of enormous potential, daguerreotypist Alexander Wolcott's innovative camera, shown opposite in the Smithsonian's collections, was patented in 1840. The National Portrait Gallery recently acquired the daguerreotype, at top, of feminist Lucy Stone, a 19th-century married woman who chose to retain her own name. H. B. Hull's daguerreotype of young Thomas "Stonewall" Jackson, above, portrays the warrior shortly before the Civil War made him famous.

draftsmen to record the finest details. Introduction of the daguerreotype was a pivotal achievement of an age of technology that began in the 19th century: after that, nothing exceeded the realm of possibility. Second, photography was democratic: anyone with sufficient manual dexterity to perform the necessary mechanical operations could quickly learn to produce a technically competent image. And virtually anyone could afford to buy photographs, made inexpensive through machine processing. Finally and perhaps most important, the impact of photographic images was so powerful, so compelling, as to seem magical.

Samuel F. B. Morse, artist, inventor, and the first American actually to see a daguerreotype, wrote of "the exquisite minuteness of the delineation," comparing "the effect of the lens upon the picture" to "that of the telescope in nature." This effect of intensified reality, especially apparent in the mirror-like daguerreotype plate ("the mirror with a memory"), gave the images—and still gives them—their particular charm.

Despite its wonder as a scientific achievement with a unique and extremely forceful aesthetic product, the daguerreotype process as it was given to the world involved imperfect technology. Insensitive films, coupled with a slow lens (about f/15) and a large plate size (6½ by 8½ inches), meant long exposure times—15 minutes or more. In short, the process was well suited for photographing buildings and monuments, but hardly workable for portraiture—early trials by Morse in New York took 10 to 20 minutes.

The commercial consequences of the daguerreotype's shortcomings were well appreciated everywhere; as a result, improvement of photography for portraiture quickly became the concern of nearly everyone who mastered the process. The French Society for the Encouragement of National Industry sponsored a competition which produced important results, and in America, Yankee Ingenuity also responded to the challenge.

Improvements were both optical and chemical. Several American innovators—William Fitz in Baltimore, Robert Cornelius in Philadelphia, and Alexander Wolcott in New York, among others—used a smaller plate size and a shorter, larger diameter lens without a stop to reduce exposure times. Daguerre's lenses were slow, consisting of a long focal length—to cover the 6½- by 8½-inch plate—and of small diameter, further reduced by a fixed-aperture diaphragm which helped sharpen the image.

Wolcott, in fact, did not use a lens at all: he invented a camera that used a fast, concave mirror to focus the light on his small (about 2½- by 2-inch) plates. With this camera he succeeded in making his first portrait—possibly the first successful portrait—as early as October 7, 1839. By March 1840 he had

Artist, inventor, and leader of American photography in the early days of its development, Samuel F. B. Morse appears in a silver print taken of him in 1872.

opened the first American portrait studio. His innovations and those of the others rapidly led to the establishment of numerous studios.

Nonetheless, the daguerreotype dominated American photography until the Civil War, although after the mid-1850s a newer technology became increasingly important. The Englishman Frederick Scott Archer invented and published the wet-collodion/glass plate negative process in 1851. His new approach was superior in many ways, but its immediate widespread adoption was delayed by Archer's legal disputes with William Henry Fox Talbot, an English photographic pioneer and patentee of the first successful negative process. He claimed that virtually all photographic innovations were covered by his patents. Finally, under great public pressure, Talbot withdrew his objections in 1854 and Archer's process became immediately available. Several years elapsed, however, before it replaced the daguerreotype.

In spite of the beauty and power of the daguerreotype image, the process itself possessed three fatal flaws. First, the physically fragile plate had to be sealed behind a protective glass and mat inside a plush-lined case, limiting convenient portability. Second, the image was visible only when viewed at the proper angle. Third, and perhaps most important, each daguerreotype was a unique original object: since the only negative was the plate exposed in the camera, it was impossible to replicate an image.

Archer's process produced a glass plate negative which could be used to print any number of identical positive images on photosensitized paper. Still, each plate had to be prepared, exposed, and developed before the collodion emulsion dried. This presented no problem in the studio, but in the field it meant carrying a portable darkroom and all the necessary materials, and preparing and developing each glass plate on the spot—no mean feat under shellfire or in the desert.

The commercial advantages of such glass negatives were obvious. They yielded positive prints that rivaled those of a daguerreotype for sharpness and clarity. The transition began with the ambrotype, a modification of Archer's process that gave an apparently positive image on the glass plate. It resembled a daguerreotype in that each plate had to be cased for protection, and this familiar mode of presentation had the added advantage of helping reduce inventories of both mats and protective cases.

Ambrotypes retained their popularity well into the Civil War, but they never competed directly with their poorer sibling, the cheap and rugged tintype, or with the small format paper prints or *cartes de visite* that were introduced by a New York photographer named Rockwood in 1859. Cartes de visite were small photographic portraits mounted on calling cards, hence the name. They could be reproduced quickly and in large quantities—studios often used multilensed cameras to produce anywhere from two to eight images either simultaneously or sequentially on one plate in one sitting—and they came cheaper by the dozen. The cards, avidly collected, were stored in albums manufactured exactly for that purpose, and album viewing quickly became a popular, socially acceptable parlor pastime. Cartes of celebrities were mass-produced and distributed wholesale nationwide; by the end of the Civil War cartes were being produced in such volume that the Federal Government began to tax them to raise revenues. Cartes de visite helped transform photography into a mass medium. For the first time in history, the names of national leaders, heroes, and villains could now be associated with tangibly human faces; they could become household familiars, collected in family albums.

Abraham Lincoln was unquestionably the first American politician to recognize and exploit the political benefits of this phenomenon: he not only allowed himself to be photographed more frequently than any previous political leader of national stature, but he is also supposed to have claimed that he owed his nomination to his Cooper Union speech and his carte de visite by Mathew B. Brady.

Carting his bulky wet plate equipment along the battlefronts, Mathew B. Brady (posing at right immediately after the First Battle of Bull Run) made arresting portraits of the fighting men, generals and privates alike, of the Civil War.

In a very real sense Brady epitomizes the entrepreneurs who dominated so much of photography's history in the 19th century. Up from obscurity—much of his biography is myth—it is a fact that between 1845 and 1860 he built from scratch a two-studio empire internationally famous for the quality of both its portraiture and its patrons. It cannot be denied that a great number of prominent figures of the 19th century are best known today from portraits taken or preserved by Brady, nor that the large-scale photo-journalistic organization he conceived and initiated produced some of the most important and impressive visual records of the Civil War.

There can be little doubt that the Civil War was a highly important factor in the popularity of the carte de visite: it created an instant pantheon of popular and unpopular political and military leaders with large public followings on both sides of the conflict. Quite obviously, cartes generated a very heavy demand for private, personal portraits of soldiers and their families. In this respect, the bulkiness, weight, and fragility of the ambrotype surely contributed to its demise, for cartes de visite and tintypes were easier to mail, lighter, and much more convenient to carry. By the end of the Civil War virtually all American photography was done on glass plates which were used to make paper prints, with the single exception of the tintype.

Hamilton L. Smith of Gambier, Ohio, patented his tintype invention in 1856. Technically it was nothing more than an ambrotype on black japanned sheet iron, but it was cheap to make, light in weight, and virtually indestructible. These virtues made it especially appealing to Civil War soldiers. After the war it became the favorite medium of the itinerant photographers who traveled throughout rural America, for whom its low production costs and instant results guaranteed sales and profits. It was also immensely popular with seaside boardwalk and amusement park

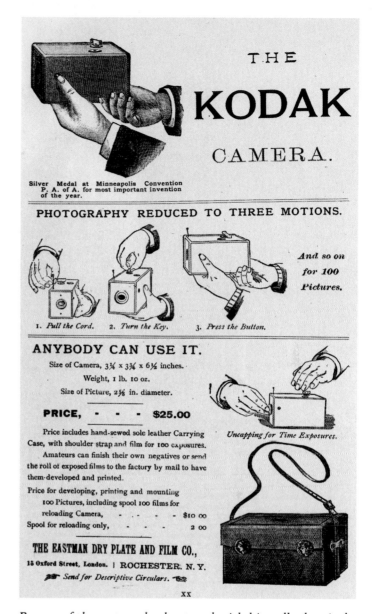

Because of the vast market he opened with his well advertised, simple technological system, industrialist George Eastman could improve his product from the original $25 box camera, top left, to the popular Brownie, which cost only a dollar. Thus democratized, photography could zoom into more specialized areas. The Kodak Graflex, center, cost $150 in 1902; its shutter speed of 1/1000th of a second (as opposed to the Brownie's 1/40th) made it popular with press photographers. The more advanced Super Kodak Six-20, bottom, went for $699 in 1938. The public responded to the challenge: today professional equipment (with automatic exposure control and electronically adjusted shutter speed) is available for less than $200. In the photo opposite, Eastman and box camera were caught by another box camera aboard the S.S. Gallia to show he practiced what he sold.

studios, where it flourished well into this century.

Until George Eastman introduced the Kodak camera in 1888, photography in America was primarily a profession, dominated by studios: if somebody wanted a photograph, he had it made or bought it. The sheer physical inconvenience of making every image almost literally from scratch, coupled with the cost and weight of all the necessary equipment and materials which had to be lugged around, was enough to discourage all but the professionals and serious amateurs. This situation began to change in 1880 when several firms introduced commercially made dry plates. Such plates were considerably more light-sensitive than the wet-collodion plates studios had used for years. Quality control at the factory guaranteed consistent and predictable results while eliminating the absolute necessity of keeping a darkroom immediately at hand and reducing darkroom work to development. Photography became a hobby as the public became increasingly more involved with making photographs.

The Kodak camera marked the first revolutionary development in photography since its invention, representing as much an innovation in marketing technique as a technological advance. Loaded with a 100-exposure roll film, the camera cost 25 dollars, including case and shoulder strap. It was simple to operate: pull a string to work the shutter, point the camera, press the button to release the shutter, and wind the film to the next exposure. When all the film was used, the camera and film were returned to Eastman Kodak for processing and reloading, which cost 10 dollars. The advertising slogan advised, "You press the button—we do the rest," and the camera scored big, creating almost instantaneously a vast new photographic market. Eastman had emancipated photography from the darkroom and integrated it into the mainstream of American popular culture, a remarkable achievement that made him a multimillionaire.

The major technological innovations and the mass-production techniques that made possible the Kodak camera ensured the transformation of photography into a consumer industry. Likewise, Kodak's lead significantly advanced the art of photography. The improved films, cameras, and lenses that began to appear on the market in the early 1890s were more versatile tools than previously known—if much more complex. They greatly extended the photographer's sphere of activity as well as his control over the entire image-making process.

Ironically, the artistic movement that emerged in America around the central figure of Alfred Stieglitz at this time seemed to reject many of the benefits of the newly advanced technology in favor of an aesthetic that sacrificed the absolute, mechanically accurate visual transcription to a romantic, impressionistic effect.

Hand-held single-lens reflex cameras like the superlative Graflex (introduced in 1907) permitted precise, yet instantaneous, composition and picture taking. Applied to portraiture by photographers like Stieglitz, Paul Strand, and Edward Weston in the teens and '20s, they were instrumental in creating a body of work that was graphically powerful, emotionally expressive, intimate, and radically different visually and psychologically from the static poses and idealized impersonal depictions of most traditional portraiture. The Graflex was perhaps the first modern American camera; it was certainly the most successful, remaining essentially unchanged for 50 years.

The years following the First World War saw rapid and important developments in the photographic industry—most of them in Europe. The trend, which had begun with the Kodak camera of 1888, turned to miniaturization combined with increased precision of optics and mechanical components. With Ernest Leitz's introduction of the Leica 35mm camera in 1925, the German camera industry seized the initiative in the design and manufacture of technically advanced and solidly constructed small cameras. American industry could not compete, simply because much higher production costs in this country would price the domestic product out of the market. The Kodak Super 620 of 1939, the first camera with an automatic exposure system; the Bantam Special, a sleek, collapsible pocket-sized camera with an f/2 lens; and the Kodak EKtra, a precision 35mm rangefinder system, were all innovative but doomed attempts by American companies to compete with the cameras made by Leitz, Zeiss/Ikon, and Rollei; yet the Leica, the Contax, and the Rolleiflex did not appeal to the mass market, and were considered "financial failures."

American industry turned to inexpensive, mass-produced cameras, making miniature photography available to an ever growing number of amateur photographers. By 1940 virtually every American home had some kind of camera and a collection of home-taken, drugstore-processed snapshot photographs.

In postwar years photography has blossomed into the democratic medium its earliest enthusiasts envisioned. The latest camera technology has made taking photographs more convenient than ever; more important, innovative design is now oriented directly at improving the vast amateur market. □

Even before modern technology allowed portrait-snapping to become everyone's hobby, men and women were trying their photographic skills. This stunning view of Alice Liddell (real-life heroine of Lewis Carroll's Alice in Wonderland) *was taken by Julia Margaret Cameron in the 1860s. Though working with cumbersome wet plates, Mrs. Cameron conquered the apparatus and depicted not a fiction but a person.*

PART 3

A Flash in the Pan

Amid the explosions of inventive genius which have produced our gadget-dependent civilization, there have also been many fizzles. But let us not stand and guffaw as Icarus falls from the sky, streaming wax and feathers (of course: what fool would try to fly?); let us not deride the doctor who would innoculate the potential smallpox victim with the germ itself. Instead, let us look at the inventor who, as the crowd laughs, cries with frustration that on the appointed day his engine has failed to start. Let us also consider the gunsmith whose new flintlock has merely flashed in the pan. His gun "hangs fire," and in that embarrassing moment he shares with other inventors—both the admirable and the fraudulent ones—a certain distance from the rest of mankind.

A potential savior on one day, a charlatan on the next, the inventor pleads for the crowd's or the king's attention. Leonardo da Vinci boasted to Lodovico Sforza that he could invent all kinds of dreadful military devices for that Milanese prince, including portable bridges, giant catapults, and the "covered chariots, safe and unassailable," that anticipated battleground tanks. Such proud vaunts sometimes lead to failure (as Leonardo discovered repeatedly), but that is the coin the inventor pays as the price for his ceaseless ingenuity.

The Industrial Revolution set the stage for technological ingenuity to take wing. And what merits particular attention, as we probe the psyches of the would-be heroes of invention past and present, is that most of the inventions were in areas of great public attention if not actual need. Man yearned to fly, he ached and craved relief; he lusted for greater (and even perpetual!) power. In response, the inventor was delighted to create tricks and/or techniques for fantasy and/or satisfaction. For instance, it had long seemed reasonable that a person could take to the air by fitting fabricated sails to his

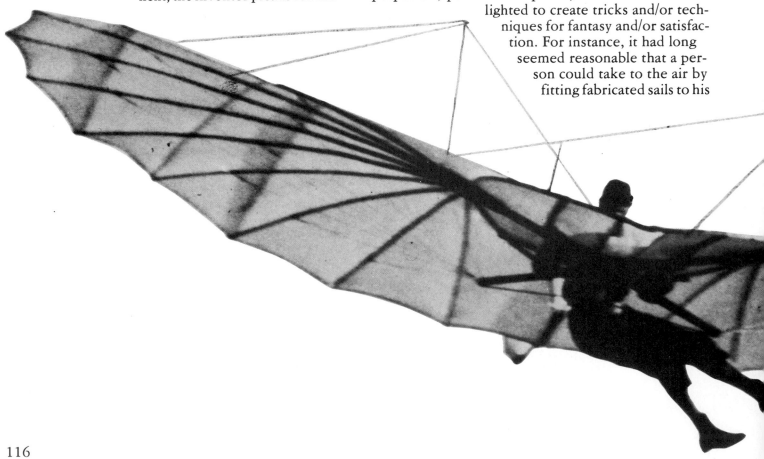

arms and flapping them strenuously. Of course, a certain technique must be involved, but why couldn't a clever man using birds as models extend himself to the sky? And thus, after myriad crashing failures, when the secret of the wing was discovered in the late 19th century, there were a few soaring successes.

Long before that, however, Leonardo had looked to birds for inspiration, sketching an ornithopter to be covered with silk. An entirely new approach for ascending into the heavens was proposed in the 13th century by the English monk Roger Bacon. He suggested launching a copper globe filled "with ethereal air or liquid fire." Within five centuries his idea had taken hold; hot air bags, pioneered by the Montgolfier brothers, were bobbing in Paris skies. Asked what use they were, Benjamin Franklin replied, "Of what use is a newborn babe?"

Searching for ways to propel their brain children, balloon enthusiasts cranked flapping wings, flailed the air with paddles, and even resorted to bird power, tethering eagles to their craft. Although none of these far-fetched schemes worked, the idea of power-controlled balloons persisted, leading to the development of dirigibles (from Latin, *dirigere,* to direct).

The success of the first balloons fired the imagination of Sir George Cayley. Almost 100 years before the Wright brothers made history, the Yorkshire baronet foresaw aircraft powered by a gas-fired engine. Lacking such a moving force, he experimented with gliders, once pressing his coachman into service as a test pilot. After a brief ride and a rough landing, the shaken servant declared: "Please, Sir George, I wish to give notice, I was hired to drive, and not to fly!"

Although the first birdman's approaches seemed foolish, fascination with flight was clearly no joke. None pursued the challenge more avidly than Otto Lilienthal, who as a lad had been intrigued by the storks alighting on the chimney tops of his home in Pomerania. He and his brother Gustav tried in vain to imitate the

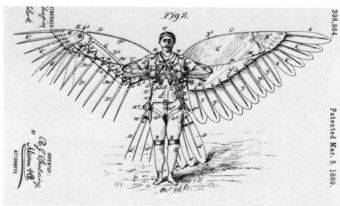

The compulsion to fly seemed so vain that 18th-century essayist William Cowper proclaimed that would-be pilots should be shot and no murder charged. Yet inventors persisted, some believing man must use birds' wings and motions—see R. J. Spalding's 1889 patent application, above. Others, including daring Otto Lilienthal, studied fixed-wing flight. He was the first to get the hang of gliding, swinging his body for control as today's hang gliders do.

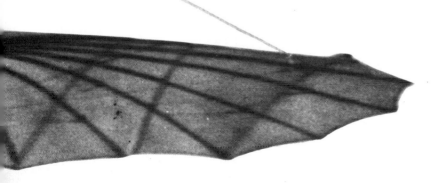

ways of the birds by strapping on six-foot wings and beating the air. They had better luck with cambered fixed wings. The daring Otto would leap from a hill into the wind and, hanging from a harness, stay aloft for several hundred feet. He executed more than 2,000 glides, finally crashing to the ground in 1896 and breaking his back. His last words before he died: "Sacrifices must be made."

Many were indeed made in fathoming the mysteries of flight. But the primal urge to soar like a bird persisted, with the unshielded body pitting itself against the air currents. Today's hang-glider athletes, leaping off cliffs and dunes to ride the wind, can dip a plastic wing to Otto Lilienthal.

Not all inventors of that daring, early industrial age aspired to such lofty goals as the mastery of flight. Many concentrated on more mundane pursuits—to ease man's transportation, enhance his comfort, and prolong his days. No matter if their efforts occasionally became targets of japery, the intent was serious.

The possibility of being buried alive was no laughing matter to the imaginative inventor of the "Improved Burial-Case," patented in 1868. Perhaps he had heard of a hasty interment and was moved to devise a fail-safe coffin. He thoughtfully equipped it with a duct to the surface, a ladder, and a bell. Thus, "should a person be interred ere life is extinct, he can, on recovery to consciousness, ascend from the grave and the coffin by ladder; or, if not able to ascend by ladder, ring the bell, thereby giving an alarm." A number of patents for such coffins were awarded in the 19th century, eloquent testimonials to the state of the medical arts during the period.

Another proposed lifesaver was a fire-escape parachute, to be worn in conjunction with thickly padded shoes. If these items were unavailable, a pair of improved suspenders, "with a cord so secured thereto or formed therewith as to constitute a part of the same," would work just fine. While the building burned, the trapped person would methodically tear off his improved suspenders, unravel the cord, then lower it to the ground, where a fire-escape rope could be attached and hauled up.

The uncertainties of the times sired many such aids to safety, as the "Combined Plow and Gun" of 1862 attested. A piece of light ordnance at the prow of the plow would be "ready charged with its deadly missiles of ball or grape." Thus armed, the farmer could till his fields with confidence. If attacked, all he needed to do was to remember to unhitch his horses, take aim, and fire the plow.

While engines of war engaged some imaginative minds, others turned toward more tranquil pursuits in the home. Inventors tinkered endlessly with furniture and household appurtenances, ever striving to make

life more comfortable. Upholstered sofas sprang, in part at least, from furniture designer Thomas Sheraton's "chamber horse." His original idea consisted of layers of springs arranged in a hassock, upon which a gentleman could simulate riding a horse, in the privacy of his own home and regardless of the weather.

A later invention incorporated bellows into the rocking chair. When the occupant rocked, blasts of air rushed upward through a tube to cool his brow. The lady of the house might have chosen the more fashionable "Pedal Zephyrion" to keep her cool. A tubular stand with a ribbed fan at the top and a pedal at the base, it required only the press of a foot to stir up a refreshing breeze.

For privileged Victorians who put a premium on privacy, there was nothing quite so relaxing as a steam bath in bed. Lying in one's four-poster, the recipient snuggled in a bag cinched at the collar while steam was funneled in at the feet. Yet, drowsy after taking the vapors, a person might slumber through dinner if he failed to hear the jingling of his alarm clock. No need to worry. The "Device for Waking Persons from Sleep" was guaranteed to bring one to his senses. A series of wooden weights suspended above the sleeper's face and connected to a wall clock would fall at the predetermined time and "strike a light blow, sufficient to waken the sleeper, but not heavy enough to cause pain." Not forgotten was the rail passenger, deprived of a Pullman, trying to sleep in a lurching coach. From Germany came a head-and-shoulder harness that, suspended from a hook, allowed the wearer to doze in comfort while sitting. The rig was said to be

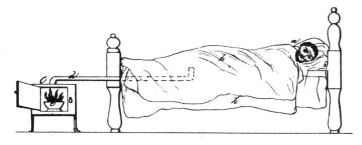

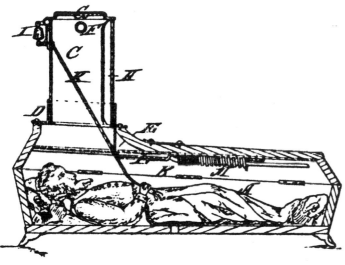

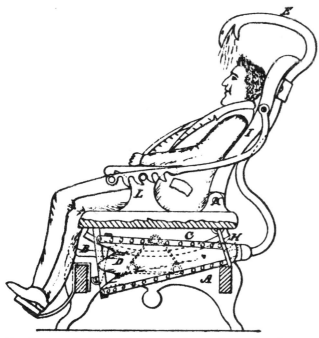

Quaint, comical to modern eyes, the products of 19th-century inventors' imaginations eased the strains of life—or death. Want a warm-up? A vapor bath patented in 1814 would steam your sleeping bag. Want a cool-off? An 1869 rocking chair salved your brow as you rocked. For those with a fearful sense of misdirection, Prof. Mayer's Topophone, opposite, promised "quickly and surely the exact direction" of some elusive sound. And for those worried about premature burial, F. Vester's patented coffin offered a late warning system.

especially useful to persons suffering from asthma.

There was also an appliance to relieve headaches. In 1912 a wire hat frame supported by shoulder braces was invented "to provide a hat which will permit of free circulation of air entirely around and over the head of the wearer, thus to prevent headaches caused by the weight and close fitting of the ordinary hat." Speaking of hats, one was devised to tip automatically when the wearer bowed. A pendulum apparatus in the crown did the trick.

Mad hattery persists; and it's a good thing. Steel combat helmets might fry their wearers but for a tricky sling frame that allows air to circulate. Football helmets have lately been equipped with radio receivers, allowing coaches into the huddle. One tropical explorer dons a sun powered pith helmet. The hotter the sun the greater the blast of cooling air from a tiny electrical fan inside, run by a raft of solar cells on the brim.

Inventing things just for the fun of it has also been going on for several thousand years. For instance, the toy bird that tips over to drink, commonly sold in dime stores, originated with the ancient Greeks, who also invented slot machines. When a coin was dropped into one, a measure of sacrificial water squirted forth. It was inevitable that the holy device would be followed by vulgar imitators—that salted peanuts would ultimately be dispensed in a similar manner.

Royal displays and carnivals for the mob have long called upon the inventor's talents. Consider the contrivance called "A Machine for Sensational Emotions," the grandfather of space capsules at carnivals today. Monsieur Carron, inventor of this sensational machine, proposed that a bullet-shaped chamber, large enough to hold 15 passengers comfortably, be built and suspended from the top of the Eiffel Tower. Seated in padded armchairs in the upper portion of the missile, riders would experience the thrill of a lifetime when the projectile, released from its mooring, plunged down into a pool of water with the configuration of a long-stemmed champagne glass. At impact no one would feel a thing. A thick mattress underfoot was supposed to absorb the shock. The modest fee quoted for the ride would surely have attracted eager throngs had the machine been built; alas, M. Carron died before he could profit from his invention.

Hopes of obtaining great wealth motivated many inventors. Unfortunately, their passion for fame and fortune often led them to make far-fetched claims for their creations, particularly those purported to have perpetual-motion capabilities. Trading on the widely known successes of such geniuses as Thomas Edison and Alexander Graham Bell, they promised more than they could deliver. Long before the formulation of the laws of thermodynamics, Leonardo da Vinci had seen the futility of the quest, railing at this species of folly:

"Oh speculators on perpetual motion, how many vain projects in this search you have created!"

Heedless of warnings, the suckers came, cash in hand, to back the miracle machines of such self-proclaimed geniuses as John Worrell Keely, who in 1872 announced the "greatest scientific discovery of the century," a revolutionary motor that harnessed "etheric force." With this force, he declared, a train could cross the country on a quart of water. At his laboratory in Philadelphia he demonstrated his machine to stockholders, scientists, and journalists, dramatically triggering the device by playing a few notes on his violin. He then poured a glass of water into his "hydro-pneumatic, pulsating vacuum" engine, which exerted such pressure that heavy cables were snapped, iron bars were twisted in two, and bullets slammed through foot-thick timbers. Such displays, combined with Keely's apparent earnestness, brought him millions of dollars over a span of 26 years. In that time the Keely Motor Company never marketed a product of any kind or secured a single patent. After Keely died in 1898, investigators found in his workshop a maze of hidden pipes and, buried in the cellar, a three-ton steel tank. His "etheric force" was nothing more than compressed air piped into a centrifugal chamber. What galvanized the engine into action was not the "harmonic vibrations" of his violin but the pressure of his foot tapping on a concealed spring valve.

Keely was not the last to claim he could work wonders with plain water. One Gaston Bulmar tried to con General Electric executives into paying him $100,000 for a few aspirin-sized pills. In his hotel room he demonstrated that one of these could transform a bucket of water into gasoline. His ruse, discovered before GE paid the money, was to prime the plumbing by pumping gasoline into the bathtub faucet. Thus, when he turned the spigot, he drew gas instead of water.

A variation on the same theme motivated con inventor Louis Enricht. In 1916 he called a press conference to announce that he had discovered a substitute for gasoline that could be produced for a penny a gallon. Staging an elaborate demonstration, he mixed a green liquid with water, poured it into his car's empty tank, then started the engine and drove the reporters around town. Before Enricht was exposed as a fraud—his car had a secret gas tank—he had bilked railroad president Benjamin F. Yoakum out of thousands of dollars and had aroused the interest of Henry Ford, who considered buying the fuel formula. But of course there was none.

A few years later Walter Hohenau was boasting that the "world will never be without power again, and it will cost practically nothing to provide fuel purely from water, all achieved with my marvelous hydro-atomizer." After demonstrations of his gadget-studded machine, which produced a flame fueled by hydrogen from a hidden tank, investors closed their minds and opened their wallets. By the time the truth dawned, Hohenau had skipped out, usually to another country where he practiced his deceit on other victims. So persuasive was he that scientists applauded him, and public figures—Mussolini, Mexican President Calles—hailed him as a genius. Although Hohenau was a fraud, he could be considered, perversely, as a harbinger of today's atom-splitting technology. In the breeder reactor, which creates more fuel than it consumes, he might have recognized the answer to his perpetual-motion dreams.

A contemporary, Victor "The Count" Lustig, made his fortune by selling perpetual-money machines. A box with a crank, his invention ostensibly turned out new $20 bills from blank paper––after an overnight wait for the process to "take." The Count's ruse was to plant the money in a false bottom, cranking it out when the time was ripe. Such a day's—and night's—work netted him up to $100,000 per box. By the time the buyer waited for his batch of blank paper to be transformed into crisp greenbacks, Lustig had departed. He finally got into trouble with the U.S. Treasury Department when he teamed up with an engraver and did what his machine couldn't—manufacture money. It was "some of the most skillfully executed" counterfeit money Federal agents said they had ever encountered. In Leavenworth Lustig became known affectionately as King Con.

For sheer audacity, his money box was equalled if not exceeded by the magic diagnosing box of one Dr. Abrams, who called his invention the "occilloclast." Claiming that it could treat just about any illness known to man, he sold the machine by the hundreds to doctors, cautioning them not to open the sealed cabinet. He also did a brisk mail-order business, needing only a drop of the patient's blood on blotting paper to diagnose in his marvelous machine. Handwriting samples would work just as well, and it didn't make any difference if the person examined were dead or alive. Using his extraordinary technique he determined that Edgar Allan Poe and Henry Wadsworth Longfellow, among other notables, had suffered from syphilis. The machine also diagnosed religious affiliation.

His downfall began when he confidently revealed that a drop of blood sent in by a physician indicated the presence of cancer, diabetes, and several other diseases. The physician sent the report to the American Medical Association, explaining that the blood analyzed came from a healthy rooster. After several such cases, a team of experts, defying Abrams' admonition about tampering with the box, opened an occilloclast and found a meaningless jumble of electronic

To hustle a perpetual motion machine, an inventor needed a firm visage and a lot of machinery. Master fraud John W. Keely thought he had both when photographed in 1889, top. Legitimate inventor Robert Fulton, artist as well as steamboat builder, exposed another fraud's machinations of 1813 with his sketch, above.

components in a nest of wires. Soon after, Abrams, exposed as a fraud, fell ill and died. His machine had lost its magic.

Such men are forthrightly condemned for their perfidy. But even they, it may be argued, have occasionally made contributions to modern science. There are, after all, "magic boxes" today to detect all sorts of flaws in man and matter. And many recent innovations are more astonishing than any dreamed up by the con men. Experiments have shown that automobile mileage can be improved by emulsifying water and gasoline. Water in the gasoline? But it works. □

Wayne Barrett

4
PART

Revolutions of Science

The greatest of inventions have been models—theoretical models to describe reality in hitherto unperceived ways. Copernicus was such an inventor, showing mankind for all time that the Earth is not the center of the universe. Newton was another, finding in the models that crossed his mind's eye formulas that explained the essentials of motion and gravity. Darwin, too, pondered models, living models—ultimately placing man in his proper place in the long continuum of life forms. Einstein's synthesis brought the universe within our grasp.

The scientific process of hypothesis-and-test continues today as physicists, employing instruments called particle accelerators, look for infinitely small and evanescent units of existence that may further illuminate our understanding of the universe.

Other new tools to test new hypotheses are developing at a rapid rate: lasers (those at right are in use in California, gauging the minute motions of the Earth's crust along the San Andreas Fault); computers that help scan the brain's mysteries; space satellites armed with cameras that minutely scrutinize the Earth's surface and atmosphere, and peer deep into the universe; telescopes that can piece together an image of the surface of a star.

Some say that we are now on the brink of "the biological century," during which the most awesome invention of all may be made. It will arise from exquisitely fine techniques for surgically altering our own genetic material. We may penetrate the secrets of life, making a working model of the forces of evolution. Then perhaps the time will come for a new species of humankind. . . .

Merchants of Light

Bern Dibner

The importance of passing events can be measured by their life span in the minds of men. Gutenberg, quietly shaping punches to be replicated to form his stock of movable type, stirred greater ultimate activity than the winning of a war or the coronation of a king. Copernicus, plotting the motion of the planets in distant Torun, came to conclusions that shifted the center of the then-known universe from the Earth to the sun. With logic and mathematical precision, Newton bound up all matter in space, from a falling raindrop to a moving planet, by universal laws that all the world soon accepted. Darwin observed plant and animal life on five continents and formulated an explanation for the variation of species and their survival or extinction that has become the key to understanding all of biology and much of geology. Though not trained as a physician, Pasteur, by exacting observation and courageous dedication, founded the science of bacteriology. To him we owe mastery over plagues and diseases of fermentation. To this calendar of giants must be added Einstein and Fermi, whose fertile minds provided the key to the convertibility of energy and matter.

In the 10,000 years since the great change wrought by the invention of agriculture, mighty civilizations have risen and faded. While wood and stone remained the basic engineering materials for dozens of centuries, bronze slowly evolved from copper to be formed into tools and weapons. With these, tribes became nations, and nations empires. Among these, the Greek city-states developed brilliant intellectual societies whose literature, architecture, ethics, and science continue into our day. Yet the Greek intellect never developed the arch; its brilliant architecture was limited to post-and-lintel construction. The Mayan and Incan civilizations, evolving independently, constructed great cities of stone and stucco, yet used the wheel only as a child's toy.

The Middle Ages witnessed a revolution of sorts—but a very gradual one. Progress was made by degree: cities grew larger, spires taller, armies mightier, life more secure, and better at least than it had been since the fall of the Roman Empire. Yet wars and pillage still threatened every community, and shifting alliances provided constant uncertainty of the future. The study of nature was scholastic, and invention was empirical. The Crusades enlivened intellectual curiosity by exposing many younger minds to new lands, other cultures, and the competitive challenge of conquest and survival. Crusaders brought back to Western Europe neglected Greek classics and works of Arabic and Ottoman literature and science.

The Renaissance saw an explosive release of energy pent up for centuries by tradition. In art, science, commerce, and culture, Europe exuberantly burst forth from its medieval chrysalis and emerged as the world's dominant force. To illuminate the Renaissance, let us consider the hundred years between 1450 and 1550. At the beginning of that period Europe had recovered from the Crusades and the Black Death and was comparatively tranquil. There were many regions and city-states, but few nations as we know them today. In the city of Mainz in Hesse, Johann Gutenberg, a metalsmith, invented a process for producing books using movable type. His great work was the Bible, printed in Latin and bearing no printer's name, place, or date of issue. Gutenberg probably printed 200 copies, of which 47 are extant. So successful was this work as a commercial enterprise that, in spite of his wish to keep the process secret, more than eight million volumes were printed, albeit slowly and clumsily, in the first 45 years of production (1455-1500). Gutenberg had to invent not only the mechanism of type founding but also the proper type metal (lead-tin-antimony) and printer's ink, which has a different consistency than writer's ink. Historians consider this not-so-simple invention to be one of the three most important events in all human history, the other two being the discovery of America and man's walk on the moon. Printing democratized knowledge, led to mass-produced books (the United States alone prints over two billion a year), and made much of mankind literate.

In 1452, as Gutenberg was printing his Bible in Mainz, Leonardo da Vinci was born in Tuscany, the illegitimate son of the secretary to the Signoria of Florence. Leonardo was apprenticed to a craftsman painter in Florence, became a master painter, and served in several courts. His masterpiece, "The Last Supper," is probably the most famous religious work of art; the portrait, "The Mona Lisa," the most famous secular painting in existence. Yet, to judge by the 7,000 surviving manuscript pages of his work, he was at heart a scientist and engineer. He died in 1519, leaving a vast hoard of unfinished work in manuscript. It was not until 1651 that his first publication, a *Treatise on Painting*, appeared, and none of his technical work was published until 1797. Since then, times have moved to catch up with his brilliant prescience, his mechanical ingenuity, intense curiosity, and unmatched skill in reducing his thoughts to clear, instructive drawings. His 650 anatomical drawings in the Royal Library at Windsor remain the unmatched illustrations of their kind. The recently discovered 700-page codices of Madrid place Leonardo among the most inventive mechanicians of all time. Courtly, scholarly, prodigiously creative, he served two dukes and a king as military engineer and clearly embodied the Renaissance man.

Gutenberg and Leonardo are but two examples of the Renaissance people who changed the world by setting it on a course dominated by reason, science, learning, and tolerance. We turn to yet another figure who extended man's horizons and enriched his own life on Earth: the mariner Christopher Columbus. Driven to

Bern Dibner, Chairman of the Electrical Historical Foundation, founded the Dibner Library of the Smithsonian in 1975. He holds 25 U.S. patents.

Composed of type, the commemorative medal, opposite, hails Johann Gutenberg, who turned on the printing presses of the Western world with his invention of movable type.

sail beyond the horizon, he organized a frail expedition to face the vast ocean in order to reach Asia by sailing West. His discovery of unknown lands, which he mistakenly thought were part of India, opened the New World to future exploration and colonization. Then, in 1519, Ferdinand Magellan and 264 crewmen in five ships sailed west to circumnavigate the globe. Magellan was killed in the Philippines; all his ships save one were lost. After nearly three years of shipwreck, desertion, mutiny, and starvation, the 85-ton *Victoria*, manned by 18 famished crewmen, limped into her home port in Spain. They had confirmed the spherical form of the Earth, the immense breadth of the Pacific, and the indomitable spirit of man.

While fleets of mariners followed Columbus and Magellan, conquering, colonizing, exploring, and reporting, European university centers flourished, spreading new knowledge, examining fresh scientific discoveries, and formulating the disciplines with mathematical rigor. Schools at Bologna, Padua, Wittenberg, Oxford, and Paris attracted thousands of scholars who explored "natural philosophy" and increasingly observed and reported on the ways of the material world.

In 1543 there appeared a book in Latin, *De Revolutionibus Orbium Coelestium*, by the Polish astronomer Nicolaus Copernicus. Years of observation of the heavens had led him to conclude that the sun, rather than the Earth, was the center of the planetary system. His book contained a diagram showing "SOL" in the system's center, next the two inner planets, Mercury and Venus, then the Earth with its moon, and finally the three then-known outer planets, all in circular orbits, and all within the sphere of the fixed stars.

Copernicus's heliocentric hypothesis generated conflict between observable celestial motion and Biblical doctrine. A period of 36 years passed before Copernicus permitted his disciple Rheticus, a young Protestant mathematician from Wittenberg, to announce in Danzig in 1540 the essence of heliocentrism. This new doctrine, so universally accepted today, did more violence to traditional thought than any other single idea, including such momentous proposals as evolution and relativity. Copernicus's book was proscribed in the Roman *Index* in 1616, and was not to be removed from this list until 1822.

Though the significance of heliocentrism was at first not widely seen or accepted, some cosmologists quietly recognized the new concept. Among them was Giordano Bruno, who, for this and other heresies, was burned by the Inquisition in Rome in 1600. Galileo Galilei also shared Bruno's conviction, but was more cautious in expounding it. His involvement with heliocentrism has made him a symbol of the shift from classical speculation to scientific empiricism. Combin-

ing classic logic with novel experimentation, Galileo was able to arrive at an opinion and then to confirm it.

At age 17, using his pulse as a timing device, he determined the isochronous oscillation of the bronze lamp in the Pisa Cathedral. He questioned Aristotle's belief that the velocity of falling bodies is related to their weight, and, as tradition has it, demonstrated the law of falling bodies by dropping objects of different weights from the Leaning Tower of Pisa. Galileo's break with the tradition of Aristotle led to friction with the Scholastics, and he moved from Pisa to seemingly more tolerant Padua, where his interests turned to astronomy. Having heard of a new, perhaps Dutch, optical instrument that could enlarge a distant object, he designed and built one, demonstrated it to the Doge of Venice, and in early 1610 turned his telescope toward the heavens. Galileo improved the magnifying power of the instrument from three- to 30-fold and within a short period of time made nine major astronomical discoveries, among them the rugged surface of the moon, the countless stars in the Milky Way, the phases of Venus, and the four largest satellites of Jupiter. Of these moons Galileo said that they had "never been seen from the first beginning of the world until our time." Aristotle's concept of immutable heavens yielded to the idea of revolving spheres—did this not confirm the heliocentric theories of Copernicus?

The case for a rotating, sun-orbiting Earth, vigorously ridiculed by Martin Luther, Melanchthon, and other Reformers, was supported by Johannes Kepler and René Descartes, and proved by Isaac Newton. A copy of Galileo's *Siderius Nuncius*, published in Venice in 1610, containing his telescopic discoveries, reached Kepler, who subsequently published two works in its support. Kepler constructed tables of planetary motion based on the many observations that were given to him by Tycho Brahe, his colleague and patron; these superseded the inaccurate tables of the time. By changing the shapes of planetary orbits from circles to ellipses, Kepler profoundly altered the Copernican system, introducing orbits considered "nonperfect" by Aristotelian standards and resolving complex planetary motion with geometrical harmony and mathematical precision based on observation. Kepler had already formulated his three laws of planetary motion, which described the shapes of the orbits of the planets, the variations in the velocities of planets in their orbits, and the relationship between the average distance of a planet from the sun and the time required to complete one orbit. These demonstrable conclusions were not just exercises in mathematical sophistry; they comprised the ruling laws of the solar system, open to anyone who would observe and be trained in the truths of mathematics. Kepler's conclusions and Galileo's astronomical discoveries led to the celestial mechanics of Newton.

The *De Revolutionibus* of Copernicus, presented in the final decade of that revolutionary 100 years between 1450 and 1550, appeared concurrently with two other books of profound significance. One was written by Andreas Vesalius, a 28-year-old anatomist of Brussels, and author of the large folio *De Humani Corporis Fabrica*, Basel, 1543. Based on his own dissection of many bodies, he presented a series of detailed and accurate views of the body's structure from the full figure inward to the skeleton. This didactic masterpiece greatly advanced the knowledge of anatomy and physiology. The final volume to close that century in which science came into its own was Fuchs's *De Historia Stirpium*, Basel, 1542. A botanical breakthrough, this herbal described 400 central European and 100 foreign plants. Appearing as it did at the first swelling of the exploring fever that followed Columbus, the 500 illustrations introduced exotic plants that altered the European diet and pharmacopoeia, including Indian corn, pumpkin, potato, and foxglove.

The period 1450 to 1550 was followed by centuries of increasingly intensive cultivation of the fruits of the explorers, investigators, scientists, and engineers. Luther and the Reformation stirred change in the realms of the spirit, and the introduction of artillery altered the technology of war in the massing of armies and the design of fortifications. In Italy the first science academy, the Accademia del Cimento, was founded in 1657 as a platform for the disciples of Galileo. After 10 years of rigorous activity, however, theological pressure forced it to close its doors. In France and Germany, noble courts supported scientific investigation—especially those experiments dealing with devices that promised improved military or navigational potential. England offered the heaviest backing to those concerned with scientific trends, men such as Francis Bacon, Baron Verulam.

Bacon had acquired from Aristotle the ideal of accomplishing great good for mankind through the discovery of truth. Bacon proposed the reorganization of the sciences based on an ordering of all human knowledge, especially those trends that had resulted in discovery and invention. Man was to further extend his domination of nature by using the skills of science. "Is truth ever barren? Shall man not be able thereby to produce worthy effects, and to endow the life of man with infinite commodities?" asked Bacon. With knowledge comes power, with truth utility. This practical lord chancellor not only proclaimed the aims of his new philosophy, but also outlined the means of attaining them in his *Novum Organum*, published in Lon-

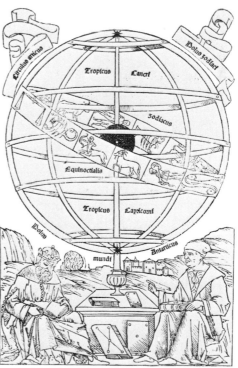

Nicolaus Copernicus published his revolutionary work on the orbits of the spheres in 1543. He appears at top holding a model with Earth circling the sun—a radical departure from the accepted Ptolemaic view of Earth at center, above.

127

Sir Isaac Newton discovered in 1666 that white light really consists of all the spectrum's colors; thus light broken into its compo- *nent colors by a 17th-century prism falls on Newton's monumental volume,* Opticks, *published in 1704.*

don in 1620. Reviewing the fallacies in past philosophies, Bacon classified the concerns of knowledge as being with nature, with natural philosophy (meaning heavenly matters), and with man. "First of all we must prepare a natural and experimental history, sufficient and good; and this is the foundation of all." Argument and syllogisms were to give way to experiment and observation. Facts were to be accumulated, changes observed, knowledge systematized, and conclusions drawn and applied. To be valid, a result must be verifiable by repetition. No room remained for unique

phenomena, miracles, or supernatural intercession. The discipline of the experimental method grew with its application. Truth was not to flow from authority; dogma would be alienated from science. Theological questions would be transferred from the province of reason to that of faith; Bacon turned to experience and observation as the basis of his new philosophy. He therewith originated the empirical school of inductive reasoning—the threshold to science. Bacon had created a new man, the research scientist, and he named him the "Merchant of Light."

The greatest of Bacon's "Merchants," Isaac Newton was born the year Galileo died. Thus, four minds—Copernicus, Tycho Brahe, Galileo, and Kepler—provided the chain of ideas that led ultimately to Newton's synthesis of the physical world. Newton developed the binomial theorem and the calculus in mathematics; he determined the composite nature of white light—the spectrum—and devised the reflecting telescope. In one of the greatest triumphs in the history of science, he described the universal nature of gravitation and formulated his three laws of motion, the basis of practical, or Newtonian, mechanics. He predicted that the Earth would be found to be a flattened rather than a true sphere, due to its rapid rotation, and was the first to postulate the elliptical orbits of comets. He experimented in chemistry; was elected professor at Cambridge University, member of Parliament, and president of the Royal Society; and was appointed master of the mint.

Newton's most important publication, the *Philosophiae Naturalis Principia Mathematica*, London, 1687, contained his law of universal gravitation (all bodies, of whatever size, attract each other in proportion to their mass and in inverse ratio to the square of the distance between them), deduced from Kepler's third law. Of the three books that constitute the *Principia Mathematica*, the first two concern mechanics, the third, the solar system. Mass, momentum, and force are defined, and the corpuscular theory of light is presented. The three laws of motion are then stated and applied to gases and liquids. The second important book by Newton is his *Opticks*, London, 1704, which treats the rainbow, "Newton's rings," double refraction, and the prismatic dispersion of white light into the spectrum of colors.

Newton's work not only benefited his nation and generation, but his clarifying discoveries continue to enlighten all mankind. The light of understanding that he provided has guided succeeding generations of scientists who have, in their turn, added to the sum of knowledge of the physical world and its forces. The world became part of the universe, bound by common laws. Other scientists supplemented Newton's proposals, but he provided the great physical synthesis.

A dramatic and convincing demonstration of the heliocentric doctrine developed by Copernicus and ultimately articulated by Newton was provided by French physicist Jean Bernard Leon Foucault in 1851. Foucault suspended an iron-ball pendulum from the dome of the Pantheon in Paris and set it swinging. The ball swung in a single plane while the floor turned beneath it, convincingly demonstrating that the Earth rotated on its axis. In the following year Foucault devised the gyroscope and further demonstrated Newton's laws of inertia and gravitation. Today, a great Foucault pendulum swings gracefully at the Smithsonian, and others are displayed in science museums elsewhere. The gyroscope became a most popular toy and, much more importantly, the heart of the gyrocompass, automatic pilot, and inertial navigation systems.

The colonization of America transplanted the societies of western Europe and, in reduced magnitude, the scientific activities of the mother countries. One American whose interests were consonant with Europe's scientific progress was Benjamin Franklin, printer, postmaster, founder of the Junto (later the American Philosophical Society) and of the University of Pennsylvania, the Free Library, and the Philadelphia Hospital, charter of the Gulf Stream, ambassador, signer of the Declaration, and inventor of the lightning rod. The last benefaction alone would earn him the world's gratitude and place him among the immortals. But as a founding father of the electrical science he originated the one-fluid theory of electricity, demonstrated the identity of friction electricity and lightning, discovered the principle of the conservation of charge, and promulgated the method of grounding lightning's destructive force by installing a simple device—the lightning rod. A deceptively simple device, its realization required a knowledge of electrical phenomena, and a Newtonian aptitude for translating meteorological data into electrical terms. The lightning rod also required that its inventor have the courageous ingenuity to design a device that would drain so destructive a force; he must be willing to demonstrate his theory by risking his life in an experiment against nature. No wonder that the tale of the kite has inspired generations of admirers.

All this Franklin did, and at age 82 he wrote, "I have been long impressed with . . . the conveniences of common living, and the invention and acquisition of new and useful utensils and instruments; so that I have sometimes almost wished it had been my destiny to be born two or three centuries hence. For invention and improvement are prolific and beget more of their kind. The present progress is rapid. Many of great importance, now unthought of, will before that period be produced; and then I might not only enjoy their advantages, but have my curiosity gratified in knowing what they are to be."

The heritage of science from the 1700s is so rich that only one more instance of its fecundity can be included in this short essay. It concerns the Italian Alessandro Volta and his discovery of the electric battery. Interest in electricity before Volta was directed mainly toward static electricity, best exemplified by the experiments of Jean Antoine Nollet and the lightning rod of Franklin. In 1800 the *Philosophical Transactions of the Royal Society* of London carried an announcement by Volta, a physics professor at Pavia, of a method of generating a constant flow of electric current from a stack of alternating copper, zinc, and brine-soaked cloth discs. This "Voltaic pile" provided a "perpetual" flow of current which was soon used effectively to decompose water into oxygen and hydrogen, to electroplate metals, and to produce a brilliant arc light. In 1820 Hans Christian Oersted, working in Denmark, discovered the magnetic vector of the electric current, a magnetism intensified by winding the insulated conductor on an iron core. Pursuing this principle, Joseph Henry, later first Secretary of the Smithsonian Institution, developed the efficient electromagnet. The electric telegraph was then devised, followed by dynamos, motors, lights, telephones, hoists, and myriad other devices. The electrical age was upon us.

The biologic world witnessed no revolutionary changes to parallel those from Copernicus to Newton in the physical world. In 1628 the English physician William Harvey published a small tract advancing the belief that the heart was the pump in a complete circulatory system of the blood, contradicting the earlier opinion that the blood moved in the veins like a tide. The complete circulation could not be observed until 1661, when Italian anatomist Marcello Malpighi, using the recently invented microscope, discovered the fine capillary vessels joining the arteries and veins. Dutch microscope maker Antony van Leeuwenhoek observed and published the earliest views of blood corpuscles, the compound insect eye, microorganisms, and living spermatozoa. Then, at the end of the 18th century, British physician Edward Jenner developed an effective vaccine against smallpox, an age-old scourge now practically eradicated.

Two giants appeared in the 1800s who lit up the obscure and complex realm of living things—Darwin and Pasteur. The English naturalist Charles Darwin spent five years observing living and geological evidence on the circumnavigating voyage of the *Beagle*, during which he visited nearly every continent and studied the natural history of isolated islands. The vast material gathered was, after 30 years, formed into a doctrine and presented in 1859 as *The Origin of Species*

Honoring the physicist who formulated the laws of relativity, this crystalline mirror-and-prism box at the National Air and Space Museum shows Albert Einstein's portrait engraved in glass from an original photographic portrait by Yousuf Karsh.

by Means of Natural Selection. This book introduced his theory of natural selection, or evolution. In 1871 Darwin published *The Descent of Man*, suggesting that man had evolved from primate ancestors. The old doctrines of special or divine creation declined as paleontological, anthropological, and genetic studies contributed to the understanding of human evolution. This most important single work in biological science brought man to his true place in nature.

A friend of Darwin, the geologist Charles Lyell, supplied a reconstructed measure of time into which the complex changes suggested by Darwin's tenet of evolution could be extended. Conflict between Victorian England's strong attitudes toward Biblical dogma and the evidence gathered by growing numbers of searching geologists, zoologists, and paleontologists, stirred unrest in the more conservative quarters. How could one reconcile fossils of dinosaurs, other extinct forms, and the similar morphology of man and ape with the constrictions of Biblical time? The mounting evidence called for eons, not centuries, of time, and Lyell's *Principles of Geology*, London, 1830-3, helped provide the key to geologic time. The 6,000-year period of scriptural time has since been extended into the present estimates of from eight to 20 billion years for the universe's calendar.

The bacterial origin of many diseases was revealed by French chemist Louis Pasteur, who turned to biological studies when his investigation of the fermentation of milk, beer, and wine led him to discover the roles played by bacteria, yeasts, and molds in the fermentation process. To kill harmful bacteria, he proposed a simple and effective process of heating that became familiar as "pasteurization." Convinced that air was the medium for carrying bacteria, he then discovered bacterial forms that flourished without free oxygen (anaerobic bacteria). Biological chemistry, the wine and beer industry, and the silk industry owe Pasteur eternal gratitude, and for his work in the conquest of major infectious diseases he has rightfully been called the greatest benefactor of mankind. He triumphed over anthrax and rabies and pointed the way to the conquest of diphtheria, cholera, yellow fever, and tuberculosis. His work has saved the lives of millions of people and animals alike.

We have now reached the 20th century—the century of science and its applications. The spirit of inquiry and experimentation has moved through the formulation and consolidation of the rules governing the structure and mechanics of the material world. We have passed through the Age of Reason, the Enlightenment, the Industrial Revolution, and the Electrical Age. A chance observation by Wilhelm Roentgen in 1895 led to his discovery of X-rays. Antoine Henri Becquerel and the Curies shared the 1903

Nobel Prize for their investigations of radioactivity. Max Planck and Ernest Rutherford unleashed a flood of fresh ideas in the structure of matter and the nuclear forces involved. Finally, Albert Einstein's postulation of the theory of general relativity effected the most profound revolution in scientific thought since Copernicus. By relating light and gravity, the dimensions of space and time, the invariable velocity of light, and the interconvertibility of mass and energy, Einstein guided scientific thought into new dimensions. His formula for the relationship between energy and mass, $E=mc^2$, became the symbol of science.

We now live in the electronic and nuclear age with uncountable miracles at our command. We may see various worldwide events "live" or select, at will, any form of sound—music, drama, instruction, oration, news, or a President's fireside chat. We move in comfort—locally, across nations, continents, and oceans; we rendezvous in space or walk on the moon. With computers we store and retrieve knowledge in quantities and at speeds far beyond the capability of the human mind. By growth, by investment in capital-creating plants and equipment, by inflation, and by improved science and technology, this nation now generates two trillion dollars worth of goods and services a year. It required 193 years to attain the first trillion and only seven years to add the second.

With pride in our accomplishments, I would pause to reflect on some red ink on the ledger. Two debits cry out immediately—wars and over-population. The resort to terror and violence, whether by individuals or by armies, for whatever reason, displays a barbarism not worthy of mankind in this century. To blame politics, chauvinism, racism, or any other "ism" provides no solution. Beyond the obvious human costs of war, the uncertainty of outcome, vast expense, waste of resources, and poor return on investment clearly argue in favor of the abandonment of armed power to settle differences. It is my hope that "open sky" politics, "hot lines," the United Nations, and other forums will provide mechanisms to reduce the tendency to resort to armed attack. We must learn to replace conflict with cooperation—or all the glories of science and invention will be just another billow in a mushroom cloud.

The world's problems can be solved, and some—though by no means all—of the solutions to those problems may come from scientists seeking, in the tradition of Copernicus, Newton, Darwin, Einstein, and all the others, to provide us with a better understanding of ourselves, the world, and the universe. □

The Atom Smashers

Paul Forman

Fifty years ago no such device as an "atom smasher" yet existed—except in the minds of imaginative physicists. Twenty-five years ago none was yet so large that it could not be housed under a single roof. Today the most powerful atom smashers are miles across and cost hundreds of millions of dollars. The largest, most expensive, and most sophisticated instruments of pure research, they are the indispensable means for advancing the frontier of knowledge toward the infinitely small, and thus toward the fundamental and the universal.

High-energy accelerators—atom smashers—produce high-velocity beams of subatomic particles. They first made possible the systematic probing and disruption of the central cores (nuclei) of atoms. Now, enormously increased in energy, they probe and disrupt the elementary particles of which these nuclei are composed.

Atom smashers must not be confused with nuclear reactors. Indeed the *only* thing that these two very different types of machines have in common is that they both work upon the nuclei of atoms. Particle accelerators—atom smashers—are complex machines that use electric and magnetic fields to steer and accelerate individual subatomic particles moving within a vacuum, in order to cause collisions between these high-speed particles and the nuclei of a target. They are not only expensive to build, but they consume

M. A. Tuve's million-volt Van de Graaff accelerator of 1933 looms over a replica of C. T. R. Wilson's 1912 cloud chamber.

A reconstruction of E. O. Lawrence's 1936 cyclotron and "Rad Lab" includes the original vacuum chamber, right foreground.

large quantities of energy. They were invented, and continue to be developed, not for any practical purpose but to produce knowledge of the most basic sort—although, incidentally, they continue to produce a most valuable kind of technological know-how.

But why was it just 60 years ago, not sooner and not later, that physicists began dreaming of such machines—and dreaming of ways to build them? The answer begins some 25 years earlier still, in Paris in 1896, with H. Becquerel's discovery of radioactivity. Physicists and chemists had speculated throughout the 19th century about the composition of the elements, and the possibility of breaking them down into fewer, smaller constituents. But radioactivity, and the discovery of the electron by J. J. Thomson at Cambridge University in the following year, created for the first time an experimental basis for speculation on the constitution of elements.

By 1902 Marie and Pierre Curie had isolated polonium and radium, two totally new elements much more radioactive than the uranium with which they were found. Ernest Rutherford—born in New Zealand, trained by Thomson, and working in Montreal—showed in a series of investigations that radioactivity was actually a spontaneous production of such new elements by successive transformations of uranium atoms, with the ejection of radiations that could penetrate most materials.

At first the least regarded, but soon the most important of these newly discovered particles, were the "alpha rays." Rutherford and his collaborators showed these to be positively charged helium atoms moving with terrific velocity—terrific for so heavy a particle. He made them his special tool, and probed the interior of other atoms with them. Alpha particles emitted by a quantity of radium were directed at a thin metal foil. Placing behind the foil a screen that scintillated or sparkled where struck by an alpha particle, Rutherford could observe the portion of the particles that deviated by various amounts from their initial direction.

The number of alpha particles scattered through wide angles was perplexingly large. In 1911 Rutherford argued that these and other data could be best explained by the hypothesis that the matter of which atoms are composed is not spread evenly throughout the whole volume of the atom, but rather that most of it is concentrated into a very, very small, positively charged central kernel. Around this kernel the negatively charged electrons swarm through the vast empty

Photographs by Ross Chapple

Paul Forman, a curator of modern physics at the National Museum of History and Technology, devoted three years to the preparation of the "Atom Smashers" exhibit.

atomic volume. This was the discovery of the atomic nucleus, the seat of radioactivity.

The lightest of these nuclei, that of the hydrogen atom, could be regarded as a single, elementary particle, the proton. The nuclei of heavier atoms were thought for 20 years—until the discovery of the neutron in 1932—to be composed only of numbers of protons, plus enough electrons to neutralize the excess positive charge.

Arguments and inferences in the study of radioactivity, and in the exciting field of nuclear physics emerging from it, were disquietingly indirect. No one had ever *seen* an atom, let alone a nucleus; the best one could do—and it had greatly impressed some eminent skeptics—was to observe the tiny flashes of light when scintillating materials are bombarded by alpha particles. In order to count the number of alpha particles emitted each second by a gram of radium, Rutherford and his assistant Hans Geiger developed in 1908 a method of electrically detecting the passage of individual alpha particles through a gas-filled tube. (This preceded the famous Geiger counter for detecting radioactivity, which Geiger and his student Walter Mueller perfected some 20 years later.) But still one had no way of "seeing" the paths of these and other rays, or the results of their collisions with atoms.

Therefore it was delightful to have all these previously hypothetical processes stand forth in black and white, as it were, in the "cloud chamber" which C. T. R Wilson devised in 1912 in J. J. Thomson's laboratory. Wilson's chief interest was meteorological physics. He had long investigated, in small glass "cloud chambers," the process of cloud formation, studying in particular the formation of water droplets around ions. (Ions are atoms or molecules charged positively or negatively by the removal or addition of an electron or two.) And now he came to the ingenious idea of trying to build a chamber in which the course and collisions of individual high-speed particles would be revealed by the formation of water droplets around the ions that such radiations supposedly produced all along their path through a gas.

A flat cylindrical glass chamber, whose floor could slide up and down like a piston, contained air saturated with water vapor. When the space below the floor was connected to a large evacuated glass bulb the floor dropped very suddenly. Rapid expansion cools a gas, so the air is rendered supersaturated and cloud droplets begin to form about any available ions. If ionizing radiations have passed through the chamber an instant before its expansion, the tracks of these high-speed charged particles stand out for a moment as strings of bright beads. And these tracks showed all the hypothesized processes, including, in particular, those sharp deflections of alpha-particles through wide an-

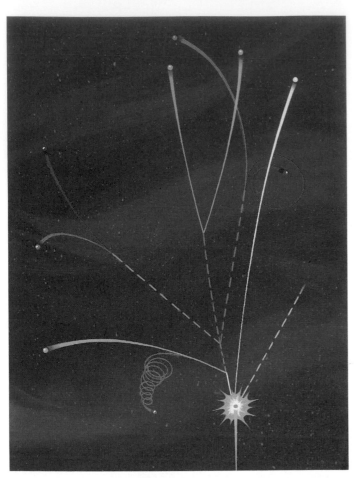

gles which Rutherford had said would result from collision with an atomic nucleus.

Collisions, yes, but, disintegration—not yet. Although physicists had the instruments to observe the results of atom smashing, they did not yet have the smasher. Indeed the very idea of building a machine to smash atoms had to wait until Rutherford showed in 1919 that such artificial transmutations were possible: very rarely, but yet occasionally, he found one of his alpha particles colliding with a nitrogen nucleus and energetically throwing out a proton. Soon after this astonishing discovery, physicists began to wonder how they might produce much more intense, and, if possible, more energetic beams of particles than could be ob-

In an artist's rendition of the high-energy collision in which an omega particle was first detected, left, protons accelerated by the Brookhaven synchrotron to 33 billion volts plowed into a metal target, ejecting a cascade of particles. Negative K mesons were separated and led into a liquid-hydrogen bubble chamber where a negative K meson (bottom) collided with the nucleus of a hydrogen atom, producing the omega particle (short white track at left) and others. The omega particle traveled about one inch in a 10-billionth of a second, then spontaneously transformed into a negative pi meson (long, curving green track) and an invisible xi particle. In the lower illustration, as ions (blue dots) are accelerated in a cyclotron, the magnetic field (represented by green arrows) curves the ions' path into a spiral.

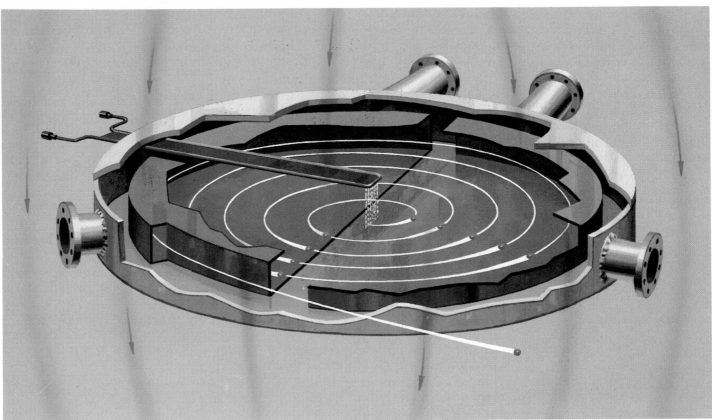

tained from natural radioactive substances. By the end of the next decade ambitious high-voltage programs had been started at a number of laboratories in Europe and the United States.

The first success in atom smashing with artificially accelerated particles was achieved at Cambridge University, where Rutherford had succeeded Thomson as director of the physics laboratory. There James Cockcroft and E. T. S. Walton

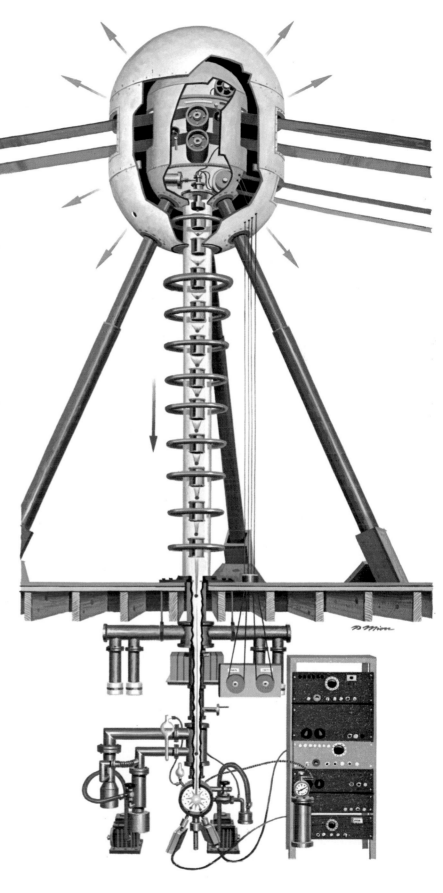

gambled on a completely novel phenomenon predicted by the new quantum mechanics: a proton, even though it had insufficient energy to force its way into the target nucleus against the electric repulsion of all those other positively charged protons, still had a chance—a small chance, but a chance nonetheless—of "tunneling" into the nucleus under that repulsive barrier.

The idea worked, and Cockcroft and Walton's gamble paid off handsomely. But the type of high voltage generator they invented, although it has proved extremely useful as the first stage of all present-day ultra-high-energy accelerators of protons and heavier ions, enjoyed only a brief vogue as an atom smasher in its own right. It could not reach into that region above a million volts where excitation and disintegration of the lighter nuclei were no longer just a lucky chance but, rather, a high probability.

Robert Van de Graaff, a former Rhodes scholar from Alabama, had an extraordinarily simple solution to this problem. He conceived of generating extremely high voltages by using a nonconducting conveyor belt to transport a static electric charge into the interior of an insulated metal shell. If the charge were to be drawn off the belt inside the shell, it would accumulate on the metal surface, raising it to ever higher potentials—until, finally, the insulation of the air or of the supports would break down with a lighting-like bolt and crack.

At Princeton University Van de Graaff sought to

In the first Van de Graaff accelerator, right, built by Merle Tuve in 1933, protons were produced at the bottom of the inner gray shell when hydrogen gas was leaked into an electric arc. Positively charged protons (red dots in tube) issuing from the bottom of the brass discharge tube were repelled down the evacuated glass acceleration tube by the positive charge built up on the shells by the large belt (the repulsive force is represented by blue arrows). The protons were focused and accelerated in the gaps between the brass cylinders through which they passed on their way down the tube. In the circular "scattering chamber" (at bottom) filled with hydrogen gas, some of the million-volt protons collided with hydrogen nuclei (protons); one or both protons were then scattered into the electrical detectors.

put his idea into practice. His efforts were followed and encouraged by Merle Tuve at the Department of Terrestrial Magnetism of the Carnegie Institution of Washington. Since 1926 Tuve had been at work on the problem of producing atom-smashing voltages with laboratory-sized apparatus. Indeed, his was the earliest of the systematic programs for developing such machines, and also for developing the vacuum tubes in which electrons and protons could be held in a tight beam while being accelerated by enormous electric fields. Tuve's attempt to harness the very high alternating voltages produced by a Tesla coil had ended in failure, and so he was on the lookout for an effective and affordable high-voltage machine.

In the autumn of 1931, as soon as Van de Graaff had made the front page of the *New York Times* with a seven-foot demonstration model of his method for generating high voltages, Tuve set to work on the first of the electrostatic—or Van de Graaff—accelerators. Completed in 1933, it reached just over a million volts, but with such precision and stability in energy that it remained a useful instrument long after all the rest of this first generation of atom smashers had been retired. One of its early and most important accomplishments was to provide the first experimental evidence that when two protons approach each other sufficiently closely, their electrical repulsion is overcome by an attractive force between the two particles. This is the force which holds a nucleus together.

But even more exciting than the Van de Graaff accelerator with its bolts of artificial lightning was the cyclotron of Ernest Orlando Lawrence—*the* atom smasher of the 1930s for scientist and layman alike. By 1929 he had become convinced that atom smashing was the frontier in physics. But Lawrence, then professor at the University of California, Berkeley, could see no new solution to the problem—until, one day, in the library, he ran across an article by Rolf Wideroe.

In this important paper Wideroe, a Norwegian working in Germany, described two types of accelerators he had built, one without success and the other with a degree of success. In the first of these, electrons circulated in a doughnut-shaped vacuum tube and were accelerated by a curling electric field. The second type of accelerator, whose principle Wideroe demonstrated experimentally after failing with the first, is the linear accelerator (contracted to linac when it came into its own two decades later). In this device the charged particles pass along the axis of a line of hollow metal cylinders contained within a vacuum

A neon tube has been inserted along the path of the beam of accelerated particles in this section of the interior of the first linear accelerator of protons (1947), exhibited at the Museum of History and Technology.

tube. Alternate cylinders are connected to opposite terminals of a high-frequency oscillator. The cylinders increase in length in proportion to the increase in velocity which the particles receive from the electric field when they cross the gaps between cylinders. Thus the particles remain in step with the oscillating field and are accelerated to higher and higher energies.

Lawrence was taken by the notion of producing high energies without the use of high voltages. He saw in a flash how to combine elements of Wideroe's two types of accelerator—circular and linear—in a single device basically much simpler and more promising than either. In a flat, pillbox-shaped vacuum chamber place two hollow, flat, D-shaped metal boxes back-to-back—but with the backs of the two Ds open, and a small gap between them. Place the pillbox between the poles of a magnet and connect the Ds to opposite terminals of a high-frequency oscillator.

If, then, ions—e.g., protons—are produced in the center of the apparatus by bombarding the slight residual gas with electrons, the oscillating electric field in the gap between the Ds will pull the ions into one or the other D. Those ions with just the right speed and direction are bent around in a semi-circle so as to arrive again at the gap just when the electric field has also reversed its direction. Thus these ions are again sped forward with increased velocity.

The faster the ions move, the larger the semicircle into which the magnetic field curves them, so that they always require the same time to return to the gap. If the strength of the magnetic field and the frequency of the oscillator are correctly adjusted to each other and to the type of ion being accelerated, the ions, once in step with the oscillating electric field, will stay in step, gaining energy each time they cross the gap and gradually spiraling outward. Thus it appeared that the only limit to the energy of the cyclotron was the size of the magnet one could afford.

Lawrence and his student M. Stanley Livingston were able to demonstrate the validity of the principle early in 1931 with a pillbox four inches in diameter. In the spring of that year, even before his second cyclotron—a mere 11 inches that produced a million volts—had been completed, Lawrence's imagination was fired by the sight of a huge World War I surplus magnet. The Federal Telegraph Company was persuaded to donate this remnant of an obsolete method of transoceanic radio-telegraphy. Lawrence then raised money from private foundations to convert it into a six-million-volt cyclotron, and persuaded his university to give him an old building as a radiation laboratory to house it and his team of enthusiastic young "cyclotroneers." Their cyclotron (the H.M.S. *Cyclotron*, E. O. Lawrence, Master, as they called it in their logbook) is illustrated here as it appeared in 1936

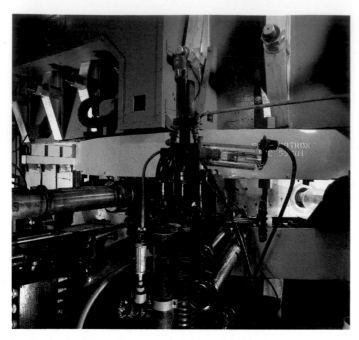

E. M. McMillan's electron synchrotron of 1949. A vacuum pump in the foreground evacuates the ring-shaped acceleration tube, while the brass pipe at left carries radio waves to impart energy to the electrons circulating in the tube.

when spruced up with a couple of coats of battleship-gray paint.

The construction of this centerpiece of the Berkeley "Rad Lab" had required about $10,000 in cash. In the five years remaining before Pearl Harbor, Lawrence completed a $100,000, 16-million-volt cyclotron, and started on the "definitive" million-dollar cyclotron, which was supposed to reach 100 million volts. Fortunately the Second World War halted its construction, for here Lawrence had overreached the limits of applicability of his cyclotron principle.

After the war and its acceleration of research, the whole atom-smashing game was changed—new goals, new rules, new strategies, and a lot more players. To smash atoms, that is, to excite and disrupt atomic nuclei, was no longer enough. It now became a question of smashing the nucleons, the protons and neutrons, the particles composing the atomic nuclei. The goal was now not millions, but billions of volts. The war had taught physicists to think big, to think as Lawrence did. Federal Government money, not previously available for atom smashing, now flowed into the laboratories, and physicists now knew how to use it. Moreover, the war years had produced the new ideas, and war research the new technologies, which gave physicists confidence that they could reach so high.

Wartime developments in radar offered one of these new opportunities. The boldest in exploiting it was Luis W. Alvarez, one of Lawrence's young cyclotroneers. As early as 1943 Alvarez had conceived of using military radar equipment to power a billion-volt linear accelerator. As the war was coming to an end, Lawrence used his influence to secure nearly 1,000 military surplus radar sets. In fact only a few of these were ever used, and the project was abandoned late in 1947 with the completion of the first 40-foot section of the accelerator (see photograph, page 136). The proton linac gave way to the synchrotron as the front-line high-energy accelerator, but the type of machine that Alvarez and his team had invented has retained to this day its value as the indispensable injector of particles into the high-energy synchrotrons, and also as an accelerator of heavy ions.

The synchrotron principle was conceived toward the end of the war by V. I. Veksler in the USSR and Edwin McMillan in the United States, as a way to overcome the limits set by the theory of relativity to the applicability of Lawrence's cyclotron principle. They showed that particles circulating in a doughnut-shaped vacuum chamber form stable bunches that can be shepherded to arbitrarily high energies by gradually increasing the strength of the guiding magnetic field and the frequency of the accelerating electric field.

Immediately after the war McMillan at Berkeley and physicists at several other laboratories built synchrotrons to accelerate electrons. These machines, of about 300 million volts, both demonstrated the principle and got physicists quickly into the energy region then of greatest interest—the energies at which mesons, the particles embodying the strong attractive nuclear force, are liberated from the protons and neutrons and thus become observable.

By 1947 physicists were ready to tackle the much larger and more complex problems of the proton synchrotron. The British were the first to start—a one-billion-volt machine. But the first in operation was the three-billion-volt Cosmotron at Brookhaven National Laboratory on Long Island, completed in 1952. In the following quarter century, the second half, as it were, of the career of the atom smasher, synchrotrons have grown progressively more powerful, larger, and vastly more expensive.

Currently the highest energy accelerators are the proton synchrotrons at the laboratory of the European Organization for Nuclear Research (CERN), in Geneva, Switzerland, and at the Fermi National Accelerator Laboratory west of Chicago. This latter laboratory holds the record, 500 billion volts, and aims to keep it. In their four-mile-in-circumference ring, a second ring is being threaded through the support legs of the original. This uses superconducting magnets to bend the accelerated protons around the circle, and will boost their energy to 1,000 billion volts.

In the years since the Second World War, since the advance from smashing atomic nuclei to the study of the elementary subnuclear particles, physicists have devised a variety of techniques for detecting and following the behavior of these short-lived entities. That which commanded the field in the late 1950s and the 1960s, when the new multibillion-volt proton synchrotrons were producing new particles almost as fast as the physicists could name them, was the bubble chamber. This device, whose function and principle of operation is closely analogous to that of the cloud chamber, was conceived in 1952 by Donald A. Glaser.

In a bubble chamber a liquid is held below its boiling point by the application of pressure. If the pressure is suddenly released the liquid is rendered superheated, just as in the cloud chamber sudden reduction of the pressure renders the air supersaturated. Just as the cloud droplets need something around which to form, something to precipitate the condensation of liquid out of the vapor, so the bubbles in the bubble chamber need something around which they can form, something to precipitate the evolution of vapor out of the liquid. In the bubble chamber as in the cloud chamber, ions produced by the passage of speeding subatomic particles supply that something. Thus the tracks of these particles are revealed for a brief moment, and may be photographed.

Bubble chambers were just what was needed for experiments with the high energy synchrotrons. The liquid itself is the target as well as the detector. For this reason, physicists—with Luis Alvarez in the lead—soon developed bubble chambers filled with liquid hydrogen (pure protons, plus electrons, of course) cooled to within 30 degrees of absolute zero. As the density of a liquid is greater than that of a vapor, so is the advantage of the bubble chamber over the cloud chamber greater. But still, as the energy of accelerators increased, the size of the bubble chambers had to increase also if they were to arrest the ever more energetic and penetrating particles. The largest are now about 15 feet in diameter—and they are not likely to be built any larger.

Unfortunately, as the energy of accelerators increases, their effective energy against a fixed target increases proportionately less and less; the marginal return on the investment declines. At the energies now attained by proton synchrotrons, only five percent of each additional billion volts is available for the disruption of the colliding particles and the creation of new ones. This problem is entirely eliminated by causing two equally energetic beams to collide head-on. However, the density of particles in an accelerator beam is so low that the chance is very small of a particle actually undergoing a collision with a particle coming toward it in the other beam. Since the probability of a collision increases as the square of the number of pulses stored, the answer is storage rings, in which hundreds of

Brookhaven National Laboratory's 80-inch, liquid-hydrogen bubble chamber of 1963, seen here in the "Atom Smashers" exhibit at the Museum of History and Technology, was used to observe the tracks of subatomic particles in collision.

pulses from an accelerator are accumulated in each of two counter-orbiting beams.

Since 1971 there has been a large proton storage ring operating at the CERN laboratory in Geneva. A second machine of this type, but with 10 times the energy, is being built at Brookhaven National Laboratory. Electron-positron storage rings were the first to be built, and have been the most productive of discoveries in recent years. New and much more powerful machines are nearing completion at Novosibirsk, Hamburg, Cornell, and Stanford.

These yet more powerful accelerators (storage rings are essentially synchrotrons) are expected to answer many questions about the constituents of the scores of elementary particles brought to light by previous generations of atom smashers. Perhaps the hypothetical quarks will finally be liberated from the nucleons and mesons they're supposed to compose. Perhaps the mesons embodying the weak nuclear force, which are correspondingly heavier than those mediating the strong, will themselves become observable. But whatever the new particles may be, they are not "machine-made," not artificial, not unnatural. As Francis Bacon said, Nature shows her true nature only when we twist her tail. □

New Tools for Science

The 1960s brought to mankind spectacular achievements in space exploration, electronics, and medicine, advances that strongly shaped research in the '70s. But now the '80s are upon us. So stand at the threshold of the future for a Smithsonian-eye view of important areas of innovation that will help determine our scientific destiny in the 1980s and for many decades beyond.

Space probes give us panoramas of the planets that no earthbound telescope could provide. In 1976 the first Viking probe broadcast back to Earth an awesome sunset on Mars. Voyager 1, on its way to Jupiter, transmitted the first scene of the Earth and the moon sailing together in the blackness of space.

Now that lunar-landing astronauts and our mechanical Magellans have turned astronomy into a field science, scholars grow ever more anxious to answer the central riddle of space: is there life out there? Or are we, by some infinite irony, alone in the cosmos?

To gain hints of life on Mars, NASA scientists equipped the Viking probe with sophisticated analytical and sensing devices for measuring surface and atmospheric composition. What they found, or didn't find, left the question of life unresolved. Images of the polar ice caps confirmed the presence of water. Photos of channels suggest that Mars once held mighty rivers. Yet today the red planet's atmospheric pressure is insufficient to support water in its liquid state. Voyager 1 is bound out past Mars toward Jupiter and Saturn. Information sent back in 1979 could shed some light on scientific speculation that Jupiter's atmosphere may support some kind of life forms, even though the planet is far different physically and chemically from Earth and Mars.

Satellites and space probes transmit pictures that transport viewers to the frontiers of space. Viking 1 sent back a startling sunset

from Mars, below. Opposite, Voyager 1 caught Earth and the moon together, backdropped by the starry void.

Sky Eyes

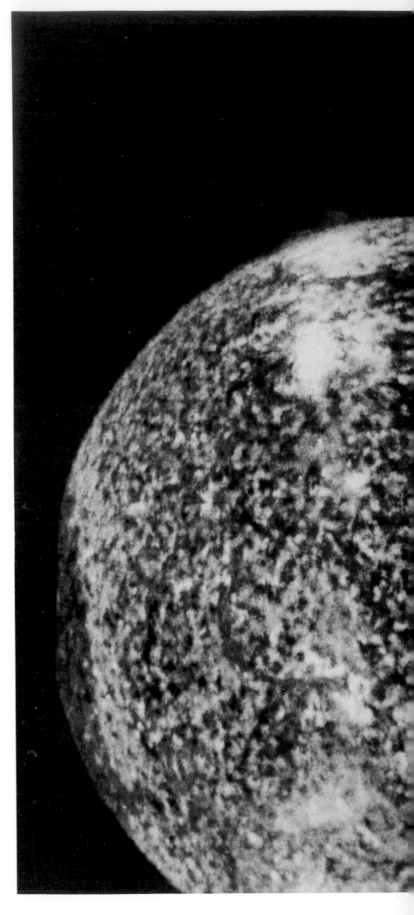

Vaulting nearly 380,000 miles across the face of the sun, one of the most spectacular solar flares ever recorded erupted before the watchful eye of Skylab 4. The solar event occurred in December 1973. A picture taken only 17 hours earlier revealed the feature as a large quiescent prominence. Such time-lapse photography may help scientists explain the sun's activity both on its surface and within its heart. Clues thus gained from our neighboring star may also help scientists solve the mysteries of distant galaxies.

Enterprise, our first space shuttle, approaches a landing field at Edwards Air Force Base in California. Such a craft will carry Skylab's more advanced successor, Spacelab, into orbit by the early 1980s. Built by a multinational European consortium, Spacelab is designed to fit the 60-foot-long cargo bay of the *Enterprise*—a spaceship as big as a DC-9 airliner.

Manned by a crew of three, one of the space taxis should perform perhaps 100 missions, each of a month's duration, during its projected lifetime. Such craft will shuttle between Earth and orbit to set out and bring back more than 90 percent of the space satellites currently envisioned. Much more work in space can be scheduled due to the far lower investment needed to fly one reusable shuttle with many payloads rather than one expendable rocket with one payload.

A complement of four "payload specialists" will operate Spacelab's sensitive information-gathering equipment. Like its namesake, the ship in TV's "Star Trek," today's *Enterprise* will boldly explore and expand the boundaries of our knowledge.

Enterprise, *the space shuttle orbiter, will economically deploy satellites and retrieve them from space in the '80s.*

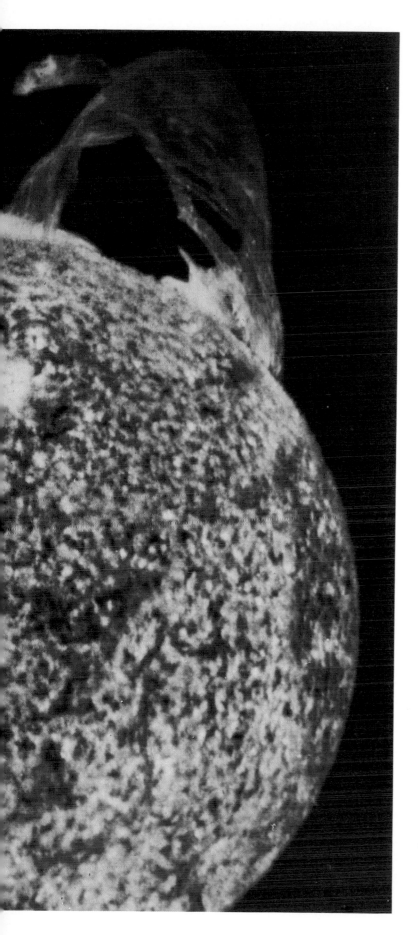

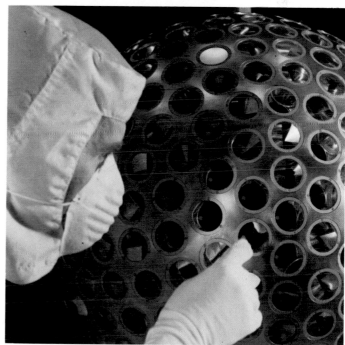

A huge solar flare appears in an ultraviolet-spectrum image taken aboard NASA's Skylab 4. The arch of superheated gas and ions erupted in less than a day, spanning 380,000 miles. Space eye also snapped a portrait of Washington, D.C., top. LAGEOS, short for Laser Geodynamic Satellite, undergoes prelaunch evaluation at the Goddard Space Flight Center in Maryland, above. The reflector ports will bounce back laser light shot from Earth, enabling scientists to measure tiny movements in the Earth's crust and perhaps predict earthquakes.

Seeing the Stars

The innovative tools with which we extend human eyesight have opened up the heavens. These devices enable us to resolve features of, for instance, almost any of the closer stars we choose of the perhaps 200 billion stars in our home galaxy, the Milky Way. And we can now see and analyze myriad other galaxies as well.

In 1976, astronomers at the Kitt Peak National Observatory in Arizona, using the 158-inch Mayall Telescope and a computer, took the first photograph which showed the true disk shape and some of the surface features of a star other than our sun—Betelgeuse, below. A red supergiant in the constellation Orion, Betelgeuse is 800 times larger than the sun, 12,000 times more luminous, and about 500 light years away. Nevertheless, viewed from Earth with the unaided eye it appears no bigger than would a 25-cent piece seen from a distance of 50 miles.

To make this amazing photograph scientists employed a technique called speckle interferometry. First, large-scale images in nearly monochromatic light were exposed at 1/125th of a second, a speed which "freezes" the ever-changing atmospheric disturbances that ordinarily smear the disk. In such a photograph Betelgeuse appears as a blob composed of countless bright speckles, each an image of the star formed by part of the telescope mirror. By scanning this photograph with a densitometer and then using a computer to superimpose and combine the speckles, a single limited-diffraction image of the star is produced without blurring or distortion.

The surface features of a star are not so easily visualized as those of Earth. On Betelgeuse they show up as barely recognizable dark and bright regions, cooler in blue, warmer in red. These variations may be caused by the rise and fall of gas convection currents in the star's hugely extended and tenuous atmosphere.

Another of the inventive tools used at Kitt Peak to collect information from deep space is the astronomical diffraction grating. The grating itself is a flat piece of optical glass that has been coated with aluminum and engraved with a ruling engine.

In actual use, starlight from a telescope falls on the minute parallel grooves of the grating and is broken into a rainbow of colors. A magnetic tape records the intensity of each color. Computerized plotting of the information creates a precise spectral graph for the star. Analysis of such stellar spectra led to the discovery of the famous "red shift" which indicated that all galaxies in the universe are receding from each other. This in turn led to the formulation of the Big Bang theory of the origin of the universe and yielded clues to its age.

The first photo of a star other than our sun to reveal a disk shape, below, was made at Kitt Peak National Observatory in Arizona. The rim of red supergiant Betelgeuse is revealed through a new technique called speckle interferometry. With beams of colored laser light, a researcher tests a diffraction grating, opposite. The device breaks starlight into a spectrum for chemical analysis.

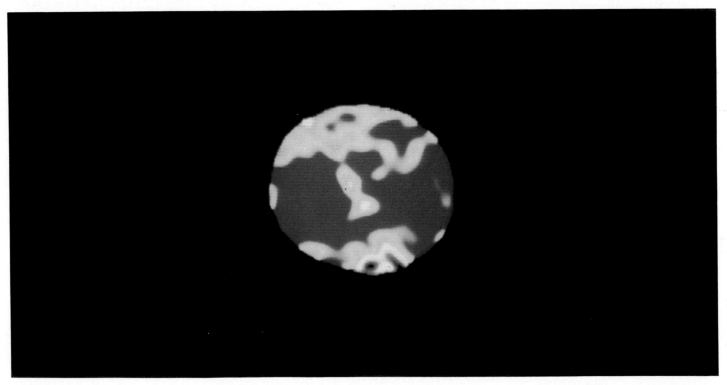

Hearing

When you pick up your telephone a few years hence, your voice may travel with as many as 33,000 others on a laser beam through a glass fiber thinner than a human hair and stronger than a like-sized strand of steel. Optical fibers can carry laser-light pulses at a rate equivalent to one million words a second. And while the basic principles of light and radio transmission are the same, light covers a far greater range of frequencies than our usual Hertzian waves.

A barium sodium niobate crystal can convert infrared laser light to visible light by a process known as harmonic generation. This technique adds still more frequencies for communication.

For calls at distances beyond 100 miles, an orbiting satellite will probably relay your voice. INTELSAT V, scheduled for launch before 1980, will join the host of communication satellites that already handle more than two-thirds of all transoceanic communication traffic and bring live television to one-fourth of the world's population.

Fingers grasp light at Bell Laboratories. Bundles of such tiny spun glass cables may soon replace expensive metal phone lines. At right, a Bell scientist basks in the rosy glow of a new solid-state laser. The cube sitting on such a laser, bottom, is a single grain of table salt, included for scale.

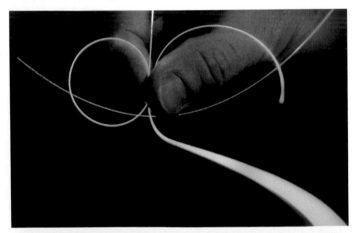

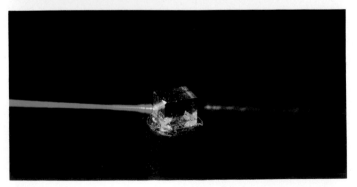

Healing

Computerized Axial Tomography (CAT) sounds like the kind of gobbledygook often associated with unproved devices and theories. But CAT is already at work saving lives. With it, technology and medicine join to take a colorful look inside a human skull.

While computers seemingly threaten to engulf us, this application has made possible the diagnosis of a deep-seated disease without invasive surgery. First, thousands of low-dosage X-ray measurements create a cross-sectional picture of the skull case and its contents. The computer processes the raw data and stands ready to present on a TV screen any three-dimensional view that a surgeon may desire. The ventricles of the brain and even the eyes can be viewed at will.

Conventional X-rays do not permit discrimination of structure composed of soft tissue, like tumors or organs. They pass through flesh and portray only bone. CAT, however, can detect a one-percent difference in the X-ray absorption rate of tissue and thus reveal inflammation and both benign and malignant tumors. Previously, diagnosis often required complicated and sometimes painful tests.

CAT is only one of a whole range of growing applications of computers in graphic display. Donald P. Greenberg of Cornell's Program of Computer Graphics forecasts that within the next decade small computers the size of notebooks will plug into television consoles to provide anybody with his own choice of graphic environment. Processed information could help plan your vacation. Computer-generated pictures of your own tennis game might help solve problems with the backhand shot. In fact, the only hitch seems to be to raise human intelligence high enough to take advantage of all that computer capacity. □

David Bridge

New three-dimensional imagery of the human skull and the living brain within allows diagnosis of a tumor or other disease without exploratory surgery. CAT for short, the acronym stands for Computerized Axial Tomography. Within five seconds a harmless bombardment of X-rays describes bone and tissue data that a computer can store and later transform into pictures. The large tomogram, above, gives a side view of a skull and its hollows. A wire-line drawing, lower left, displays bone measurements from eight tomographic cross sections. Middle, the front of a skull with eye sockets. Tomogram at far right depicts eyes and brain within that skull—rendered transparent through selective visualization techniques.

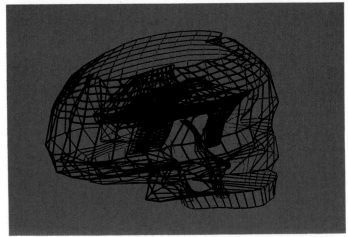

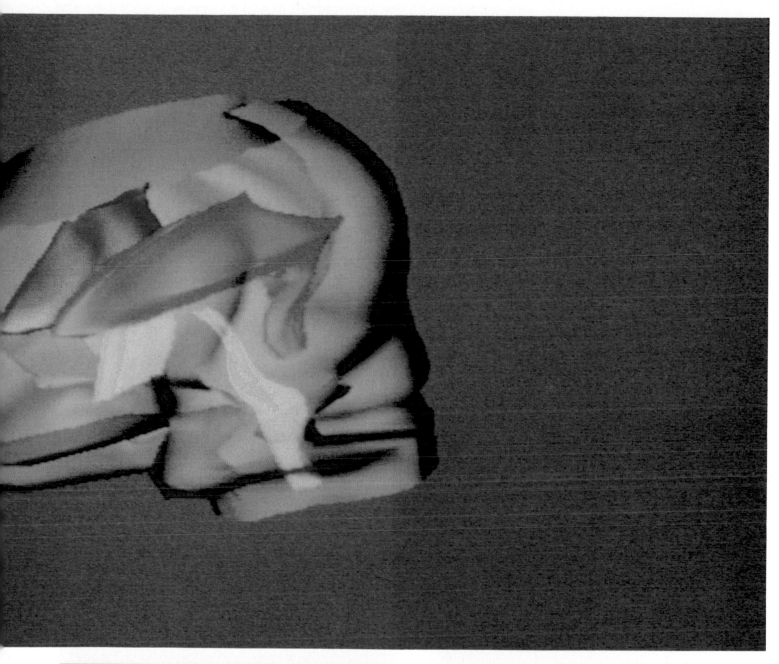

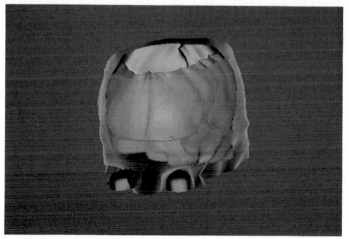

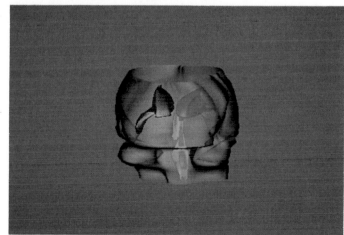

Tinkering with the Genes

Nicholas Wade

The most important inventor in the history of mankind is one whose name has not been recorded. It was the person who first learned how to bring wild plants under cultivation. Through the archway of that seemingly simple achievement, man passed from a precarious existence as a hunter and gatherer to life as farmer, herder, villager, and city dweller. Other Neolithic inventors domesticated most of the plant and animal species that remain in use today, thus laying the agricultural foundation upon which urban civilizations rest.

The newly developed art of genetic engineering is a biological invention which may prove just as far-reaching as the art of domesticating plants and animals. The two achievements are widely separated both in time and in concept. The Neolithic inventors of 9,000 years ago did not create new species. They selected, and enhanced by breeding, the traits they desired from within the natural genetic potential of existing species. After that brief flowering of biological invention, a long pause ensued. The next steps could be taken only when the nature of life was better understood.

"Nature proceeds little by little from things lifeless to animal life in such a way that it is impossible to determine the exact line of demarcation, nor on which side thereof an intermediate form should lie." So stated the Greek polymath Aristotle in the fourth century B.C. With the idea that no sharp distinction existed between the living and the non-living, Aristotle had perceived an important truth, one soon lost sight of. To later thinkers it seemed evident that there had to be something unique about living things. The 18th-century Italian scientist Luigi Galvani believed that a simple fluid held the essence of life. It was a brilliant albeit wrong idea. Life is not a fluid, but in the course of searching for it he discovered electricity. And the concept that the essence of life was a single, identifiable substance proved to be correct, although in a far more complicated way than Galvani could imagine.

The modern era of biology began in 1859, scarcely more than a century ago, when Charles Darwin published his theory of evolution. Under the pressure of adapting to changes in the environment, Darwin supposed, species are either driven into extinction or else gradually evolve into slightly different species. Natural selection, the motive force in Darwin's theory, needed some source of variability on which to act. It was the 19th-century Austrian monk Gregor Mendel who realized that the predictable variability in his green peas could be explained by their inheritance of discrete hereditary factors, later known as genes.

The next giant leap forward after Darwin was the discovery that genes are embodied in the chemical known as deoxyribonucleic acid or DNA. In 1953 Francis Crick and James Watson worked out the marvelously suggestive helical structure of DNA, and almost everything molecular biologists have done since has been based on this discovery. All forms of life, all the observable facts of heredity and evolution, derive

Nicholas Wade, previously Washington correspondent for Nature, *writes for* Science Magazine. *He is author of* The Ultimate Experiment.

from the physical expression of the information encoded in DNA molecules.

The 20th century has been the great age of physics, and the basic scientific knowledge so gained has laid the foundations on which modern technology is built. After the discovery of the structure of DNA, it seemed that next it would be the biologists' turn to shake the world. For the next 20 years the biologists proceeded to accumulate a vast storehouse of pure knowledge. Yet with rare exceptions, very little of this scholarly wealth has been practically applied.

The reason for this was not lack of inventiveness but a problem of scale. The DNA molecule is extremely intricate, and, though large as molecules go, it only teeters on the edge of visibility under the most powerful microscopes. Precise manipulations of the molecule, such as snipping out a gene-sized segment from the DNA of one organism and transferring it to that of another, seemed well beyond the limits of practical possibility.

Exactly such a technique was developed in 1973 by a team of four scientists: Stanley N. Cohen and Annie C. Y. Chang of Stanford University and Herbert W. Boyer and Robert B. Helling of the University of California, San Francisco (Helling is now at the University of Michigan). Known as the gene-splicing or "recombinant DNA" technique, it immediately transported genetic engineering from a science-fiction fantasy land into the realm of the possible. It began the age of synthetic biology exactly 20 years after the great analytic phase was initiated by Watson and Crick's discovery.

The Cohen team was not attempting to build a bridge to the practical world. All were research scientists whose aim was to develop a more powerful tool for analyzing DNA. But they were sufficiently aware of the practical implications of what they had done to have their institutions apply for a patent on the technique. (The application is still pending.)

The essence of the gene-splicing technique is that it at last enables the precise manipulation of DNA and the genetic information. A key feature of the technique is the use of "restriction enzymes," proteins produced by bacteria to destroy foreign DNA, such as that of invading viruses. The restriction enzymes, which cut the DNA molecule at certain precise points, are the tools that make it possible to operate at the molecular level. The technique serves as a combined scissors-and-paste and copying kit. With the scissors-and-paste part of the technique one can cut out a particular small region of a DNA molecule (the gene that codes for insulin, say) and splice it into the DNA of one of the virus-like entities known as plasmids. The copying part then exploits the cloning phenomenon, a method of reproduction common among bacteria.

Venerable propounder of evolution by natural selection, Charles Darwin led the way for other biologists.

Above, J. D. Watson, at left, and F. H. C. Crick posed with the model they built to show the structure of the DNA molecule. Their discovery earned them a 1962 Nobel Prize, shared with M. H. F. Wilkins, on whose studies their work was partially based. Opposite, George Washington Carver with his hybrid amaryllis. Director of the department of agricultural research at Tuskegee Institute, Carver improved hundreds of plants through hybridization.

When a bacterium divides it produces two genetically identical daughter cells which in turn divide, and so on and so forth, until a large number of genetically identical bacteria have been produced. If the founding member of the clone, as the group is called, has been infected with the insulin-gene-tagged plasmid, all other members of the clone will also carry a copy of the plasmid. The insulin gene is reproduced as many times as there are members of the clone.

An immediate practical application of gene splicing is to manufacture hormones, vaccines, and other biological substances of therapeutic value. Insulin, for example, needed by diabetics, is at present extracted from the glands of cattle and pigs, a source that may soon be outstripped by the demand. The gene-splicing technique should make it possible to program bacteria with the human gene for insulin. Grown on an industrial scale, the bacteria would produce, in addition to their own proteins, harvestable quantities of human insulin. Progress toward this goal has already been substantial. A team of scientists from Harvard and the Joslin Diabetes Foundation in Boston announced in June 1978 that they had succeeded in programming bacteria to produce rat pro-insulin, a protein that is the natural precursor of insulin.

A group that includes Herbert Boyer, one of the co-inventors of the gene-splicing technique, has reached a similar stage of progress in programming bacteria to produce another hormone, somatostatin, which also plays a role in controlling the metabolism of

Seeking to crack the dread mystery of sickle cell anemia, Dr. Makio Murayama of NIH built a model of the hemoglobin molecule, tinkered with the parts, and found an answer.

sugar. Vaccine production is another area ripe for takeover by the gene splicers. Flu vaccine, cultured from the flu virus in eggs, contains egg proteins which often cause side effects. By programming bacteria to synthesize the viral protein that forms the basis of the vaccine, a much purer and more effective product could, in theory, be obtained.

Programming bacteria to produce useful substances is likely to be the first fruit of genetic engineering. A more distant application may be a new assault against genetic diseases such as sickle cell anemia. "Gene therapy," as it has already been named, depends on the proposition that in diseases caused by a defective or absent gene, a properly functioning version of the gene can be inserted in working order into the patient's relevant organs. In the case of sickle cell anemia, for example, the bone marrow cells might be extracted, infected with a plasmid carrying genes for the normal variety of human hemoglobin, and reinserted in the patient.

Another category of possible applications lies in the genetic engineering of whole organisms. The most promising candidates are plants, because some, such as carrots, can be grown from a single cell. Splice into the DNA of a single carrot cell some useful genes, such as those promoting better taste or resistance to disease, and the whole carrot and all its progeny will be genetically improved. One idea often mentioned is that of equipping cereal crops with the genes to extract their own supplies of nitrogen from the air, thus making nitrogenous fertilizer unnecessary.

The invention of gene splicing makes it possible for the first time to consider seriously, or at least not to laugh out of court, the genetic engineering of man. Numerous technical and social obstacles must be considered, and yet the gene-splicing technique has already solved what may prove to be the worst of the technical problems, and it will perhaps provide the knowledge to solve all the others. The more formidable social and political barriers may yet crumble too. The benefits of human genetic engineering are going to be demonstrated first in curing genetic disease, then perhaps in ensuring that every individual reaches his full genetic potential. Once the human genetic potential has been improved a little, however, for the best of reasons, there may be no clear barrier to improving it a lot. The idea of progress is deeply rooted in Western societies; would it be true to that value to pass up the opportunity of improving the inheritance of a scarcely perfect species? Why let man's genetic future be shaped by the blind forces of genetic drift and natural selection? What is inherently wrong about creating a group of genetically improved individuals? The idea may not be as democractic as could be wished, but human societies are fully inured to elites whose claim to superiority is based on—of all absurd propositions —their heredity.

The dilemma of improving upon the human gene pool is more than purely taxonomic. Even a few genetic changes could produce a creature as different from man as man is from the apes. *Homo sapiens* would have brought to birth his finest creation, *Homo sapientior.*

Even if the future of gene splicing follows quite different lines from those presently envisaged, the technique remains in principle an intervention in evolution. Evolution moves by degrees, reshuffling the genes within species but seldom, so fas as is known, transferring genes between species far removed from each other on the evolutionary tree. A bacterium containing the human gene for insulin has yet to arise naturally. What if this or other gene-spliced organisms should escape from the factories or laboratories in which they are housed? Extra genes, in evolutionary terms, are probably rather like a random mutation, and most mutations are lethal. Almost all gene-spliced organisms would be ill-adapted to the environment into which they escaped, and would certainly perish. As for the rest, not enough is understood about evolution to say for certain what would happen. For this or other reasons, some biologists have been seriously concerned about the possibility of mishap.

As a result of such concerns, some types of gene-splicing experiments have been declared off limits; others are conducted under special safety procedures drawn up by the National Institutes of Health, a government agency that supports much of the nation's biological research. For the past two years Congress has considered making the NIH safety rules mandatory for all researchers, including those in industry, but so far has not managed to come to an agreement on the specifics of legislation. Feeling among scientists has run high, some fearing that a slew of new bureaucratic impediments would make gene-splicing research impossible, others warning that their colleagues' professional interest in playing with the new technique has blinded them to the longer-term consequences. "Have we the right to counteract, irreversibly, the evolutionary wisdom of millions of years, in order to satisfy the ambition and curiosity of a few scientists? . . . My generation, or perhaps the one preceding mine, has been the first to engage, under the leadership of the exact sciences, in a destructive colonial war against nature. The future will curse us for it," wrote Columbia University's Erwin Chargaff, whose work on the chemistry of DNA paved the way for Watson and Crick's discovery.

The consequences of gene splicing and its successor techniques may not be as treacherous as Dr. Chargaff fears. After all, we are a long way from knowing how to assemble genes so as to create a viable organ-

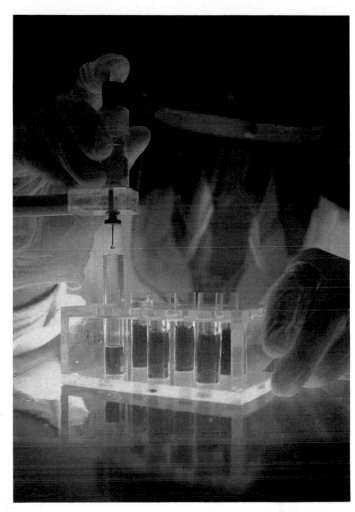

In a recombinant DNA laboratory, a technician adds a drop containing trillions of DNA plasmids to a test tube of plasmids centrifugally separated from bacteria cells. With such material, scientists make new genetic combinations.

ism. Nor do we know how to design new genes. Gene splicing should bring about a better understanding of the course of evolution, but may not suffice, even with the aid of other techniques, to penetrate the mists that surround the dawn of life on Earth. But biological inventions have the potential of being more profound in their consequences than any other kinds. Most technologies serve merely as tools to extend the powers of man's hand or eye or brain. Gene splicing offers a way of turning man's tools inward to manipulate the whole kingdom of DNA, including man himself. For good or ill, the new invention promises man a tool for manipulating the mechanisms of evolution, for controlling his own creator. □

5
PART

The Reach of Industry

More often than not, at the foundation of an industry, whether it produces television sets or screw propellers, lies a patent: that is, an exclusive right to make something. And virtually everything we use has, at one time or another, been patented. In fact, we demonstrate a madness for patenting. After all, invention has, for a famous few, been the ladder to fame and riches.

Perhaps our most important industry, for survival or profit, has always been food and its production. Not just innovations in planting, reaping, and packaging, but also the ingenuities of the chemist and the geneticist have combined to turn the United States into the breadbasket of the world. This has not been accomplished, of course, without some problematic side effects.

Just as little changed in the methods of growing food until the 19th century, so mankind worked with the same natural materials for many other products—wood, stone, ivory, iron, gold. Now, in little more than a century, we have developed hundreds of new materials. Vital materials such as aluminum, Bakelite, nylon—each has been the cornerstone of a new group of industries.

What holds it all together is one pivotal industry, the business of keeping in touch. Until recently communication was only as fast as a human could carry a message. Now, through electronics, we have turned the world into a shrinking global village where almost anyone can know almost anything, anywhere, in an instant or two. But the need to invent ways to communicate the important, rather than the trivial, remains. . . .

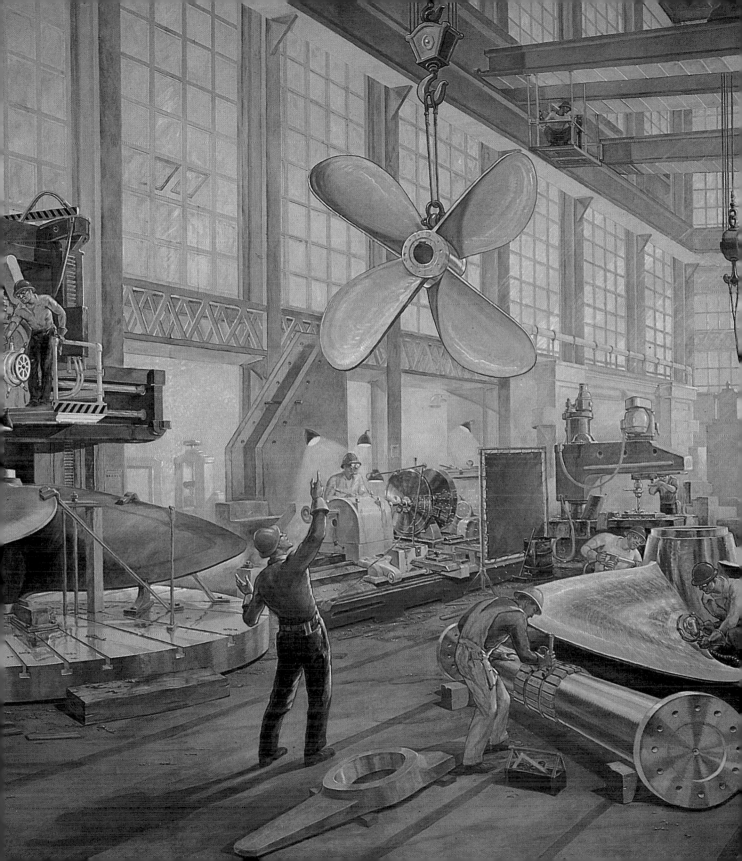

A Patent Madness

Morgan Sherwood

Just before the Civil War, Walt Whitman urged his fellow Americans to "give but a passing glance at the fat volumes of Patent Office Reports and bless your star that fate has cast your lot in the year of our Lord 1857." There was indeed by that year an impressive total of U.S. patents: 20,000. Whitman seemed right in equating U.S. prosperity with the blooming good health of the patent system.

Certainly the U.S. Patent Office itself harbored no doubts about the importance of its functions or about its part in aiding the growth of our technology-based, invention-powered civilization. It issued a pamphlet crediting patents for the flourishing state of American industry, for the employment of millions of Americans, and for the encouragement given to "hundreds of thousands of inventors." The pamphlet concluded with the triumphant vaunt that "The Patent System is one of the strongest bulwarks of democratic government today."

It behooves all of us to look more closely at the history of an institution that flashes such impressive credentials—and which still rests upon the oligarchal proposition (so upsetting to Jefferson) that government should distribute temporary monopolies to a special class of people—the inventors.

First, Americans did not invent patents. A Florentine received a patent in 1421, and Venice enacted a patent law in 1474. In the mid-16th century, England began to grant patents for inventions. During the reign of James I, 1603-25, all royal monopolies were outlawed except patents given specifically to inventors of "newe Manufactures."

Colonial Americans across the Atlantic adopted many, but not

all, of the English precedents. Several colonies granted no patents and no colony granted very many. A government might present a monetary award rather than a patent to the inventor. Private societies also awarded prizes, medals, and the like for new discoveries. The Continental Congress promised to give James Rumsey the title to 30,000 acres of public domain if his steamboat could travel upstream for a certain distance in a certain time.

By 1787, when the Founding Fathers gathered to draft a new social compact for the United States, the country had experimented with a variety of ways to reward ingenuity. In Philadelphia, James Madison recommended "premiums and provisions," while Charles Pinckney suggested Federal patents. The authors of the Constitution, without paying much attention to what they were doing (there were larger and more important problems to resolve), chose the Federally granted patent "to promote the progress of the useful arts." Even before the first patent law was enacted in 1790, Congress was asked to grant compensation or exclusive rights in exchange for revealing "an infallible cure for the bite of a mad dog," for the design of a wheeled boat to roll over river rapids, and for improved lightning rods, including "conductors and umbrellas . . . making them certain preservers from lightning." (The latter had already been demonstrated by a Frenchman, who had equipped even his top hat with a lightning rod.)

The Act of 1790 invested a patent board consisting of the Secretaries of State and War and the Attorney General with the authority "to grant patents for any useful art, manufacture, engine, machine, or device as they should deem sufficiently useful and important." After examining an application, the board could refuse to grant patents for devices that failed to meet these criteria or were not new. The authority was exercised rigorously although the rule to prohibit patents for mere changes of material was later repeatedly ignored. Patents were issued during the 19th century for concrete coffins, paper coffins, glass coffins, steel coffins, and Celluloid coffins. The substitution of rubber for leather shoe heels received a patent.

The Act of 1790 was short-lived; the ludicrous spectacle of cabinet ministers acting as patent clerks brought about a new patent law in 1793. Under the new "registration system," almost any aspiring inventor could get a patent without prior examination by simply submitting an application, specifications, a fee of $30, and an affidavit stating that he did "verily believe" that he was the "true inventor." The courts

Morgan Sherwood, author of a book on the patent system, teaches the history of American science at the University of California, Davis.

Thousands of patent models were on view, top, in 1870 in the stately South Model Hall at the U.S. Patent Office Building. Above, Carl W. Mitman, a curator in the Department of Engineering and Industries, was pictured in 1926 studying some 20 such models at the Smithsonian's National Museum. Opposite: model of an unusual scow. In 1804, Oliver Evans won a patent for a remarkable high-pressure steam engine. A year later, to rid the Philadelphia waterfront of garbage, he built the 20-ton Orukter Amphibolos, a steam dredge powered with the engine. The cumbersome scow, rumbling down Market Street to the water, was the country's first steam vehicle to travel on a city street.

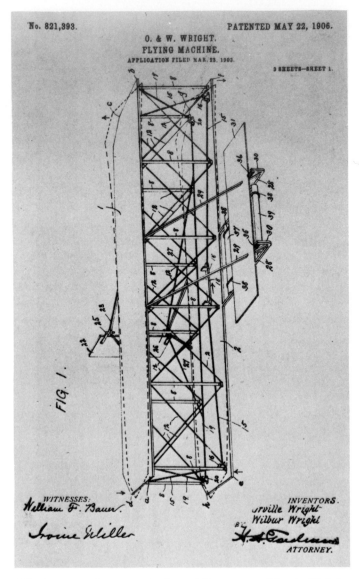

O. & W. WRIGHT.
FLYING MACHINE.
APPLICATION FILED MAR. 23, 1903.

3 SHEETS—SHEET 1.

FIG. 1.

WITNESSES:
William F. Bauer
Irvine Miller

INVENTORS.
Orville Wright
Wilbur Wright
By
H. A. Toulmin
ATTORNEY.

The drawing above was the first of five presented by the Wrights to explain their invention, the "Flying Machine," patented in 1906. Dotted lines indicate the vital "wing warping" system invented by the Wrights to permit lateral control.

would draw the fine lines if a patent were challenged. Prominent American inventors such as Eli Whitney, Oliver Evans, and Thomas Cooper actively lobbied against the new laws. The *Journal of the Franklin Institute* contained a "Modern Antiques" column, reporting age-old inventions that received new American patents and were cited by the magazine as examples of "piracy by the ancients." During this innocent but confused "registration" period, one citizen patented the fallowing of agricultural land.

Reintroduction of the examination system in 1836 and the formal establishment of a Patent Office mark the beginning of the modern patent process, and over the years the courts have created a huge and complex body of interpretive laws. Interpretation was necessary to define patentability, to determine whether the "process, machine, manufacture, or composition of matter" indeed represented a "new and useful" invention of the applicant or patentee. The complicated procedures and issues can best be explained with a case history.

John and Kate Strong of Talladega, Alabama, "put their minds together" and invented a barrier to prevent ants from climbing the legs of kitchen tables. It consisted of a flange, concave on the underside, to which a coating of chalk was applied. Ants that foolishly tried to ascend the table leg would lose their footing on the chalk and tumble to the floor. In 1875 the ingenious couple applied for a patent. At the same time, Savannah Cruikshank claimed an exclusive 17-year patent for the same kind of ant guard. "Interference" proceedings (which resulted when a claim was contested before the patent was issued) got underway in the Patent Office. The first examiner decided in favor of Cruikshank. The Strongs appealed, and the Board of Examiners-in-Chief found for Mr. and Mrs. Strong. The opinion was then appealed to the Commissioner of Patents, who decided that neither claimant deserved a patent because even children knew that chalk impeded the movement of insects, and concave flanges had been used on trees for the same purpose for years. Cruikshank gave up his claim after that, but the Strongs were not so easily discouraged. They appealed outside the Patent Office, and a court ruled the ant guard "a novel and patentable invention." Admitting to the prior use of both concave flanges and chalk to bar "the march of ants," the court said: "In this case the inventive faculty was exercised by the Strongs in combining the flange and the chalk in such a relation to each other as to produce a new and useful result," and the court found the "gist of the invention" to be "in placing the chalk on the *under side* of the flange, where it . . . prevents the passage of insects in a more effectual and satisfactory manner than it otherwise would." After nearly five years, the Strongs received their patent and the progress of the useful arts was again promoted.

To determine novelty or newness, the patent examiner is expected to search through the "prior art"—all information about all inventions made from the beginning of time to one year ago. The examiner and the court are likely to drown in such a sea of data, from which (said a judge in 1952) "one can fish out . . . any kind of strange support for anything, if he lives so long." Although patents are granted nowadays to about 50 percent of all applicants, examiners have been criticized for acquiring "a most extraordinary power of discovering resemblances," and for losing their faculty of seeing differences.

In the middle of the 20th century one particular

law disqualified a device for patent if it were obvious to someone having "ordinary skill" in the particular art or craft. The criterion had been introduced formally 100 years earlier by the Supreme Court, yet a patent was granted in 1859 for "bent, stamped or pressed seats . . . so that a form of the seat will fit and conform to the shape of the person who shall occupy the chair." Another was issued that year for a ventilated hat — a hat with holes in it. When challenged, the inventor claimed that he was only patenting the method of making the holes. Two-piece stilts were patented in 1861, and one decade later a pollution control device for horses appeared. A grapefruit shield was patented in 1928, and in 1969 a "design" patent put legs on the hot dog. For each of these non-obvious contrivances, the inventor received a government-sanctioned, temporary monopoly.

Early in the history of American patents, the courts abandoned any serious attempt to define "useful" in the way most people define the word. How, after all, can anyone predict accurately the utility of a genuinely novel device? Instead, "useful" was interpreted in 1817 by Associate Justice of the Supreme Court Joseph Story to mean *not* mischievous or *not* immoral, or *not* "frivolous or injurious to the well-being, good policy or sound morals of society."

The nuances of definition harried officials. A horrible mixture of roots, leaves, nitre, opium gum, and other such delectables was patented in 1832 as a cure for syphilis and named "The Unfortunate's Friend." The *Journal of the Franklin Institute* worried: "Should those who are so unfortunate as to be affected by the vile disease in question, depend upon the . . . Friend, 'Alas, poor Yorick!' " Inventor Daniel Harrington specialized in patented electrified suppositories. According to Fanny W. Paul, who patented a "sleep inducer" in 1885, insomnia was caused by nervous tension and a quickening of the flow of blood to the brain, enlarging the neck vessels and thus further exciting the gray cells. Her solution took the form of a leather collar with a covered spring inside and screw adjustment. At night, the insomniac strapped on the collar and turned the screw to press the padded spring "against the flesh beneath the jaw" in order to "restrict the too abundant flow of blood to the head." There can be little doubt that her invention indeed offered a cure for wakefulness; whether it might be "injurious to the well-being of society" seems to be arguable.

The modern statutes also consider operability—whether the contraption works—as a necessary part of the utility test, and, except for the registration period between 1793 and 1836, workability was evaluated by the Patent Office—with uneven results. Jacob Nollner received a patent in 1838 for movable railways, one on top of the other, to increase the speed of trains;

William Crandell got a patent in 1872 for his tipping rails, "to resist lateral strains, and cause the moving cars to gravitate inwardly instead of swaying outwardly. . . ." In 1845 a patentee recommended the use of siphon-propelled railroads, and toward the end of the century a patent was issued for a railroad train of cars covered with inclined planes at each end and a platform on top fitted with rails, to avoid collisions by allowing one train to pass over another.

Finally, in the discussion of utility, it has been determined that the discovery of a natural law does not make that species of invention eligible for a patent. A scientist cannot patent a natural principle he or she reveals—only some new application of it. Benjamin Franklin's discoveries of the nature of electricity and Albert Einstein's theory of relativity do not qualify for a reward under the patent system.

Most inventors of significant processes, machines, manufactures, or compositions of matter probably do well financially. They also probably represent a small fraction of all the patentees. For, in its nearly 200 years of existence, the system, with its promise to the uninitiated of instant wealth, has approved more than 4,000,000 patents, including a tremendous overlap and undercutting of many totally insignificant devices. On this subject, a U.S. Senator on the floor of Congress once hypothetically undressed a colleague with old, insignificant patents:

"I could go into the Patent Office and find old patents today which may be bought for a song, that would enable me to bring at least a dozen well-founded suits, against the Senator from Massachusetts himself. I suspect I could, and for a sixpence, buy up some old patent that would compel him either to pay me a royalty or to strip his boots off on Pennsylvania Avenue. And I suspect that if I were to examine his suspenders I could find they infringe a half dozen patents, and that he must take them off and run the risk of walking down the street without them, or else pay several royalties."

If not all of the patented devices were significant, they were and are, taken altogether, ubiquitous. Americans are nursed with the aid of patent baby bottles, fed patent foods from patent packages that are cooked in patent stoves. They work at patent machines with patent tools. They sit in patent chairs, sleep in patent beds, ride in patent vehicles, play patent games, live in patent houses. And when they die, they are buried in patent coffins.

Whether or not the U.S. patent system has proved to be democratic or inducive to better inventions and better procedures for inventive ideas, the Patent Office, in its gradual development, has covered the span of our earthly lives. Judging from the number of patents issued to the aerospace industry, it apparently intends to follow us into the heavens as well. □

The Farm Goes Industrial

Edward S. Ayensu

From the beginning of agriculture in Neolithic times to the early 18th century, a span of nearly 10,000 years, the individual farmer's capacity to produce food changed but little.

Hand implements—hoes, scythes and sickles, axes, and the like—originally made of wood and stone, improved in form and material through bronze, iron, then steel. Animal-drawn plows of gradually increasing effectiveness were introduced, and plowing and irrigation techniques were adapted to varying conditions of soil and topography.

The development of these implements and techniques allowed the pre-18th-century farmer to increase his total output by only a slight degree, because human muscle power remained the major energy source. Even after draft animals were joined to the plow, human energy still provided the main source of power for many agrarian activities.

In the 18th century, a number of English innovations in farming techniques coincided with the Industrial Revolution there to markedly increase the farmer's production potential. These innovations quickly crossed the Atlantic with colonists and were adapted to the varying conditions of the east coast of North America.

The United States, with nationhood achieved, entered the 19th century with a predominantly rural, agrarian population composed mainly of small, independent farmers, except in areas of the South, where large plantations worked by slaves were the rule.

Several factors combined during the first half of the 19th century to begin the industrialization of agriculture in America, a process which has since been repeated in many parts of the world. Explosive population growth, the American industrial revolution, acquisition of vast new areas of fine farm land, a railroad

Well into the 19th century, the American farm was a small family enterprise, though, one suspects, not as idyllic as this pumpkin harvest portrayed by John Whelton Ehninger in an oil titled "October" at the National Collection of Fine Arts.

transport system through the nation's breadbasket, and, paradoxically, a shortage of farm labor (many American farmers preferred to settle and till new lands rather than work for someone else), gave rise to intense pressure to make agriculture more mechanized and labor-efficient. The results were astonishing. At the time of the Civil War, a farmer could feed himself and two or three others; by the Second World War he could feed 12 others.

The mechanization of agriculture began in the United States with the introduction of plows designed for specific soil conditions. In 1819, Jethro Wood invented a cast-iron moldboard plow with interchangeable wearing parts that proved particularly suitable to the rocky soils of the East. John Deere followed in 1837 with his steel moldboard plow, which proved superior to the cast-iron type in shearing and turning over the rich, moist soil of the Great Plains. More significantly, Cyrus K. McCormick introduced his horse-drawn reaper in 1831, and Jerome I. Case began to manufacture threshing machines which efficiently separated wheat from chaff. These machines were refined and merged; toward the end of the century, giant combines pulled by teams of dozens of horses or mules swept across the great wheat farms of the Midwest, harvesting grain at previously unimaginable speed and efficiency. With draft animals replaced by the advent of steam- and then gasoline-powered tractors in the early 20th century, the mechanization of agriculture assumed its modern form.

We are told that today the farmer feeds himself and nearly 50 people. This remarkable achievement should be viewed within the context of the support facilities that are within the reach of the American farmer today. The fantastic array of industrial support includes farm equipment supply houses, the fuel, fertilizer, and pesticide industries, and seed multiplication and improvement centers.

Looking at agricultural productivity from another angle, we find that in 1910-40 it took 35.2 man-hours per acre to produce 26.0 bushels of corn. By 1962-66 it took only 6.2 man-hours per acre to produce 68.0 bushels of corn. Similarly, between 1910 and 1940, 15.2 man-hours were needed to produce 14.4 bushels of wheat. By 1962-66 only 2.9 man-hours were needed to produce 25.9 bushels of wheat.

Viewing this remarkable achievement from another perspective, W. F. Buchele noted that ". . . if the total time required to build a combine is 300 man-days and the combine, doing the work of 1,000 men, is used 30 days per year for 10 years, the ratio of labor efficiency is 1,000 man-days saved for each day expended."

Let us examine some of the factors that have made the industrialization of food possible in the United

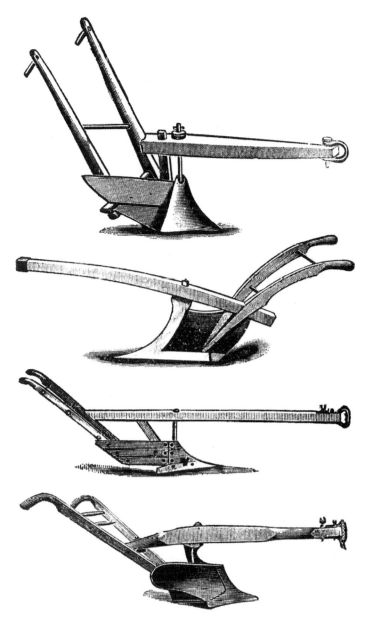

Progress of the plow: changing designs for a growing land. From top to bottom: early wooden moldboard from Pennsylvania; quite close to European designs, this plow type furrowed Eastern seaboard farms during Colonial and Revolutionary eras. Charles Newbold's patent of 1797—America's first cast-iron plow. First steel plow, 1833. James Oliver's patent plow of 1873, with replaceable parts, is a forerunner of new models and designs that revolutionized farming on the Great Plains, a region of heavy sod that needed breaking before agriculture could thrive.

States and have since affected food productivity throughout the developed and many of the developing countries. The primary technical innovations of the 19th century that affected agriculture, particularly in the United States, were mainly those that made the farms less dependent on large numbers of farm hands, but at the same time increased the acreage that each farmer could handle with various mechanical devices. The mechanization of agriculture enabled the average farmer to command more horsepower than the average factory worker. Machines such as the Acreater can plow 100 times more land than a battalion of ox-drawn carts. Similarly, a self-propelled combine can harvest a corn field that would require more than 80 people to harvest by hand.

However, such purely technological innovations permitted only the increase of agricultural output of each farmer, who had seemingly unlimited farm land, not the productivity per unit area of land. As land became scarce and stiffer demands were placed on the farmer to produce more food from his land, a series of alternatives had to be sought. With the replacement of horse-drawn plows by engine-powered machines, over 90 million acres which had been the source of "fuel"—oats and hay for the draft animals—were added to the regular farm lands. This land was soon used up as more food was demanded by the rising American population and the rest of the world. Many factors had to be combined to increase substantially the yields per unit of land. To achieve this goal, scientific researchers endeavored to improve seeds for planting, develop chemical fertilizers in sufficient and correct quantities to upgrade the soil, and to perfect many plant protection devices such as pesticides and herbicides. In addition, certain farmlands were irri-

BAILOR MOTOR CULTIVATORS

Have you placed a Sentimental Value on your Horses out of proportion to the work they are able to perform?

The introduction of the inexpensive cultivator brought machinery within the reach of the small, low-yield farmer.

gated to extend the acreage of usable land, and such irrigation sometimes permitted double and triple cropping. Indeed, the full potential of fertilizers cannot be fully realized without improved water management, including irrigation and drainage practices.

The development of chemical fertilizers led to many remarkable innovations in food production. Their manufacture involved the chemical processing of raw materials capable of converting the nutrient elements into forms that could be used more readily by plants. In addition, micronutrients such as boron, copper, iron, manganese, molybdenum, and zinc were incorporated as needed into otherwise regular grades of fertilizer to help soils produce more food.

Plant breeding is a major biological innovation in the history of food productivity. While not thinking of food per se, an Austrian monk, Gregor Mendel, began a series of experiments in 1857 to explain the nature of inheritance. Working with the green pea flower, he transferred pollen from a tall variety to the stigma of a short-stemmed variety. The resultant seeds were planted, and they produced new plants whose characteristics explained for the first time the relationship between parents and offspring, or heredity. The application of this experiment, which became the backbone of the principles of plant genetics, has been refined into sophisticated scientific and technological methods used in plant breeding. Mendel's initial discovery, and the extension of his work by researchers throughout the world, is among the miracles of the 19th century and, in the broader sense, a modern miracle as well.

The crop that opened new vistas in plant breeding techniques for mass food production was maize, or corn—a plant that the Mexican Indians had domesticated thousands of years before the white man landed in America. The development of hybrid corn during the past 30 years has demonstrated man's ability to improve the quality of crops.

Studies by geneticist G. H. Shull in 1906 produced important information on the reduction in vigor caused by inbreeding and the restoration of vigor by crossing. D. F. Jones, head of corn research at the Connecticut Agricultural Experiment Station, suggested in 1918 that the way to remove the limitation imposed by poor vigor of inbred parents was to double-cross hybrids with four inbred parents. This led to the first commercially produced double-cross hybrid, Burr-Leaming, which was released to the farming public in 1921. Several individuals and experimental stations participated in the development of this new hybrid by crossing hundreds of inbred lines and isolating the desired hybrid.

At first some farmers were reluctant to plant the new hybrid, but when they saw the results from vari-

Drawn by 24 horses, a Holt combine (combined harvester and thresher) plies the dry wheat fields of Walla Walla, Washington.

Invented in the 1880s by Benjamin Holt, it was in use into the early 20th century. Holt's firm became the Caterpillar Company.

ous demonstration plots, the Corn Belt's demand for the hybrid seed exceeded the supply. From 1935 the seed industry began to flourish; today nearly all corn acreage is planted with hybrid corn. The beneficial effects of this new seed have enabled farmers to produce at least 20 percent more corn on 25 percent fewer acres than was the case in 1930.

Improving the nutritional quality of crops is yet another significant contribution man has made in this century. To improve the protein quality of corn, for example, scientific research has enabled the breeding of high-lysine strains for the nourishment of humans and non-ruminant animals such as pigs and poultry.

The combined use of agricultural engineering, fertilizers, and breeding techniques has brought about a vast assortment of food mechanization practices. The tomato industry offers a spectacular example. In 1947 tomato researchers at the University of California, Davis Campus, headed by G. C. Hanna, conceived the idea that eventually the tomato would have to be harvested by machine. With this idea in mind, he and his colleagues began to develop a variety having the right skin thickness, with fruits that would all ripen at about the same time, and which also could withstand the rigors of machine harvesting. After much effort a suit-

able harvesting machine was produced between the early and mid-1960s. Today, more than 90 percent of all tomatoes are mechanically picked and loaded into tractor-drawn trailers for automated packaging.

Equally interesting was the "invention" of the all-purpose potato. The Kennebec variety, developed by R. V. Akeley and his colleagues at Beltsville, Maryland, is now grown throughout the United States because of its adaptability and versatility. The Kennebec has been described as the "variety that can be baked, pan-fried, French fried, boiled, mashed, chipped, and even used as starch in bread or pancakes."

Livestock improvement also took a dramatic turn early in the 20th century, when animal breeders began skillful selection and crossing of different varieties to produce breeds that yielded large quantities of milk and meat when bred in different climatic zones. Actually, the livestock in the United States were mostly descendants of nonpedigrees from Europe. Initially not much effort was put into the improvement of the animals, but by 1900 the development of purebred cattle, sheep, and American-bred swine was well under way. Although breeds of beef cattle imported from the United Kingdom continued to dominate the markets in most of the country, the cattlemen of the

Old Red, International Harvester's automatic cotton picker, appeared in 1943, just in time to free the South's sharecropping labor force to move north to the factories of war. It also permitted cotton growing in the Southwest and California, where labor was scarce. Bottom, techniques have changed in Walla Walla. Staggered procession of combines permits the harvesting to be done with locust-like thoroughness. Overleaf, air-conditioned, CB radio-equipped combines sweep across a Texas wheat field.

southern states found that they lacked resistance to heat and insects that abound in the South, and could not feed well on the coarse, tropical type of forages. Dewlapped, hump-backed Zebu cattle introduced from India survived the southern climate better, but the quality of meat was not up to the required standard. By interbreeding several Indian Zebu breeds, the American Brahman was created—an exercise that could be truly characterized as an "invention." The interbreeding of crossbred British and Zebu cattle was followed by crossings of the American Brahman and shorthorn breeds, culminating in the development of the Santa Gertrudis which has become so popular in many countries. Following this development, several other breeds were produced to fill specific needs of farmers and consumers.

Another milestone in the quest for improved animal production was the development of artificial insemination. In 1938 New Jersey dairymen organized the first cooperative in the United States for the artificial insemination of cows. The process involved the introduction of semen into females without natural mating. By using the best bulls in artificial insemination programs, thousands of cattle have been produced in a way that natural breeding could not accomplish. The cattle industry has both brought about and benefited from a remarkable efficiency in the production and distribution of meat.

The production of poultry was initially a backyard operation for many rural American families. In fact, it was the duty of many housewives to keep the chickens for their supply of eggs and the occasional chicken dinner. With the introduction of breeding programs and the invention of the forced-draft incubator, the complexion of chicken production changed dramatically. For example, it used to take 13-14 weeks to produce an adult broiler after supplying it with four to five pounds of feed. With various technological innovations, including a carefully regulated, well-balanced diet, it now takes about eight weeks and only two pounds of feed to produce a full-sized broiler. The national average of egg production in 1940 was 134 eggs per hen; by 1962 each hen was producing well over 200 eggs. Today, highly mechanized egg-producing installations handle well over two million hens and produce several million eggs a day.

Industrialization of food, especially in America, has not been based on biological research alone. It has embraced other industrial components such as food additives, spoilage retardants, tenderizers, preservatives, food coloring, and advanced techniques for processing, storage, packaging, transportation, and marketing. All of these enterprises have historical roots in the preparation of food for consumption. We know, for example, that food was preserved in ancient times by salting, sun-drying, pickling, smoking, and different fermentation processes. The ancient Egyptians and the Chinese used food coloring to improve the appearance of certain dishes. Today, both artificial and natural colors and other additives are used to improve the appearance of various foods and to give them the required taste.

Processing of food began some 6,000 years ago with the grinding of cereal grains into flour and its subsequent transformation into bread. But the basic processing of wheat into flour did not change materially until mechanization of food products became a commercial venture. Increased production of perishable crops, coupled with greater marketing areas and improved transportation, necessitated research into spoilage by microbes and adverse chemical change. The canning process, invented by Nicholas Appert of France and handsomely rewarded by Napoleon, increased the shelf life of various perishables. In addition, mechanical refrigeration showed its impact on the food industry by the early 1900s. By 1865 New York had its first cold storage facility, thus enabling the wide distribution of perishable fish, poultry, vegetables, and fruits. It was not until the 1920s that Clarence Birdseye developed the modern quick-freezing methods used in the food industry today.

Sun-drying as a means of food preservation is a practice begun even before the earliest civilizations, probably a serendipitous discovery. With the industrialization of food the natural drying process has been replaced largely by artificial dehydration. Since most of our whole fresh foods are 75 to more than 95 percent water, the process of dehydration has lowered the cost of packaging, transporting, and storing large quantities of food. The concentration of orange and other juices has now made it possible to expand the marketing of fruit crops from large plantations.

Another invention that had an impact on the American food industry was the production of condensed milk, begun by Gail Borden in the 1850s. Like all experiments in the food industry, condensed milk was initially viewed with apprehension, but after it had been supplied to Union forces during the Civil War it became acceptable. Prior to Louis Pasteur's discovery of the basic principles of sterilization, many products were manufactured under unsanitary conditions. Today, all the States have compulsory pasteurization laws, the first being enacted in Chicago in 1908.

Marketing is an important branch of the food industrialization process, involving as it does the transportation of varieties of produce to the consumer in the desired forms and conditions at the lowest possible cost. Marketing has been developed into a "science" to meet American consumers' expectations for a system that keeps food items flowing continuously without unnecessary interruptions.

The increase in productivity of various food items, and the creation of new products to satisfy the market, are all indications of Americans' concern to produce more of everything. But varietal improvements of both plant and animal products, and the effectiveness of the fertilizers and pesticides that have contributed to this dramatic increase in the food supply, have not been achieved without adverse environmental effects. The introduction of fertilizers and herbicides has had deleterious effects on the constitution of soils. The development of crop monocultures has disturbed the ecological balance of many regions. With a superabundance of foods, post-harvest food losses (both on the farm and in households) have resulted in astronomic food wastage estimated to cost billions of dollars.

Agriculture remains a fragile business. The market for food products is tied inextricably to Federal regulation, subsidy, and control. And as food is the chief export product of the United States, international market developments can either benefit or hurt the American farmer.

Furthermore, the high capital costs of running an industrialized farm make it all the more likely that there will be a continuing economic tendency toward fewer, larger farms. Such a resurgent plantation system runs a kind of parallel to the creation of the "monoculture" farming of single crops that is so vulnerable to disease or climatic change.

Agronomists and economists will continue to argue over the soundness of what is called "agribusiness," but a new and ominous statistic will haunt their discussion in the years to come. The statistic has to do with energy.

By substituting mechanization for human and animal labor, we have increased our reliance upon fossil fuels for the production, harvesting, and delivery of food to the consumer. David Pimentel of Cornell University has estimated that to produce and deliver a can of corn with 270 calories of energy, the expenditure of 2,790 calories of energy is required. If the rest of the world—particularly the underdeveloped nations of the globe—were to adopt our mode of food production, the entire world's petroleum reserves, it is estimated, would be exhausted in 11 years. Clearly, it is time for increased inventiveness in that most basic of human endeavors—growing food. □

Industry's New Ingredients

Jon B. Eklund

There is more than a little of Walter Mitty in most of us. We can all dream vaguely of inventing a wonder drug, a clever gadget or widget, or, perhaps, some miraculous substance. Eureka! We hold it in our hands—the strongest, the lightest, the shiniest, the most useful *stuff* ever seen on Earth. The dream usually starts and ends there, and for good reason, since we have omitted the two really sticky problems involved with invention: (a) how did we get this strange lump in the first place, and (b) what do we do with it *now*? For the increase and diffusion of dreams let us consider four cases of the invention of materials: aluminum, Celluloid, Bakelite, and nylon.

Aluminum was very much a product of science. Metals had played a central role in chemistry since the period when the alchemists held sway, and the general properties of metallic compounds were fairly well understood and recognized by the beginning of the 18th century. Thus it was not surprising that a number of compounds containing metals were recognized as such even though the metals themselves, such as sodium, potassium, and aluminum, were not isolated until considerably later. In the early 19th century sodium and potassium yielded relatively easily to the voltaic (electric) battery, powerful new tool of English chemist Sir Humphrey Davy. However, when he turned his experimental apparatus onto the "earthy compounds of aluminum," the results were less satisfactory, and the products which he labeled "Alumum" or "aluminum" were small in quantity and poor in quality.

A substantial advance in formulating aluminum was made by Henri Sainte-Claire Deville around 1855. He modified the methods of Davy and other scientists in several ways, and actually began the production of aluminum on what should be considered an industrial scale. At the Paris Exposition of 1855, the new metal was hailed as "Silver from Clay," and exhibited both as gleaming ingots and as useful and decorative objects. In article after article in popular publications, waves of praise washed over the material and imaginations worked overtime suggesting uses to which it could be put. Yet the output, according to all available figures, rose only very slowly, and more than

a few aluminum works opened and closed during the 19th century.

Doggedly, industrial chemists sought to improve existing methods or find new ones which would effect additional economies of scale, believing that this was all that was needed to get a truly viable aluminum industry off the ground. Acting quite independently, both an American, Charles Martin Hall, and a Frenchman, Paul Louis Toussaint Heroult, succeeded in the direct electrolysis of aluminum in 1886.

If the industrial chemist's faith had been justified, the industry should have leaped forward at this point, for the Hall and Heroult processes drove the price down far lower than had the best variations and improvements on the Deville process. Thus in England the price dropped from 16 to about four shillings per pound between 1887 and 1889.

Still, the industry remained sluggish. Not until the early 1890s after what was, for that time, an intensive marketing effort, did aluminum become an acceptable material for cookware. For many years this familiar use formed the backbone of the industry—all this in spite of the fact that aluminum utensils had been made as early as the 1850s. The extensive use of aluminum as a construction material would have to await the rise of the aircraft industry, still many years away.

Thus, in spite of its novelty as a new metal, in spite of its attractive physical properties, and in spite of its success among technological *cognoscenti*, aluminum products did not enjoy widespread acceptance until the early part of this century, some 50 years after its first commercial production and almost a century after it was first seen.

Like aluminum, Celluloid had a chemical background, though not nearly so venerable. Cellulose is a natural "polymer," a very large molecule made up of many identical units called monomers. In the case of cellulose, the monomer is cellobiose, which, like our common table sugar, sucrose, is composed of two "simple" sugar molecules. In table sugar, the simple sugars differ. In cellobiose, they are identical sugars called D-glucose. Cellulose treated with nitric acid yields nitrocellulose, but when in 1838 Theophile-

For centuries mankind used natural materials such as the ivory in this piece of scrimshaw, top. In the 19th century we created new substances like Bakelite, shown in objects, above, in front of the notes of inventor Leo H. Baekeland.

Jules Pelouze treated rag paper, a good source of cellulose, with nitric acid, he called this substance "pyroxylin." More extensive researches on nitrating cellulose were carried out by Christian Friedrich Schonbein, professor of chemistry and physics at the University of Basel. Because he used mixtures of nitric and sulphuric acids, his nitrocellulose had, on the average, a higher degree of nitration. This rendered it far more unstable (most common explosives are nitrates) and, accordingly, he named the product "guncotton" and patented it as an explosive.

Nitrocellulose substances like pyroxylin with fewer nitrate groups (on the average) are soluble in a number of organic liquids, such as mixtures of ether and alcohol. The resulting liquid is viscous and syrupy. More important, it dries and hardens into a thin, smooth, continuous, usually transparent film or sheet which adheres to and takes the shape of the surface on which it dries. The solution, and sometimes the film,

was known as "collodion" in photography, where it served as a vehicle for the light-sensitive chemicals of the photographer. Both of these applications were suggestive of the materials later called plastics.

Though suggestive of the solid structural materials we now call "plastics," collodion was a far cry from the modern product, and it took a great deal of work by several men to reach that goal. Two in particular were responsible for bringing nitrocellulose plastics to maturity: an Englishman, Alexander Parkes, and an American, John Wesley Hyatt.

The approach of Parkes and his associates—which was to add oils and solvents to nitrocellulose, producing a material he called parkesine—was essentially similar to the formation of collodion: forming a solid by the evaporation of solvents. Hyatt used a quite different approach. Reputedly responding to a prize of $10,000 offered by the New York City firm of Phelan & Collender for an ivory substitute for billiard balls, Hyatt tried the well-known process of molding under pressure wood pulp and gum shellac. When this product proved unsuitable, Hyatt was soon trying pyroxylin (nitrocellulose) instead of wood pulp (primarily cellulose). In 1869 he received a patent for a method of "making solid collodion." Hyatt's own testimony admits that he had a fairly wide knowledge of previous patents for pyroxylin-based substances, probably including those of Parkes. From one or another of these, he picked up the idea of adding camphor to the mix and getting rid of additional filler materials. The resulting combination of pyroxylin and camphor, mixed in a ratio of about two to one and molded under heat and pressure, produced the first "plastic" substance in the modern sense of the term: Celluloid.

Aside from a few changes in the process during the next two years, improvements in the manufacture of Celluloid were largely mechanical, involving devices which better and more intimately mixed the main ingredients, or which heated, pressed, cut, or shaped the final product. With Hyatt's Celluloid, the later problems were not primarily scientific, nor even technological, but—as had been true for aluminum— in marketing the new product.

Although new markets developed fairly slowly, the company started by Hyatt, which became the Celluloid Manufacturing Company in 1871, was able to take over a portion of one market after another. The earliest were dental plates and billiard balls, but other small utilitarian and decorative products were gradually added and licenses were issued to more companies for producing others. The Hyatt company became profitable within a few years, due largely to its ability to cut unit costs, though a decrease in the costs of most of the raw materials in this period also helped. Combs, brushes, and knife handles provided useful

Aluminum could be produced on an industrial scale by the 1850s, but it awaited the airplane to find a major market. Energy-intensive to produce, it is far less so to recycle. Here, raw scrap, right and above center, is remelted, top, and ultimately processed into final sheets, bottom.

170

economic mainstays for the company from its early years, as did collars and cuffs somewhat later.

In one sense Celluloid enjoyed a considerable advantage over aluminum. Its general physical properties and the ease with which it could be colored enabled it to be substituted for a wide range of natural materials such as ivory, horn, bone, and shell in existing markets. A mass-produced artifact manufactured from a new material requires *three* inventions: the material, the artifact, and the market. The properties of aluminum did not allow it to replace the older metals in as many areas as Celluloid could replace the materials to which it was similar. There were simply more niches for Celluloid in the world's economy between 1870 and 1910, when it was challenged by the world's first completely synthetic material, Bakelite.

Bakelite is a polymer made of two chemical units that in themselves are quite simple molecules: phenol and formaldehyde. When reacting together under the proper conditions, however, phenol and formaldehyde link together not into simple long linear chains or even two-dimensional networks, but directly into a three-dimensional solid material which, contrary to our recollections of all those muddy brown radio cabinets and distributor caps, is a lovely clear amber color. The muddy quality comes from fillers which are added to give the pure, rather brittle Bakelite a degree of structural strength which is necessary for the objects made from it. The trick, then, lay in getting these two recalcitrant molecules to react together in an orderly manner. This was one—though far from the only—achievement of Leo Hendrik Baekeland.

Baekeland was born and educated in Belgium, earning a doctorate in chemistry from the University of Ghent in 1883 at the age of 20. After a period of academic life at Ghent, he sailed for America in 1889 and remained in this country for the remainder of his life. His first successful major invention was the photographic paper Velox, and he was successful not only in inventing the process and the artifact, but also in marketing it to photographers. Velox made him rich, for he was able to sell it to George Eastman in 1899 for an amount which, though in dispute, was somewhere in the neighborhood of three-quarters of a million dollars. He then used this money to set up a new laboratory on his estate in Yonkers, New York, where he worked on a number of projects. In 1902 he began researches in phenol-formaldehyde reactions.

As with aluminum and Celluloid, the substance we know as Bakelite had a chemical past, but a notably less encouraging one. From about 1871, chemists had reported various products resulting from reactions between phenol and formaldehyde, products that ranged from intractable solids which defied analysis, on one hand, to rather promising-looking, amber-colored syrups which several researchers, including Baekeland, saw as possible substitutes for shellac.

Baekeland worked on the phenol-formaldehyde problem off and on for several years. The difficulty was the large number of variables: relative amounts of phenol and formaldehyde; temperature; pressure; the amount of the moderating substance which was necessary to control the reaction; and even a number of possibilities for the use of other reactants chemically related to phenol and formaldehyde. By the spring of 1907, a somewhat desperate attempt to form the artificial resin directly at or near the surface of wood samples provided the key he needed to put together the rest of the pieces: the polymerization reaction is best done—and chemically understood—in stages which, somewhat tongue-in-cheek, he labeled "A," "B," "C." The final stage, "C," is the hard solid which he initially called "Bakalite" and later changed to the modern term, Bakelite. It was not chemically very different from the earlier, intractable solids, but, because the solid was created through controlled stages which hampered the sudden formation of gases but still allowed for the orderly and controlled linking of molecules, the end product was smooth and homogeneous, rather than spongy and unmanageable.

From the beginning, Baekeland sensed the potential of the new material. He succeeded in developing a good resin during three days of intensive work between June 18 and June 20, 1907. By the third day, he had not only given it a name but his mind was exploring possibilities for the new material as a substitute for Celluloid and for hard rubber.

The properties of the material surpassed those of Celluloid or the other natural polymers. To be sure, Bakelite faced two disadvantages vis-à-vis Celluloid: it was not flexible and did not take colors well. These qualities probably cost the company only the rather short-lived collar-and-cuff market, and some toy and novelty areas where bright colors were crucial. On the other hand, Bakelite was so much stronger, more workable, and chemically more stable than Celluloid (not to mention the absence of Celluloid's inflammability) that it could successfully compete in most markets that Celluloid had won over the years. In addition, it offered just the right substance at the right time for the fledgling radio industry. Besides being strong and moldable, Bakelite is an excellent insulator, and at one time almost all the nonmetallic structural parts in most radios were of Bakelite.

Bakelite and Celluloid, however, shared one limitation among their useful physical properties: neither of them could be drawn into long fibers.

The first truly synthetic polymer with major fiber applications was nylon, the invention of Wallace Hume Carothers in the mid-1930s, shortly before his

"Hit the silk!" paratroopers shout. But since WWII it's been nylon that floats them to earth. First synthetic fiber of a large family, nylon was patented by Du Pont in 1937.

death at the age of 41. Carothers was born and educated through high school in Iowa, and earned his Bachelor's at Tarkio College, Missouri. His natural bent for science led him to the University of Illinois. Carothers received his doctorate in 1924, and after teaching at Illinois and Harvard, was named head of the organic chemistry section of the Du Pont Company's new fundamental research program at their Wilmington experimental station. It was there that he began his work on various aspects of polymerization.

Carothers was interested in understanding the details of how polymers are formed in "condensation" reactions. In this type of reaction, the basic units (monomers) which make up the polymer each *lose* some of their atoms when they link up with other monomers. Perhaps the classic example of this type of reaction is that which takes place between an acid and an alcohol to form a molecule known as an "ester." In theory, at least, a chain could be made of alternating acids and alcohols, called "polyesters," and Carothers succeeded in making a number of the polymers which were larger than any previously produced. He and his assistant, J. W. Hill, were able to synthesize very large molecules with molecular weights of up to 25,000. To distinguish these from the relatively small polymers which had very different properties, Carothers called them "superpolymers."

Although ultimately the large polyesters would become a familiar component in textile blends, the "superpolyesters" which Carothers was able to make at that time had some undesirable qualities. Thus he turned to a related, though somewhat different kind of polymer made by joining an "amine" molecule to an acid rather than an alcohol molecule.

Carothers tested a number of acids, amines, and related molecules to find polymers of this type that yielded good fibers. In 1935 Carothers created a polyamide which produced excellent fibers. It was given the name "nylon."

As usual, the problem was to break into the market. This time, however, there was a pool of experience in marketing techniques to draw from and a large and respected chemical company to underwrite the effort. The fiber's properties made it a natural for stockings, and the first pair was produced in the laboratory in early 1937. By the fall of 1938, other fiber products such as toothbrush bristles had been fabricated. The new plastic was announced in October 1938, and the following year there was a marketing trial of the new nylon stockings. On May 15, 1940, nylon hosiery was introduced at department and dry goods counters nationwide, and in the first year some 64 million pairs were sold.

The properties of the fiber made it ideal for many applications during World War II, when the problem

The first plastic-like substance, Celluloid, found early use in billiard balls. In the intervening century, plastics have become ubiquitous in a host of products from auto parts to a nylon bicycle wheel introduced in 1978.

was not how to successfully market the product, but how to procure enough raw materials and build enough production capacity to meet the demand—a far cry from the struggles of the aluminum pioneers to gain acceptance, or even the cautious product-by-product upward movement of Celluloid. The consuming public was now geared to the new.

If materialism presupposes a tendency to preoccupy oneself with material goals and concerns, it would seem that man is by nature a materialist. Like a number of other animals, we pick up natural objects to employ them for our own ends. Like a very select group of animals, we modify these objects into primitive artifacts for better employment. But like no other species, we seek endlessly not only to shape naturally existing materials, but also to find and, quite recently,

to create new materials which have properties still more advantageous to our endless shaping of artifacts.

It is surprising that almost all materials used in technology up to 1850 were known before 2000 B.C. The applications of these materials have required great ingenuity, to be sure, and acquiring the skills and techniques for working wood, fiber, stone, ceramics, glass, and other material groups took a long time and a great effort. Such accomplishments must be admired. Yet the number of materials—mostly synthetic polymers—which have been invented in the years since 1850 overwhelm the number which preceded that date. We live and work immersed in a sea of materials. What is perhaps most surprising of all is that we have maintained some sense of selectivity in the face of the brilliant blandishments of the innovator. □

Keeping in Touch

Bernard S. Finn

Nowhere is the ability of the inventor to transform society more apparent than in communications. The links that hold us together are forged of information. To change the amount of that information, or the speed with which it flows, is to make a fundamental alteration in the social order.

During the past century and a half these changes have all been in the direction of enormously increasing both the amount and the speed of communications. The effect on society has been radical, involving us all with more and more external events, increasing the speed with which a variety of decisions must be made, and generally accelerating the pace of life. It is a revolutionary process that has not abated; inventions being made now may easily have as much impact on us as all of those mentioned in the following pages had on our ancestors.

The premise has always been that the more we know, and the sooner we know it, the better off we will be. Knowledge brings understanding, and understanding brings peace. However, a good argument could be made that improved communications systems have more often served the cause of war than that of peace. But no matter. From earliest times the impulse has been to speed up rather than slow down, and, as is so often the case in invention, the demand for speedy communication has been stimulated by war.

During the great 18th-century struggle between England and France, optical semaphores were brought to a high degree of sophistication, the most important invented by Claude Chappe in France in 1792. His system consisted of a series of towers, each with a pair of arms which could be placed in a variety of coded positions to spell out a message readable from the next tower. Chappe lines spread out across France. One, between Paris and the Rhine, was about 150 miles long and had 14 towers. A message could be transmitted over it in six minutes. From the Rhine to Berlin was 15 minutes more. Napoleon made good use of Chappe's

Bernard S. Finn is Curator of the Division of Electricity and Modern Physics at the Museum of History and Technology.

semaphore to control his European conquests, keeping in constant touch with his commanders in different territories and responding rapidly to trouble wherever it might occur.

But for most people at the beginning of the 19th century, communications moved no faster than they themselves could. Furthermore, the speed of travel —by foot, by horse, by ship—was not noticeably faster than it had been in the time of Columbus. Traveling from London to New York could take three weeks to two months, depending on the winds. Internal travel in the United States was much more difficult. Rivers provided the best routes. The trip by flatboat from Pittsburgh to New Orleans, a distance of 1,950 miles down the Ohio and Mississippi Rivers, took four to six weeks. The return trip, accomplished by poling, rowing, and being towed against the flow of the water, took four months or more. Roads outside of towns were little more than passageways through the wilderness, as indicated by an Ohio law that required stumps in rural roads to be cut so that they were no more than a foot high. Even after a period of road building that was stimulated by the War of 1812, it took 75 days for a wagon to get from Worcester, Massachusetts, to Charleston, South Carolina, a distance of a little less than 1,000 miles.

Some attempts were made to improve road surfaces. One popular technique was invented by John McAdam, a Scot who spent the Revolutionary War years in New York and then returned to Britain. He experimented extensively with various means of building roads, concluding that it was of prime importance to keep the roadbed dry and thus determining that it should be constructed above the ground level, in contrast to the common practice of digging a trench for the road's foundation. He built up a relatively thin layer (about eight inches) of broken chips, with the top surface fitted and compressed so that water would run off. Chalk, dirt, and anything else that would absorb moisture were excluded. He emphasized the importance of using small stones (less than an inch in any direction) to lessen the possibility of their being dislodged. His ideas became widely appreciated in the 1820s, and by

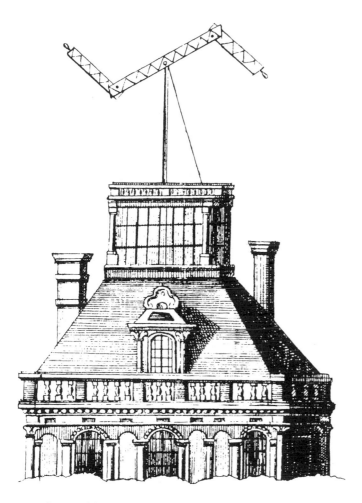

Napoleon could communicate with his far-flung generals using a string of semaphore towers, above. A message could pass 150 miles from Paris to the Rhine in six minutes. Below, an exhibit at the National Museum of History and Technology shows an 18th-century American postmaster greeting the post rider.

the end of the century 90 percent of the principal British highways were macadamized. American engineers studied the results, and the techniques were applied successfully to many roads in the United States, beginning with the Hagerstown-Boonsboro road in Maryland in 1823. A measure can even be given to the value of a macadam road: a horse could pull on it better than twice the load possible on gravel.

Speed on even the best roads, however, was still limited to that of the horse. It was elsewhere that steam was applied with dramatic effect to the ways people could keep in touch.

Robert Fulton left his native Pennsylvania for Europe at age 21 in hopes of becoming an artist. His underlying inventive talents were soon roused, however, by the flurry of activity around him. He tried unsuccessfully to sell a submarine to both England and France. He was then persuaded by Robert Livingston, at that time American Minister to France, to build a steamboat for use on the Hudson River. His design of the 100-ton *North River Steamboat* (later known as the *Clermont*) had no significant new features. But his decisions to use paddle wheels and to order his engine from the experienced Boulton & Watt firm in Birmingham, England, were keys to success. The *North River* started from New York to Albany on August 11, 1807, making the 150 miles in 32 hours; the return trip took 30 hours.

Meanwhile, John Stevens, who earlier had had an agreement with Livingston, was experimenting with steam engines operating at higher pressures than customary at that time. His first large boat, the *Phoenix*, started service on the Delaware River. Proliferation of the steamboat was rapid. By 1830 there were nearly 200 operating on the Mississippi and its tributaries —many of them side-wheelers with high-pressure, noncondensing engines. (This was not without danger: in the period 1815-30 there were 35 explosions, killing 250 people.)

These steamers provided dependable and relatively rapid service (often reaching 20 mph), and with the expansion of the canal system, much of the nation's interior could be reached by waterborne commerce.

When steam was applied to ocean-going vessels, mainly by the British, the external world also became compressed. By mid-century dependable mail service between New York and London by steamer took as little as 12 days. And passenger service was attractive enough to encourage Thomas Cook, in 1866, to begin tours from England to the former colonies to see such wonders as Mammoth Cave, Niagara Falls, and Civil War battlefields.

Early American railroad builders also looked to Britain for the basic technology, but differing conditions—notably the rougher terrain—made changes

Morse's first telegraph receiver, one of the earliest inventions to use electricity in communications. An artist, he made this device from a modified canvas stretcher.

necessary. For instance, American trains needed to be lighter and able to negotiate tighter curves. By 1840, after only 10 years of development, the United States had laid over 3,000 miles of track—double that of Britain—and by 1860 this network had reached 30,000 miles. In 1869 the East and West coasts were joined by a transcontinental railroad link. The impact on personal travel was considerable, especially over longer distances, for the cross-country trip now took less than two weeks, as opposed to about three months by ship or by wagon.

Thus, late in the 19th century, Americans could send messages or travel themselves at speeds that would have seemed miraculous 50 years earlier. In the meantime, however, even more rapid means of keeping in touch had been devised, with even further reaching consequences. The agent here was not steam, but electricity, available from chemical batteries since 1800. Significantly, the magnetic effects of an electric current, reported by the Danish experimenter Hans Christian Oersted in 1820, led to the independent in-

vention of electric telegraphs in Germany, England, and America. The American version was, of course, developed by Samuel F. B. Morse, an artist who fell into conversation about recent electrical experiments when returning from Europe in 1832. If electricity could be carried apparently undiminished through a wire, why couldn't it be used to carry a message? The public answer to this question would be 12 long years in coming, for an essential element still to be learned was that the electricity wasn't undiminished—that there was a relationship between the intensity (voltage) of the battery, the length of the wire (resistance), and the current that flowed. We know this as a law described by Georg Simon Ohm in 1827 but not generally understood for another decade. In 1837 Morse learned of the experiments of the American physicist (and later first Secretary of the Smithsonian) Joseph Henry, in devising efficient electromagnets. Henry's work showed that the problem of resistance in the line could be practically overcome by using a high-intensity battery at the end of the line, and a more efficient and powerful electromagnet at the receiving end. Morse then added another vital element—the code that still bears his name.

These improvements allowed Morse to complete his invention and to perform a series of demonstrations for potential financial backers. Morse himself had no money, and he struggled to make a living while pursuing the vision of a practical telegraph over the next half-dozen years. Finally, in 1843, he was successful in obtaining $30,000 from Congress to construct a line between Washington and Baltimore which was completed on May 22, 1844. That event marked the beginning of a revolution in communications in the United States. In 1847 a line ran from New York to Washington, in 1848 to New Orleans, in 1860 to San Francisco, in 1866 to London. Distance was no longer the determining factor in establishing the time taken to deliver a message. Places that had been weeks, even months, apart were suddenly separated by minutes and seconds. The effect of this transformation, this annihilation of distance, is difficult for us to understand today. Immediacy brings a familiarity, an involvement, that becomes a part of our lives. If we read news that is a month old it no longer involves us emotionally in the same way it would if our knowledge were immediate. We cannot affect the outcome, even by prayer, because the consequences—still unknown—have to an extent already occurred. Yet this is the way people knew the world prior to the telegraph. Then, very quickly, newspaper columns appeared headed "by telegraph from . . ."; there were even names for newspapers like *The Daily Telegraph* and *The Telegrapher*. Individuals could also use the wires for business, for family, for keeping in touch.

176

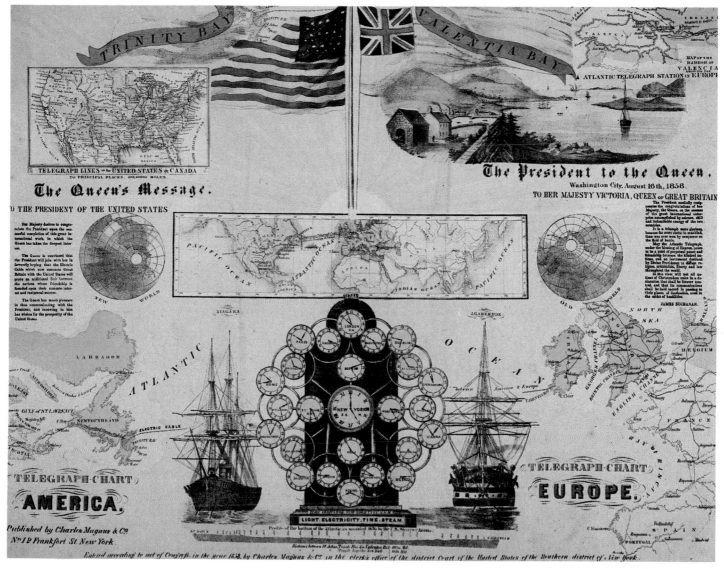

The second transoceanic telegraph cable was laid a year after the first attempt failed in 1857. This new cable, commemorated in the poster above, carried messages for a month before it too failed. Finally, in 1866, promoter Cyrus W. Field succeeded.

The Morse instrument, as introduced in 1844 in a form that owed much in design detail to Alfred Vail, was simple and rugged: a transmitting key to make and break electrical contact, a relay which was simply a sensitive magnet (in Henry's fashion) that could respond to the weakened signal strongly enough to open and close a switch (or second "key") controlling the current from a second battery. This current would then energize the receiver, which would make marks on paper or otherwise register receipt of the message. The simplicity and ruggedness were well suited to the American situation, where stations were far apart and trained mechanics were not easily found. But improvements could of course be made, and it was typical of 19th-century Americans—or perhaps of all people at all times—that a host of inventive solutions arose, some of them useful, most doomed to obscurity.

There was, for instance, the unknown operator who noticed around 1850 that he could read the dots and dashes of the message by simply listening to the clicks that the receiver made as the magnet pulled the armature against the recording paper. This meant that the paper was unnecessary and that the instrument could be further simplified, resulting in a series of designs for "sounders," or receivers in which this mechanical clicking noise was emphasized.

There were other, more ambitious modifications. In particular, a number of people tried to devise an instrument that would print the message automatically in letters, thus eliminating the need for an experienced operator and also permitting faster transmission. One of the few who succeeded was English-born David Hughes, who was a Kentucky schoolteacher when he devised his machine in 1856. The American rights to

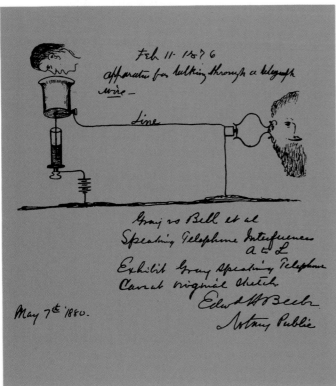

A replica of Alexander Graham Bell's liquid transmitter, top, which he devised in 1875 and sent to the 1876 Centennial Exposition in Philadelphia. Below, a page from the inventor's notebook showing a preliminary description of the telephone written the day before the famous message: "Watson, come here."

Hughes's telegraphic printer were purchased by a group, including Cyrus Field, involved in laying a telegraph cable across the Atlantic. They needed a land system which could not be challenged by the Morse patents. The Hughes instrument was used on lines between New York and Newfoundland when the first (temporarily successful) cable was laid in 1858. But after consolidation of American telegraph lines took place, the Hughes printer was relegated to limited use, primarily on heavily trafficked routes between large cities. Hughes himself went to Europe, where his printing telegraph was very popular.

Attempts to perfect a method of sending several messages over a single wire simultaneously led Alexander Graham Bell, a young Scot who, like Morse, was untutored in the field of electricity, to design a device that could transmit the human voice. Unlike a contemporary, Elisha Gray, who was independently proceeding along the same path, or a predecessor, Phillip Reis, who had experimented with an instrument that was technically capable of speech transmission, Bell had the foresight to realize that the urge of people to keep in touch was sufficiently strong to ensure that this new invention could be made profitable. And, of course, he was right.

Bell's telephone, patented in the U.S. Centennial year, might be said to have marked a watershed in the history of American invention. Before that, the typical inventor was a lone tinkerer. Afterwards he (or, occasionally, she) was increasingly likely to be part of a laboratory with its many resources, or teaching at a university with its intellectually stimulating influences. Thomas A. Edison provides the best early example of the former. With money from some telegraph inventions, he built and staffed a laboratory in Menlo Park, New Jersey, in 1876. Here he turned his mind in directions that led to the phonograph, the incandescent light, and an improved telephone. Soon after Bell had shown that the telephone was possible, Edison devised a much improved transmitter that depended on the way in which the resistance of packed carbon granules varied as the pressure on them changed. Others had similar solutions about the same time, although Edison eventually received patent credit. But his inventive genius and the capabilities of his laboratory were perhaps best illustrated in late 1878. While in the middle of work on the incandescent light, Edison received a cable from his agents in England pleading for a new receiver design which could be used to circumvent the Bell interests, who were rightly claiming violation of their patents. Edison considered the problem, had some models made, and within three months had a receiver that gave a response substantially better than Bell's. It consisted of a stylus resting on a rotating chalk drum. Friction between stylus and drum varied with the current and reproduced the voice sounds. The new models were delivered in the nick of time, allowing the Edison company to arrive at a profitable compromise with the holders of the Bell patents.

The telephone was fundamentally different from the telegraph, of course, because it transmitted speech. But of even greater importance was the fact that it reached into individual homes. And how rapidly it did so: 54,000 telephones were in service in the United States in 1880; 234,000 in 1890; 1.3 million in 1900; 7.6 million in 1910. People clearly liked to talk to one another.

There was no practical mechanical relay for the telephone like the one used for the telegraph (though one was devised and used on a few lines early in this century). Therefore some method of long-distance transmission became an increasing concern. In the 1890s conversations could be held over a few hundred miles (like New York to Boston) with a great deal of shouting and careful listening. At the turn of the century, Michael Pupin at Columbia University and George Campbell at the telephone company, working independently on the theoretical calculations of English physicist Oliver Heaviside, devised proper methods for placing loading coils at intervals along the line to improve its electrical properties to the extent that conversations could be held over distances upwards of 1,000 miles.

But this was still just conserving energy, not increasing it. The problem of amplification was solved with the application of a new device which had its origins in an effect observed by Edison: that negatively charged particles seemed to be given off by his light bulb filaments. He experimented with some modified light bulbs in 1883. These inquiries were pursued in England by John Ambrose Fleming, a teacher and

Out of courtesy and a well-honed sense of public relations, Bell demonstrated the telephone to Queen Victoria, then had an elaborate ivory model, like this one, made for her.

Early radio messages were received by headphones, as demonstrated by this anonymous pioneer of the plugged-in generation, from the Museum of History and Technology.

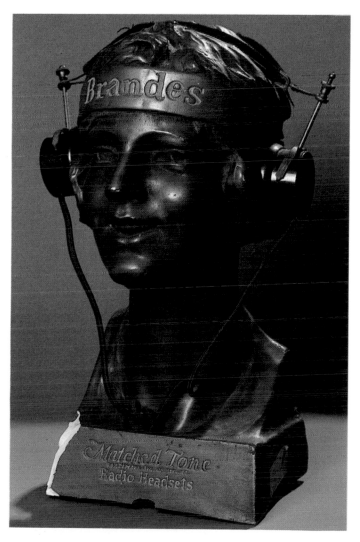

sometime consultant to Edison and later Guglielmo Marconi. In 1904 Fleming devised a two-element valve (vacuum tube) which could be used to detect radio waves. In New York, Lee De Forest, who was determined to make his living as a radio inventor, added a third element to Fleming's valve to form what he called an audion. When modified—notably by Irving Langmuir at General Electric, and Harold Arnold at Bell Laboratories, who evacuated the tube to a much higher degree—the tubes turned out to have remarkably fine amplifying properties, and were used on the first transcontinental telephone line in 1915.

The vacuum tube, which was so important for the telephone, also had enormous impact on radio. Previously treated like, and indeed called wireless telegraphy, radio had the advantage that it could reach places that the ordinary telegraph couldn't, such as ships at sea. Skilled inventors like Edwin Howard Armstrong and Alan Hazeltine built radio receivers which made broadcasting a commercial possibility after the First World War. Although these two men worked largely alone, most of the work in this period was done in university or commercial laboratories. The combined effort brought the radio into increasing numbers of homes: 60,000 in 1922; 2.75 million in 1925; 14 million in 1930; 28 million in 1940.

As if it weren't enough to be bombarded with telegrams and voices from around the world, the forces of invention were providing a feast for the eyes as well. A primitive form of television was actually broadcast in London by John Logie Baird in 1929 and in Washington, D.C., by C. Francis Jenkins the following year. Both systems used a spinning disc with a spiral pattern

of holes which "scanned" the scene in front of a photocell; the impulses from the photocell were broadcast by radio to a neon tube in the receiver, which in turn was scanned by another disc. However, commercially feasible electronic devices had to accomplish essentially the same thing before such a system could be made. The two major contributors to what would become modern television were Vladimir Zworykin, a Russian emigré who first persuaded Westinghouse, and then RCA, to allow him to work on a means of sending pictures electronically. The other was Philo Farnsworth, an Idaho farm boy who confronted the same problem alone with scant financial support. Commercial television hit the United States in 1939 (and somewhat earlier in Britain), but the real take-off occurred after the Second World War, with consequences that are all too well known.

There are inventors like Bell, De Forest, and Farnsworth today, but they are becoming harder and harder to find. Even the Arnolds and Zworykins have become increasingly buried in large laboratories. Major commercial advances in communications are apt to comprise complex systems, constructed out of many inventions, some of which may have been shared by several people. For instance, we are at the edge of what is likely to be a major breakthrough in communications technology with enormous social consequences. It will be caused by a major escalation in the amount of information that can be made available electronically in the home, which in turn will be made possible by fundamental changes in transmission and processing systems. Contributing to this technological revolution are work on the laser (light can carry much more information than microwaves), fiber optics (to carry the laser light rays), computers (for storing and processing information), satellites (as relay points), and much more. It doesn't take more than simple arithmetic to realize that, given the exponential growth of communications technology, the channels for transmitting information will soon outnumber the audience on Earth.

The problem will be—as indeed it is now to some extent—not how to keep in touch but rather how to filter out what we don't want and how to digest and interpret the mass of information available to us. □

"HIS MASTER'S VOICE"

The stained-glass symbol of RCA and the vintage jukebox, brilliantly colored, resplendently nostalgic, equally "sold" Caruso and the King of Swing and remind us that music has always been a way of keeping in touch. As with all modes of communication, music is now transistorized, amplified, computerized, and all the more omnipresent. The question, now more than ever, is to determine what we want to hear and what we don't.

6 PART

The Impact of Innovation

W e have conquered Earth, explored the moon, and voyaged with automaton limbs, eyes, and minds throughout the solar system, yet we humans now sense the urgent need to contemplate our brilliantly lit cities and consider what will happen if the power goes off. What have we wrought? Are we victims or beneficiaries of our highly prized creative impulse?

To the extent that we perceive ourselves to be either victims or beneficiaries, we judge ourselves, because we as human beings invent, produce, sell, and buy the products and systems by which we benefit or suffer. We and our civilization are both tools and products of invention.

Clearly, our new industrial techniques have greatly reduced hard labor and added leisure time. But in exchange we often receive a new kind of industrial drudgery, the ennui of the endlessly repeated task. Home labor savers have liberated the old servant class, only to create a new class, housebound and dependent upon machines. Similarly, modern war has stimulated medical science and accelerated the development of myriad devices with important peacetime applications. It has also given us the atomic bomb.

It now seems increasingly likely that we will be able to control our own biological evolution, and when we do, we will then be responsible for it. Similarly, we must reflect on our responsibility for the evolutionary course of our civilization, especially as it is affected by the accumulation of the things we create. As we achieve the power to change the course of nature itself, we yearn for a way to assure that the impact of invention will be, if still unpredictable, at least gentle. . . . .

182

The Evolution of Invention

Derek de Solla Price

Invention and discovery are very different processes. When one discovers, in any age or any society, there is a feeling akin to strong constraint because there seems to be only the one world to discover. This is equally true of geographic exploration and of the intellectual enterprise of understanding the universe around us. Different people may explore places or ideas by quite different routes—by radically different means of transportation, different languages and ways of expressing what has been discovered—but they will all reach the same place. That is, what is reached and comprehended is somehow a given fact of our environment rather than an optional goal. No matter who maps the sources of the Nile and the Amazon and the terrain of Tibet on foot, by boat, or by Landsat satellite, we gradually acquire more and more knowledge about this Earth. Similarly, whether Boyle or Mariotte discovers the gas laws, the laws have then been found once and for all. Even if the little green men from a distant galaxy landed, we would somehow expect them to know the same universe of physical constants and laws, such as those of the velocity of light, Planck's constant, the wave equation, and the laws of thermodynamics.

With invention one surely has alternatives. Such basic matters as food, clothing, and shelter are handled quite differently in various parts of the world and in diverse societies. We don't expect the little green men to have spacecraft resembling our own. The point to be made here is not only that the process of invention can yield many ways to do the same thing, but also that societies can make choices between one and another of those ways of doing the same thing. That they can and do make such choices is evident in that societies frequently do not immediately accept recent inventions, while many important innovations are derived from old inventions.

In our society we often think of invention as the result of applying some new piece of scientific under-standing. Indeed, we sometimes speak of "science" as if it contained all the technical processes which benefit and afflict us. Nevertheless, to the best of modern knowledge, no simple, direct relationship exists between highly constrained scientific discovery on the one hand and the free will of socioeconomic choice in the invention and innovation of technology on the other. The interaction between science and technology is peculiarly devious and has been different at each step in the evolution of mankind. Invention and innovation have passed through several different stages, and, like a series of overlapping geological strata, each stage has run on through the present to become part of our complex world.

It is startling to realize that writing is a somewhat late technological development of mankind. About 5,000 years ago great river-valley civilizations were beginning to flourish on the banks of the Nile, the Indus, and the Yellow rivers, and in the fertile crescent between the Tigris and Euphrates. One can trace the steady growth of the craft of writing in various forms and the accumulation of a corpus of literature and accrued learning, as well as the special craft that evolved into arithmetic and then mathematics. It is during this post-literate evolution that the special business of science begins with knowledge of the calendar and the chief cycles of astronomy, with collections of information about the nature of the world and its plants and animals.

More than 5,000 years before this beginning of science, there had been dramatic, even revolutionary, technological change. When the river-valley civilizations began, mankind had already acquired the traditions of thousands of years of sophisticated skills in pottery, basketry, weaving, cooking, building, hunting, fishing, boat building, and the winning and working of iron and bronze as well as complicated constructions in jewelry with gold and silver and precious

Derek de Solla Price, Avalon Professor of the History of Science at Yale University, is author of Science Since Babylon *and* Little Science, Big Science.

Representing an early age of experimentation with scientific instruments, this anonymous American and his dog posed for a primitive artist in about 1800.

stones. The most far-reaching step had been the Neolithic Revolution itself, when mankind had, for reasons not fully comprehended today, left the Garden of Eden life as a hunter and gatherer and settled into more sizable groups of people engaging in agriculture and becoming a much more complex society. It was invention and technical change that sparked this transformation from a sort of pack animal stage into the stage known as civilization—the culture of cities.

The early inventions that produced such decisive changes before the beginning of science were not by any means naive in the sense of being simple or obvious. The craft tradition may be just as cumulative and just as much a subject of genius as the literate tradition of scientific understanding. Ancient man possessed a great deal of cunning and skill, perhaps more than is commonly found today. Extremely ingenious devices and processes are common among almost all of the so-called primitive peoples, and the most ancient jewelers' fine metalwork techniques are very similar to those used by modern craftsmen. Pottery and weaving still run the gamut from the careless to the skillful, as they always have.

An important point to be remembered is that this sort of naive invention is still with us in such objects as the paper clip and many other pieces of domestic hardware. Some of the finest crafts came from the preparation of food, the methods of cooking and baking, and the fermentation processes for beer and bread. Even machines—presses for wine and oil, for example—were developed long before people thought out the mechanical theory underlying them. Indeed, much of the early theory on the nature of chemical change proceeded from a long familiarity with such food-preparation processes, and most of the techniques of the alchemists and early chemists were borrowed directly from the kitchen.

Early in Greek and Roman civilization when the first fundamental advances were made in the foundations of science—chiefly in mathematics and astronomy—a special craft of crucial importance began to develop, that of making scientific instruments. We have a natural tendency to suppose that the early instruments were tools for doing something scientific, for taking special measurements, and so on. In fact, this was by no means the case. Early astronomy depended solely on qualitative (not quantitative) observations that could be made with the naked eye, and a great deal of theory could be derived from very little observation because the movements of the celestial bodies were regular and cyclical.

The early instruments seem to have been developed as models to assist and display knowledge derived from observation. They were, in a sense, idols of

science, tangible models that were analogous to modern theories, in that a theory is a kind of model of mathematics or hypothetical structures, rather than an actual thing that can be held and shown.

Later these models were adapted to more useful purposes. Armillary spheres became devices to measure celestial positions, and the rotating star-map became the astrolabe, most famous of ancient instruments. From this sprang a craft tradition of making beautiful instruments to illustrate the application of mathematics to problems of surveying and navigation. These devices were never quite so useful as their makers and advocates asserted. Instrumental surveys were not much more accurate than those made by rule of thumb and eye estimates, while position finding at sea was always, until the 18th century, more a matter of expert seamanship than any sort of navigation by angle measurement or magnetic compasses.

Most important for later history was the integration of the self-powered astronomical model into the mechanical clock. Clock making flourished toward the end of the Middle Ages, acting as a medium for the transfer from master to apprentice of the most sophisticated mechanical skills and ingenious mechanisms. At the beginning of the 17th century, as the craft of instrument making had grown from a few itinerant workers keeping alive an already old tradition to a healthy population of active shops in such major cities as Nuremberg, Augsburg, London, and Paris, a new phenomenon caused a vast revolution in the role of instruments in invention and discovery. Galileo's telescope suddenly showed that a simple device composed of lenses in a tube could provide one with evidence about the universe that no one had ever seen before. A whole new world opened up to a new sort of philosophy; soon the microscope revealed yet another world of tiny living beings, and such devices as the vacuum pump and the static electrical generator gave rise to physical conditions that never occurred naturally in common experience, yet were keys to further understanding of the laws of nature.

Throughout the 17th and 18th centuries there existed a virtual intoxication with the ingenuities of scientific instruments and the new worlds of learning and capability that they opened to inspection. Philosophic gentlemen like Thomas Jefferson devised ingenious mechanisms in this fashion, and the arts of surveying and clock making became showpieces of culture. Particularly ingenious craftspeople were valued for their rare talents and sought to exercise every trick of the trade to make the known instruments better and better. At this culmination of high scientific craftsmanship many artisans became famous, like Jess Ramsden, whose dividing engine brought a new accuracy to angular measurement by achieving

The automatic division of fine scales. The telescope itself remained the queen of instruments, and the process of making larger and larger lenses evolved from a craft skill into a fine art. Henry Fitz epitomized this personal growth of inventive skill. His products were sought after and with others became an essential part of the furniture of the observatories known as "lighthouses in the sky." They proliferated, springing up everywhere that money could be found to pay for this first of the sciences to depend on big and costly instrumentation—astronomy.

By about 1800 instrument making had grown from a craft guild of small workshops to a major industry of moderate-sized supply houses for a much wider public. Schools and colleges purchased increased quantities of apparatus for instruction in the new natural philosophy. Two new scientific discoveries then opened fresh floodgates for a whole new inventive spirit. Just at the turn of the century, Luigi Galvani, trying to identify the force that made the muscles in frogs' legs kick, and Count Alessandro Volta, who extended his work to produce a new sort of force from a pair of dissimilar metal plates separated by acid water, accidentally found a particularly powerful natural force—current electricity. The discovery of this force and the invention of the electric cell for producing it gave chemists the first really different agent for changing things since fire and distillation.

Science and technology were quick to apply the new tool. Its use led rapidly to the isolation of such

Developing his skills from locksmith and camera tinkerer to lens and prism maker, Henry Fitz of New York, seen below in a reconstruction of his shop at the Museum of History and Technology, epitomizes the mid-19th-century instrument maker. Fitz found the quality of women as lens crafters high, their rates low. By 1874 American instrument making produced a sophisticated telescope, above, for observing a transit of Venus.

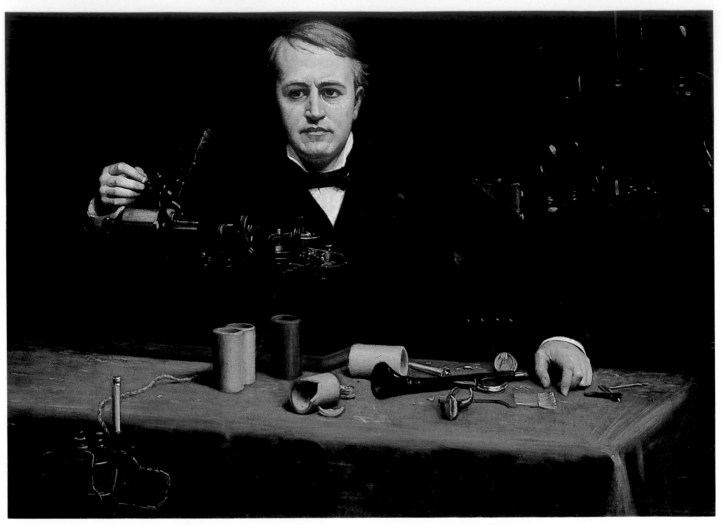

An 1890 portrait of Thomas A. Edison painted in Paris, re-created his Menlo Park, New Jersey, laboratory, and surrounded him with the fruits of invention: electric lamps behind, wax cylinder phonographs in front.

highly reactive new chemical elements as sodium and potassium, and within a few decades almost half of the chemical elements were revealed. The science of chemistry consequently reached a new level, enabling production of a whole panoply of substances that had never before been available. These substances in turn encouraged the rapid development of inorganic and then organic chemistry and opened the door to a first round of derivative chemical technologies. Electro-plating was regarded as an almost incredible transmu-tation of metals, and organic chemistry moved with unbelievable speed to artificial dyestuffs and scientific agriculture using soil-testing and fertilizers. Thus the fantastic array of scientific inventions stimulated prac-tical application of the new knowledge. Scientific and technological improvements in agriculture opened up whole continents, especially in the United States, and colleges proliferated, complete with laboratories for the study of chemistry and electricity.

During the first half of the 19th century the world was transformed not only by the twin forces of electric-ity and chemistry, but also by the advent of the railroad and by enormous changes in population patterns and mobility. It is at this point that invention began to play a new social role, becoming itself a means of social mobility. All over the world, but especially in the United States and the most industrialized parts of Europe, it became a fabulous dream of every ingenious child to experiment in some sort of home workshop-laboratory and produce the great invention that would win him fame and fortune. Real-life prototype of the mythic inventor was physicist Michael Pupin, whose autobiography *From Immigrant to Inventor* induced other aspirants to flood the patent offices with models of better mousetraps and a million and one hopeful devices, some of which became the innovations that ushered in a new age of manufacture.

Some inventors achieved the legendary success of a Ford or an Edison, while others languished or be-came, through self-education as an inventor, adept at other skills. Notable amongst this latter class was the young Luxembourgian, Hugo Gernsback, who came to the United States with a practical idea for one of the countless new types of electric battery; he stayed to become a pioneer of the pulp magazines that gave the world *Popular Mechanics* and science fiction as well as clubs of home radio experimenters and photographic darkroom enthusiasts. Much of the real innovation in radio and photography resulted from these home experiments rather than from the research of professional scientists in colleges or industry. In addition to these more scientific crafts, there was also a resurgence of the older pattern of naive invention that needed no highfalutin theory, just keen ingenuity and the persistence to try countless combinations of ideas until something worked well enough for commercialization. Of this nature were the designs for the first typewriters and office adding machines, as well as all sorts of machinery for agriculture and such industries as textiles and railroading.

Invention had reached such a pitch by the middle of the 19th century that it became an instrument of international competition and prestige—almost a substitute for the more dangerous force of war. The first great exhibition in 1851 in London's Crystal Palace, itself a triumph of new technology in glass and girder construction, was a resounding success. It set the pattern for a series of almost annual events in the principal cities of the world as nations vied for gold medals in heavy machinery and machine tools, and in all such industrial arts as the production of tapestries and fine porcelain, hunting rifles and machine guns, printing presses and household appliances. The fairs and exhibitions promoted international trade in such sophisticated wares so intensely that the wealth of nations began to move away from the traditional exports and imports and into this new trade in high manufactures. Invention became the source of the developing economy of factories. It was in this spirit that manufacture grew mightily in every aspect. Steam-engine technology gave way to the automobile and the airplane, and at each stage the technology offered a point of departure for scientists to analyze designs and production and to try to provide a basis for resolution of problems. In the way that the steam engine had stimulated a science of thermodynamics, the airplane set minds thinking about and experimenting with aerodynamics. Pure science thus moved forward investigating this arena of artifacts and processes in addition to the world of nature, while the applied sciences contributed to the improvement of manufacture and an ever increasing range of new products.

By the early years of the 20th century the new scientific industries and industrial machine building

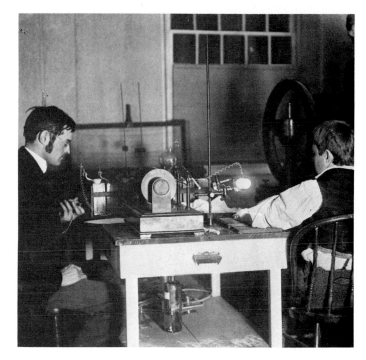

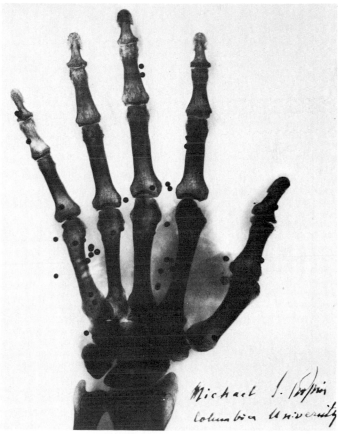

The discovery of X-rays in 1895 resulted in a remarkably rapid transfer from science to technology: within a few weeks, physics labs were photographing injuries for doctors. Top, Professor Edwin B. Frost of Dartmouth takes a radiograph of a patient's arm. Above, an 1896 radiograph of shotgun pellets in the hand of a young New York attorney.

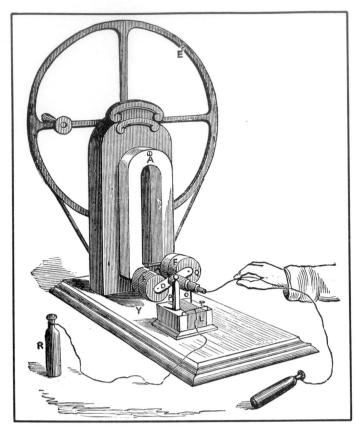

Toy into tool: shocking parlor games of 1850 employed the magneto for joltage; it soon was used to plate metals; and by 1882 a dynamo lit up New York as Edison revved up big "Mary Ann."

had eclipsed both naive invention and the patent craze. Professional and amateur inventors turned to the technicalities of electricity and electronics, organic chemistry, and experimental optics. It was an age of chemistry sets and home electrical experiments of radio and photography buffs who could buy equipment from special supply houses and develop new craft techniques for themselves. Often the amateurs acted as an interface between the professional technologists in the industrial laboratories and the consuming public. Many young people were exposed to science by such activities and accompanying popular magazines; a generation grew up with its eyes fixed on the wondrous machines of the future.

The First World War used plenty of heavy machinery but relatively little science except in telegraph, telephone, and radio communications and the often unsuccessful attempts to use poison gas. During the years between the wars an increased sophistication in both scientific theory and instrumentation produced new techniques and devices, such as X-ray crystallography for the study of the structure of materials, electronic devices for working with small particles, and the elaboration of radio into both radar and television. By the time of the Second World War this new sort of invention had matured sufficiently to herald yet another age of science and invention.

The wartime development of the atomic bomb and the rapid evolution of radar set the scene for a new sort of technology involving a high degree of scientific training and considerable investment in refined apparatus for its exploitation. These high technologies were tightly linked to the research front of science in a way in which the 19th-century exploitation of electricity and chemistry were not, and there was little place for the amateur inventor in this era. During the next decades the products of high technology extended into all areas, bringing forth radically new products of enormous social impact. The antibiotics and the steroid drugs for birth control changed patterns of life and death and the nature of the family. The transistor, the microelectronic chip, and the computer involved huge inputs of basic science and the careful nurturing of novel craft techniques of manufacture, yielding products whose side effects are as yet only beginning to be felt. The wartime use of rocketry rapidly developed into a technology that could take us into space and, again, like the telescope, tell us things about the nature of the universe that we had not known we wanted to know.

The economic, military, and social impacts of the high technologies have changed the basis of both the scientific enterprise and the nature of invention. In science today one is no longer a philosophical hobbyist. The impact of powerful new technologies is, indeed, so great that we often become afraid that unforeseen side effects may present unacceptable dangers to us all. Consequently, the art of invention is now feared as much as it is respected.

The world is not as simple as it was when ingenuity could take one from immigrant boy to inventor genius. Invention and scientific research once seemed relatively simple, noble occupations that were usually pleasing to the ingenious and philosophical mind and might even be the source of some boon that would save lives or labor, create better products or more profit, and enable mankind to extend control over nature. Now we know it is not so simple. Indeed, we discover we know very little about the way that invention and innovation really work and the way in which we have gradually gained some understanding of nature. □

Tools of the space age, technology's rockets have given scientists ever higher platforms from which they can look out into the universe, and equally important, back at the Earth. Right, "Changing Environment," by Lowell Herrera.

Labor Savers?

Joseph & Frances Gies

Labor saving is as American as apple pie—which these days is usually factory-made, flash-frozen, plastic-packaged, and ready to brown and serve. But the idea has British roots. Samuel Slater of Massachusetts pirated designs for textile machinery from England, originated some others, and by hook and by crook assembled a New Englandized spinning jenny that launched the United States' first industry.

Obed Hussey, Cyrus McCormick, and myriad others carried the newborn American industrial revolution to the land. The farmer put down his immemorial scythe and took the reins of a horse-drawn reaper.

In advanced models the operator could even sit down as the machine deftly clipped the grain. The later combine was aptly named—it combined the work of reaping and threshing.

Almost overnight an American standard of production began to emerge. At its best, the American way grew to combine efficiency, speed, and comfort. An amazing breakthrough in this direction occurred in 1785 when Oliver Evans designed, built, and operated the world's first automated factory, a flour mill. Conveyor belts, endless screws, and chains of buckets moved the grist from one processing station to

In Winslow Homer's bucolic scene, "The Morning Bell," women stroll to work, liberated from the drudgeries of the farm. Yet the bell, hooked to a clock, and the looms within the factory would create their own regulated, wearisome life.

another. Water-powered devices ground, spread, dried, sifted, refined, and packed the flour.

From its original industrial context, labor saving came to have a special meaning for the American home. As the country changed from rural to urban, women abandoned their traditional function as food and textile producers. They stopped feeding poultry, gathering eggs, milking cows, making butter, spinning and weaving, and concentrated instead on the narrower areas of housework: cooking, cleaning, and child care. In this role they became targets for manufacturers using the new mass-production system of interchangeable-parts.

The idea had been pioneered by Eli Whitney and perfected by such men as arms manufacturers John Hall, Samuel Colt, and Simeon North. Their techniques dramatically reduced the unit costs of their guns, and smoothed the way for more peaceful industries to make products the average home could afford.

One of the first nonmilitary applications of interchangeable parts was the iron stove. Introduced in the early 1800s, it was more convenient and efficient for cooking than the still prevalent medieval fireplace. The iron stove was far from labor free, but as long as wood and coal were cheap it resisted competition.

It may seem incredible to us today, but the gas range was demonstrated at the London Crystal Palace Exposition of 1851, and the electric range at the Chicago Columbian Exhibition of 1893. In 1906, General Electric marketed its first range, a wooden table with 30 plugs and switches powering 13 appliances, including a frying pan, an oven, double boilers, pots, a coffee-maker, toaster, and waffle iron. Electricity arrived in rural areas only with the New Deal in the 1930s, and even in towns the slow diffusion of central heating made families prize the iron stove. That feeling was social as well as economic—families often gathered around the iron stove on winter nights for cheer as well as warmth. However, by 1924, Robert and Helen Lynd reported in their classic work *Middletown* that two out of three houses in Muncie, Indiana, had gas ranges, and by 1935 in *Middletown in Transition,* 95 percent.

The labor saving afforded by new stoves was not restricted to the elimination of such chores as chopping wood or emptying ashes. Kitchens became easier to keep clean. Therefore they became cleaner, and the clean kitchen became a fetish. So did the clean house and clean clothes, leading to the Age of Homemaking, or the Age of the Mad Housewife.

A whole array of labor-saving devices was en-

Joseph and Frances Gies write mainly on medieval history and the history of technology. Their works include Bridges and Men *and* Women in the Middle Ages.

In descending order, a Remington No. 2 typewriter which by 1878 reached present office size, if not shape; a woman works at a Eureka loom, used into the 20th century; and "Hello Central."

GRANITE IRON WARE IS "ALL THE GOSSIP."

Major. Knapp & Co. 56 & 58 Park Place N.Y.   OVER

Mass-produced, low-priced enameled metal and crockery cookware made food preparation more hygienic and efficient.

thusiastically designed to help the new house-centered woman in her house-cleaning mission. The carpet sweeper, introduced in America in the 1870s by Melville Bissell of Grand Rapids, Michigan, was a long-handled wooden box on rubber-tired wheels, enclosing a cylindrical brush rotated by traction to pick up dirt and deposit it in a pan. Cheap, light, easy to operate, the carpet sweeper is still with us, one of the rare inventions to survive along with its technological replacement, the vacuum cleaner.

The success of many appliances, including the vacuum cleaner, awaited the development of the small electric motor. A historic achievement, the device grew in part out of the electromagnetic experiments of Joseph Henry, founding secretary of the Smithsonian Institution.

A blacksmith, Thomas Davenport, studied a giant Henry electromagnet that had been installed in an iron works to extract iron from pulverized ore. He bought a magnet and built a motor. Davenport's wife, Emily, helped in the achievement by suggesting the use of mercury as an electrical conductor.

Davenport's motors found use in his own shop and powered the world's first electric printing press (1840). But the motor's true vocation awaited the dynamo, or generator, toward which Joseph Henry had also pointed the way. When large generators began producing power, the electric motor came into its own, a genie for dozens of new and old devices.

The hand laundry was one old invention that cried for an electric motor. Elbow grease worked the typical "dolly," a long-handled tool with a head like a small stool. The operator pumped it up and down in the washtub to agitate the clothes. A few modern washing machines still incorporate the dolly principle, though in streamlined form and with electromotive power.

Electric washing machines may have saved women less labor than did the introduction of commercial soap powders, which supplanted not only the tedious 19th-century chore of home soap making, but the later task of shaving or boiling bars of manufactured laundry soap as well.

The fully automatic washer did not arrive until after the Second World War. At about the same time, the rotating hot-air dryer eliminated the final act in the old wash-day drama, the lugging of the basketful of wrung-out garments and linens up the cellar stairs and into the back yard for pinning to the clothesline.

Washday Monday—blue Monday—was followed by another day's drudgery—Tuesday ironing. Irons were massive, heavy, and heated by coal in a compartment or on an iron stove. Finally, after World War I, a light, inexpensive, practical electric iron appeared and within a decade almost every household owned one.

One labor-saving device after another hit the market. Yet an unexpected effect of labor savers was the decline in status of housewives. Where the 19th-century middle-class housewife acted as manager, supervising a staff of servants, her 20th-century granddaughter—though flattered with the title "homemaker"—managed only her own labor. That loss of prestige, as much as the freedom conferred by technology, may be responsible for the movement of women from home to office—which is, in fact, a return to woman's historic role as producer.

In the office, technology yielded another paradox: it gave women something and took away something. For example, a new role for women was on its way to becoming institutionalized when the YWCA graduated a class of eight typists in New York City in 1881. Up until then, offices had been as masculine as battleships. Women worked a little in factories, some in shops, but mainly as nurses, servants, and teachers.

Christopher Sholes was quite proud of the social effect of the typewriter he invented. "I do feel," he told his daughter, "that I have done something for the women who have always had to work so hard. This will enable them to more easily earn a living."

J. M. Barrie, author of *Peter Pan,* dramatized the typewriter's beneficence in the *Twelve-Pound Look.* Lady Sims plotted her escape from a bullying husband via the typewriter. Neither Sholes nor Barrie foresaw a time, a few generations hence, when the typewriter—like so many other historic innovations—would metamorphose from a young liberal into a crusty reactionary and be reviled for its part in restricting women to lower-level office jobs.

In the march of advancing technology, there is always much to cheer, but inevitably—or so it seems—some grass and flowers get trampled. □

The 1870 Howe sewing machine, top left, incorporated Elias Howe's patented lock stitch, a breakthrough in machine sewing. A marketing revolution occurred when Singer inaugurated a program of installment payments. Soon electricity became the thing in labor-saving devices. At first it was merely tacked on to existing machines such as the early toaster, above, and the 1912 Speed Queen washing machine, little more than the old model with an electric motor added. On the other hand, the Hoover suction sweeper of 1908 called for a wholly new design. Within a year, such pneumatic sweepers were also being promoted as hair-driers, "using the current of pure fresh air from the exhaust." As labor-saving devices became available, household hygiene became more important, thanks to guilt-provoking advertising, and household chores like laundry and vacuuming expanded to fit available time. Result: continuing drudgery.

The Pace of War

Harold D. Langley

Between the first use of gunpowder and the development of the atomic bomb, no invention changed warfare so dramatically as the machine gun. Despite its enormous impact, the inventor of the automatic weapon is largely unknown.

Maine-born Sir Hiram Stevens Maxim (1840-1916) possessed a remarkable inventive genius in the tradition of Thomas A. Edison and Alexander Graham Bell. In his youth he worked at a series of odd jobs as bartender, boxer, wood-turner, and brass-fettler. When he was 24 he went to work in an uncle's engineering firm in Fitchburg, Massachusetts, where he learned drafting and pursued technical and scientific studies. For his uncle he invented a gas lighting machine, improving the device before the first version could be manufactured. In 1866 he asserted his inventiveness by taking out his first patent—for an improved curling iron. About two years later, while working as a draftsman in New York City, he invented a locomotive headlight that

was widely used. He also invented an automatic sprinkler type of fire extinguisher. His interest in gas led him to establish the successful Maxim Gas Company. It also led him to invent a density regulator for equalizing the illuminating value of gas, but he soon saw the limitations of gas and began working on an electric light. In 1878 he became the chief engineer of the United States Electric Lighting Company, the first such organization to be established in the country. He next introduced an electrical pressure regulator, which, when exhibited at the Paris Exhibition of 1881, won him the Legion of Honor decoration from the French government.

Maxim spent some time in the early 1880s sightseeing in Europe, and in Vienna he met an American to whom he related his recent triumph at Paris. The acquaintance was not impressed. "Hang your chemistry and electricity!" he said. "If you want to make a pile of money, invent something that will enable these Europeans to cut each other's throats with greater facility." Heeding the message, Maxim moved to London and by 1884 he had a model automatic gun ready for demonstration. On hand for the occasion were the Prince of Wales, the Duke of Edinburgh, and Sir Garnet Wolseley, one of the most prominent British generals of the day. Lord Wolseley was delighted with the gun's performance and potential.

The gun that Maxim had invented was the first successful automatic weapon—that is, it would fire continuously, as long as the gunner held the trigger, until the ammunition was exhausted. In a sense, the Maxim gun could be said to be another kind of internal combustion engine: a machine that would continue to operate as long as fuel—in this case, cartridges—was supplied. It was therefore fundamentally different from the hand-cranked, multiple-barrel Gatling gun, developed during the American Civil War. An unfortunate marriage between the rifle and the engine, the machine gun efficiently and impersonally performed what had previously been hand work. It presaged the coming mechanization of war, the turreted, steampowered warships; the tanks and armored personnel carriers; the airplanes; the breech-loading, self-propelled artillery pieces; the increasingly clever missiles; and all of the other appurtenances of modern war. As weapons became increasingly mechanical, warfare became industrial. Mass armies comprised of technicians as well as the more traditional cannon fodder, equipped and fed by the agricultural, technological, scientific, and industrial resources of entire nations, confronted enemies similarly backed and equipped. The result was mass death, accompanied by dehumanization of the participants on a scale hitherto inconceivable. At the same time, paradoxically, concern for the welfare of the individual combatant increased in proportion to the frightfulness of battle, at least in Western armies. Hospital care, leave policy, recognition of battle fatigue, entertainment, even training and preparation for battle all reflected the rising importance of the individual soldier, sailor, or airman in the eyes of the nation he stood for.

The British Army adopted the Maxim gun in 1889, and the Royal Navy in 1892. In 1893 the Krupps of Germany obtained the Maxim patents and began manufacturing a German version. Immediately, the Russians, the Austrians, the Italians, and other powers became interested in the gun.

Others entered the competition to produce better machine guns using various modes of operation. Nonetheless, professional military men were slow to appreciate the significance of the machine gun. That the British had used Maxim guns in Africa in the Matabele War of 1893, in the Sudan in 1898, and in the Boer War of 1899-1902 tended to make many officers think that the weapon was useful in a colonial setting, but of limited value in a European war. As a result, the tremendous losses inflicted by machine guns during the first months of World War I came as a rude surprise. Very reluctantly, professional soldiers came to admit that the machine gun had changed both the tactics and the nature of warfare.

The machine gun did prove to be the most formidable defensive weapon of its time. However, as advanced defensive weapons have always stimulated development of more advanced offensive weapons, the machine gun provoked the invention of its great antagonist, the armored tank.

Machine guns also played an important part in transforming the airplane from an observation craft to a new weapon of war. A French aviator, Roland Garros, developed a device that allowed him to fire a machine gun through the propeller blade of the plane. The Germans discovered the secret and Dutch aircraft designer Anthony Fokker devised a better system. Then the Allies captured a German plane and adapted the device for their own aircraft. Casualties increased. Though brutally dangerous, air war led to popular acclaim for a new breed of heroes, the flying aces.

Perhaps it was understandable that the public would associate aerial combat with the code of chivalry. But on the ground, tanks, hand grenades, artillery shells, flame throwers, poison gas, and automatic weapons had long since ended any possibility of gentlemanly warfare. To meet the needs of the World War I foot soldier, U.S. Colonel J. T. Thompson invented a compact machine gun that he called the "trench broom." The war ended before it could be produced, so Thompson tried with some success to interest the military and the police in his invention. In 1925 Chicago gangsters began using it, and other underworld characters followed suit. Perhaps the most dramatic incident linking the Thompson sub-machine gun with crime took place in Chicago in 1929. Two men dressed as policemen, who were employed by gangster Al Capone, lined up members of a rival gang and killed them with machine-gun fire. This incident, known as the St. Valentine's Day Massacre, shocked and fascinated the American public. In real life and on the

"A visible wave of death swept over the advancing host" when the British used Maxim machine guns in the Sudan in 1898. Here Sir Hiram demonstrates his machine gun.

Harold D. Langley, a curator of naval history in the National Museum of History and Technology, teaches history at Catholic University.

197

Following World War I slaughter, the machine gun went on to movie roles: Hollywood (and real-life) gangsters wielded it, above. A throwback to the Gatling gun, the Vulcan 20mm revolving barrel cannon, opposite, is used by jet fighters; it fires up to 6,000 rounds per minute from its six barrels.

screen, the "tommy gun" was associated with gangsters. Laws were passed forbidding individuals from owning a working machine gun. To combat crime on a national level, the Federal Bureau of Investigation was created, with FBI agents using the tommy gun against gangsters. Given the tools of mass warfare, street combat flourished.

In the post-World War I years the public's fascination with airplanes and heroic pilots was furthered by the barnstormers. Using surplus aircraft, the barnstormers did stunt flying at outdoor events throughout the country. By bringing the airplane and entertainment to fairs and small towns, the barnstormers gave hundreds of ordinary people a personal experience with an invention that was transforming the world. The public read about the growth of scheduled commercial airline service from 1925 onward. In 1919 a U.S. Navy flying boat had made the first trans-Atlantic flight. Then, in May 1927, much of the world rejoiced when former Army pilot Charles A. Lindbergh made the first nonstop solo flight across the Atlantic. Army Air Corps pilots had already achieved the first round-the-world flight.

The airplane increased in speed, size, endurance, and flying range. World War II brought a whole range of bombers and fighter types into military use and public awareness. Propeller-driven craft gave way to jets. Conflicts in Korea and Vietnam were largely fought with jet-propelled fighters and bombers, but in both those wars the rotor-driven helicopter emerged as the work horse of the modern Army. Used as a personnel carrier, an ambulance, a gun ship, a rescue device, or a

hovering guard force, the helicopter gave the Army a new mobility and striking power.

The side effects of 20th-century total war were far-reaching. After World War I, the doughboys' return to civilian life was marked by a number of interesting changes, some of which were short-term matters. In men's clothing the waistlines narrowed, coats flared below the waist, and buttons reached higher. Checks, plaids, loud ties, and bright socks were favored. More lasting results could be seen in shoes. Before the war men wore low shoes in summer and high in winter. But leather shortages during the war, as well as the experience with leggings and puttees, made men prefer free ankles, and low-cut shoes became the year-round choice. During the war the wrist watch proved more convenient than the pocket watch, and remained popular with returning servicemen, who regarded it as a symbol of virility. Wearing wrist watches soon became a dominant fashion, first among men and later among women.

Fabric shortages during World War I dictated that women's skirts would be shorter. But after the war skirts did not return to the earlier peacetime lengths. In the 1920s skirt lengths for younger women rose above the knee, and to a few inches above the ankle for the more mature types. Wartime shortages of cotton and wool forced women to stop wearing stockings of those fabrics and to substitute silk. The wearing of silk stockings continued after the war until rayon and later nylon became the basic component in women's hose. High-button shoes also became a casualty of shorter skirts and changing styles. New materials, scantier skirts, and looser clothing led to briefer styles in underclothing.

Overseas service had a long-range effect on how American women treated their complexions. Before leaving France, many a soldier sent his wife or girl a duty-free package of perfume and cosmetics from Paris. To meet the growing demand, French firms began to do a brisk cosmetic business with the United States, inspiring American companies in turn to produce less expensive items more competitive with French products.

The war changed other social patterns; for many soldiers, living with men of different economic and national backgrounds under the extreme stress of combat broke down old prejudices. Marriages made amid the tempo of war frequently could not withstand the everyday demands of peace; couples drifted apart and divorce rates soared.

Veterans of World War I effected major changes in medicine and health. In 1924 veterans' groups won from Congress the right to free hospitalization for all veterans of all wars whether their disabilities resulted from war injuries or peacetime accidents. By 1942, 93

Making up for over 12 million tons of Allied shipping sunk by Axis forces in World War II, U.S. yards helped win the war using mass-production techniques: the three ships above were launched at 12:30 a.m., noon, and 4:30 p.m. of the same day.

percent of the annual admissions to veterans' hospitals were for non-service-connected disabilities. The various bureaus dealing with veterans' problems were consolidated in 1930 to form the Veterans Administration, an independent Federal agency. It was still coping with the long-range effects of World War I when the U.S. entered World War II.

On the combat front, World War II was fought predominantly with improved versions of the weapons used in World War I. With combat in every climate, and the wide distribution of troops, few places in the world escaped the impact of war, a large part of which involved the dissemination of war-related products, techniques, procedures, and inventions. One such invention was DDT, widely used in the tropics to kill malarial mosquitoes. While making an area safer for troops, the DDT spray also improved the crops and the quality of life of the native inhabitants. In postwar years farmers in the United States and other countries relied on DDT to control crop-devouring insects, and many homeowners used it on their gardens. After the war Rachel Carson warned of the dangers of continued widespread distribution of DDT in her book *The Silent Spring* (1962), many of her predictions coming true in the following years. Not only did the chemical change the patterns of nature, but large amounts of it ingested by humans posed a substantial threat to health. In addition, the insects that it was designed to kill developed greater and greater tolerances for the chemical. However, DDT is still used in many parts of the world.

Radar was another invention that saw extensive use in the war. Prior to World War II, various countries had information on the method of detecting metallic objects by electromagnetic radiation. Just before the outbreak of the war, the British secretly deployed a number of primitive radar sets that signaled early warning of German air attacks, an inestimable advantage during the crucial Battle of Britain. During the war the major combatants achieved giant strides in the improvement of radar. Aside from locating the enemy, radar played a conspicuous role in bringing planes through bad weather to safe landings. This important service made an easy transition from the needs of war to peacetime use. Today, improved radar is a vital part of ships, military installations, planes, and airports. The war-induced production of radar sets made it possible to bring down the cost of oscilloscope tubes and thereby promote the sale of televisions. Although TV had been invented well before World War II, it was too costly for most families. Radar not only helped to win the war, it gave television to the world much sooner than would otherwise have been the case.

Many servicemen brought home with them fond memories of the ubiquitous, general-purpose vehicle called the jeep. Some ex-soldiers bought surplus jeeps and used them for outdoor work and recreation. The popularity of the design led its manufacturer to market a successful civilian version, the Jeep, and a host of similar vehicles have since been introduced.

Military clothing such as Army field jackets, Air Corps and Navy leather flight jackets, Navy pea coats, and Army officers' gray trousers or "pinks" also became a part of the civilian scene. Sometimes olive drab trousers were dyed a darker color, but the lack of cuffs, common in civilian clothing, betrayed their military origin. The most popular items of clothing were the cotton khaki trousers of ex-soldiers; the demand became so great that manufacturers began to market slacks that were designed to look like the Army versions. Khaki pants remained popular on the college scene for many years before giving way to new styles in blue jeans and other garb. In this way, military clothing became civilianized.

Male headgear also changed permanently as a result of World War II. All servicemen were required to wear hats during their time in uniform, and it was assumed by some hat manufacturers that this habit would lead to a fresh demand for hats in civilian life. Instead, there was a widespread rejection of headgear by almost all veterans.

The war's impact on American society ran far deeper. Manpower demands led to plans to use women in a limited and temporary capacity in the armed forces as had been done in World War I. Special units for women were established by the Army, Navy, Marines, and Coast Guard. Women with aviation experience, organized into the Women's Air Force Service Pilots (WASP), ferried planes from manufacturing plants to airfields in this country. The WASPs were disbanded late in World War II, but the other women's organizations became a part of the peacetime armed services. Later, after a separate Air Force was established, a women's organization was created for that service. So successful was the experiment of using women that by the late 1970s they were outgrowing their separate organizations and becoming an integral part of the regular armed forces.

World War II saw the incorporation of a number of blacks into the armed forces, but mainly in the Army. Only a small proportion of those in uniform saw combat, despite the efforts of black leaders to give black citizens a full and equal participation in the war effort. When the Army commissioned its first Negro general in 1940, he commanded segregated troops. It was not until the Korean War that segregation ended in the armed services. Thereafter, individual black soldiers fought side by side with their white comrades in Korea and in even greater numbers in Vietnam. There was also a growing number of blacks in the officer corps, some graduates of the service academies. Still, it was not until 1968 during the Vietnam War that the Air Force commissioned its first black general. The

WWII Germany's vaunted mechanized armies, most of which actually relied on horse-drawn transport, were ultimately de- *feated by wheel-and-track-propelled Allied forces, typified by the jeep-mounted G.I., below, churning by a dead horse in 1945.*

Tom Lea's portrait of a WWII Marine with a "2,000-yard stare" depicts war's difficult-to-repair inner injuries; Vietnam War Navy surgeons, below, fight to save a shrapneled leg.

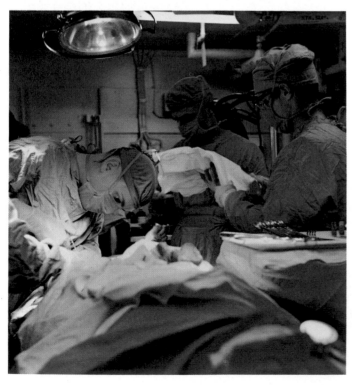

Navy commissioned its first black officer in 1942 and selected its first black admiral 30 years later.

War was a great mixer of our pluralistic peoples. A good part of the American army in World War I came from rural and small-town backgrounds, many of them gaining their first and sometimes their only glimpse of life in a foreign land. In World War II the population mix and the exposure to diverse cultures was much more intense. Northerners and southerners, easterners and westerners, Protestants, Catholics, Jews, and atheists from virtually every ethnic background had to learn to live together. They were transplanted by the military services into foreign experiences ranging from the jungles of the South Pacific and Burma to the highly civilized societies of western Europe. Most of the men and women exposed to such experiences were changed in whole or in part. Earlier prejudices, attitudes, and points of view founded on ignorance gave way to more tolerant outlooks or at least a willingness to suspend judgment. Significantly, this transformation was taking place at a time when the United States was assuming a position of greater world leadership.

For some men in uniform this exposure to foreign lands led to marriage with women of other nations. The war brides, and those who were married as a result of occupation duty or peacetime service overseas, usually settled in the United States. To their communities and their circle of friends and acquaintances they brought their own special contributions to America's ethnic and cultural mix. They were also a part of the broadened horizon and renewed strength of the American people.

No weapon of World War II bore more shocking implications for the future of humanity than the atomic bomb. When the United States dropped the first atomic bomb on Hiroshima on August 6, 1945, an estimated 100,000 people were killed immediately, and tens of thousands of others died later of radiation poisoning. Among the victims were two U.S. Navy fliers who were being held in a local jail. Three days later more death and devastation struck Japan when a second atomic bomb was dropped on Nagasaki. Japan promptly sued for peace, and World War II ended.

In the years that followed the war, Americans and the rest of the world learned about the details of the development of the bomb and the decision to use it. It was revealed that not all of the scientists who worked on the project were convinced that a bomb should be made. Once it was made, there were others who argued that its power should be demonstrated before enemy witnesses on an uninhabited island rather than

An undersea hunter, the 360-foot-long, 6,900-ton nuclear attack submarine U.S.S. Groton *dramatically emphasizes the high technological level of modern naval vessels.*

by dropping it on a Japanese city. Such concerns were swept aside amid fears that an enemy might develop the bomb first, and belief that its use would save the lives of soldiers destined to invade Japan in October 1945. Yet Secretary of War Henry L. Stimson, who was involved in the development of the bomb and the decision to use it, called it "the most terrible weapon ever known to human history. . . ." The Secretary was not blind to the dangers that lay ahead. "War in the twentieth century has grown steadily more barbarous, more destructive, more debased in all of its aspects," he wrote. "Now, with the release of atomic energy, man's ability to destroy himself is nearly complete."

Horrible as the first atomic bombs were, the destructive potential of modern weaponry was increased by the development of the hydrogen bomb and by the building of intercontinental ballistic missiles with nuclear warheads. The United States and the Soviet Union came close to a nuclear confrontation in 1962 over the Cuban missile crisis. When diplomacy and reason triumphed in that situation, there was a tendency for many of the American people to feel that nuclear weapons, like poison gas, would never again be used in warfare.

American military men also understood that an exchange of intercontinental ballistic missiles with nuclear warheads could destroy more people in a few hours than all the wars in history. Faced with such a prospect, war lost all of its meaning, forcing military planners to think about the possibility of future wars without resort to nuclear weapons. While the United States and the Soviet Union built, maintained, and improved their nuclear arsenals, much attention was focused on the development of more advanced conventional weapons. The Korean conflict and the Vietnam War accelerated such work.

Korea and Vietnam were wars in which the traditional concepts of victory and defeat were discarded. These were limited wars with limited objectives that fell far short of the unconditional surrender formula of World War II. Limited wars with limited goals were more like the wars of the 18th century than those of the 19th or 20th centuries. Yet for a number of Americans, including many military men, Korea and Vietnam seemed like case histories of victory denied for political reasons. They argued that in waging war there should be no restrictions on military commanders, including the choice of weapons and terrain. Still other Americans both in and out of uniform believed that it was proper to restrain military leaders. For modern warfare, even when waged with conventional weapons, was a terribly destructive experience for all concerned. Vietnam brought that home to thousands of civilians through their newspapers, magazines, television, and conversations with men in uniform.

While American military leaders tried to anticipate the problems of future wars, they could not forget some of the lessons of past conflicts. One disturbing lesson was that you could train a civilian to become a soldier; you could give him the best weapons and teach him how to use them, but you could not make him kill. In World War II and Korea it was discovered that only one out of every three or four soldiers would fire at an enemy in plain sight. Thus the potential fire power of a given unit was drastically reduced. American soldiers preferred to do their killing in circumstances where they could not see whom they were hitting. Aerial, artillery, and naval bombardment were the preferred forms of delivering death. In an infantry fire fight, the modern American infantryman preferred to shoot in the direction of the enemy rather than take aim at a particular soldier. Under such circumstances no one could know just whose shot hit an enemy soldier.

As a result of this approach to combat, the cost of killing an enemy increased astronomically. In World War II and Korea, to wound an enemy soldier took an average of 10,000 rifle bullets, to kill him 50,000. The wasteful pattern continued in Vietnam. It was estimated that for every guerrilla killed in 1966, some 27,000 rounds of ammunition were expended. Likewise, the United States dropped an average of eight bombs for every Vietcong guerrilla killed. Even conventional warfare was becoming too expensive to wage for very long.

Still another mounting expense of warfare involved the medical and pension expenditures for veterans and their dependents. The last dependent of the American Revolution died in 1911, and the last dependent of the War of 1812 in 1946. Benefits are still being paid to a small number of widows and dependents of Civil War veterans of both sides. Time is thinning the ranks of the World War I veterans, but many of those who served in World War II now require extensive hospital care. With the statistics of our past wars in mind, it is clear that some Vietnam veterans and their dependents will be drawing benefits through much of the 21st century. Both military and civilian planners are realizing that the expenditures for the care of veterans and their dependents, and the rising costs of arms and warfare, must somehow be stabilized or the nation will go bankrupt. It is a situation fraught with economic and social perils, and in a large measure it is the ultimate cost of warfare in the 20th century. Money, rather than weapons or men, may be the ultimate means of outlawing war. □

Straight up into the wild blue yonder zooms an F-15 Eagle. Probably the world's best fighter plane, its design is so specialized that civilian aircraft technology can borrow little from it.

6
PART

Seating Everyone

David A. Hanks

Frank Lloyd Wright once complained that too much intimate contact with the furniture he had designed gave him a certain "discontent." Nonetheless, the contributions of this master architect to the techniques and qualities of American furniture were both eye-catching and profound. His basic innovative idea was that furniture should be "organically" related to the surrounding space, that all design elements should reflect a central concept.

Fortunately for the development of modern design in this country, Wright's career bridged the most recent two centuries of our nation's life. He was aware of both the remarkable innovations made by the Victorians—at a time (1870-1900) when inventiveness here was an end in itself—and of the technological opportunities for industry in the 20th century. Designers had devised furniture that folded, expanded, and changed its form for diverse purposes; they had struggled ingeniously with the materials at their command to meet the needs and the whims of those who wanted to be better seated. The early 20th-century manufacturers pursued new markets no less avidly, bringing about major changes in the way our grandparents sat and reclined as the industry responded to mass-production machinery.

It seemed to Wright, whose architecture is known today as the Prairie School style because of the way his houses hugged the typically low-lying Midwestern terrain, that houses should be built of natural materials with rooms that opened expansively into each other. He designed both built-in and movable furniture to complement these spaces, using harmonious materials and forms to create a pervasive sense of unity and repose. The house Wright designed for Frederick C. Robie in 1908 presents an outstanding example of this unification of built-in and free-standing furniture: the slatted chairs of the dining-room ensemble, placed within the wide-open, horizontal space of the dining area, seem to fence off a special place, a kind of shelter from the prairie's seemingly limitless expanse.

An equally important component in this aesthetic was Wright's desire to have the furniture, for all its elegance, simply manufactured from indigenous materials. The Robie House furniture, of natural oak, was produced as a series of rectilinear forms by a Milwaukee manufacturer. As may be seen in the interior view of the Robie House, which still stands near the University of Chicago campus, the chairs, the table, the lamp stands . . . everything is designed to be a working part of the total architecture. Wright wrote in 1910: "In Organic Architecture then, it is quite impossible to consider the building as one thing, its furnishings another and its setting and environment still another. The Spirit in which these buildings are conceived sees all these together at work as one thing. All are to be studiously foreseen and provided for in the nature of the structure. All these should become mere details of the character and completeness of the structure. . . . The very chairs and tables, cabinets and even musical instruments, where practicable, are of the building itself, never fixtures upon it. . . ." Indeed, the Robie house is a grand and appropriately styled dwelling for the age of industrial inventors and forward thinkers.

Wright's simple, elegant lines contrasted sharply with the typical furniture of the period. The chairs were not elaborately carved; instead, the slats, integral to the chairs, served both as back and as ornament. Wright found it difficult, though, to design chairs that were architecturally pleasing and fit for human use.

Even more indicative of the pivotal age in which Wright lived and worked was his design for the 1904 Larkin Building in Buffalo. Office buildings at that time were a relatively new architectural conception.

David A. Hanks organized The Decorative Designs of Frank Lloyd Wright *for the Smithsonian Institution's Renwick Gallery in Washington, D.C.*

Frank Lloyd Wright created a new approach to seating Americans at their work and leisure. His swing-out desk chairs for the Larkin Building, opposite, built workers into the industrial design; his chairs, lamp stands, and flower holders for the Robie House (displayed at the Renwick Gallery, above) integrated the dining room "organically" with the mansion's structure.

This great hall with its lofty, light-filled central space looks as fitting for Renaissance princes as for workers in tight collars and shirtwaists. The desks and chairs that Wright devised for the Larkin Building were the first pieces of steel office furniture and the first to express in form the nature of their material. Attached to the desks, the chairs could be folded and swung into them, creating compact and efficient units that made work more pleasurable and cleaning easier. The same integrated, industrialized principle appeared in the toilet Wright conceived for the Larkin Building, the first instance of a hung plumbing fixture in Western civilization. The entire building was designed to be a clean, light, well ventilated working environment for employees who would thus be screened from the unpleasant, surrounding factory area.

In designing furniture for such carefully wrought environments, Wright was constantly, universally inventive. Why he never took out patents on his many creations remains a mystery. However, whatever his status as a member of the inventors' fraternity, Wright's works continue to beguile us with their uncompromising style and progressive flavor.

In the 19th century that Wright left behind, mechanically innovative furniture was the order of the day. Never mind that some of it looks naive now; then, it delighted the mind with its witty manipulability and its easy handling of iron, bamboo, horn, or whatever. This is not to say that previous generations of Americans (like Duncan Phyfe) lacked innovative genius, but rather that the demands of an emerging middle class after the Civil War gave new furniture production a notable boost; the bourgeois yen for comfort demanded fulfillment.

The mahogony library chair on page 210 offers a splendid example of the 19th-century fascination with movable parts and the awareness of everyman's needs. Possibly you remember one something like it in your great-uncle's den. The arms move on brass ratchets as the back reclines; the paneled front-seat rail is actually the front of a drawer that pulls out to make a footrest. Underneath the footrest pad is a tattered label of furniture dealer William Hancock of Boston, a bold and enterprising manufacturer.

Some of the most incredible furniture designs of the 19th and 20th century resulted from early experiments in the simple process of molding and bending wood—a technique in which Americans pioneered and still excel. Technical virtuosity in the bending of wood can also be seen in the richly carved ornamented furniture of John Henry Belter, America's leading exponent of the rococo revival style popular in the mid-19th century. In the 1930s and '40s Charles Eames, in collaboration with architect Eero Saarinen, also experimented with bending molded laminated surfaces.

208

Victorian furniture manufacturers produced ingenious pieces from bizarre materials. The "camper" below, of artificial bamboo and ornate fabric, took the parlor into the field. Rococo designer John Henry Belter, working with wood laminations, submitted a patent model application for a chair in 1858, bottom. His techniques allowed replacement of the chair's usual rail-and-stile with a back composed of laminated wood sections bent to shape and glued together in overlapping layers. His grand drawing-room table at left was produced by the same method, with the wood elaborately carved and pierced in floral patterns.

Wood molding for chairs had always been in just one direction; the Eames-Saarinen plywood chairs, however, were molded in two directions. Still, their technique resembled Belter's in that they used thin laminated veneers alternated with layers of glue.

The back and seat of the handsome chair Eames designed in 1946 are two separate wooden forms bent, as described, in two directions. They are joined to the spine, or back support, and to the legs by means of rubber shock mounts, increasing resilience and at the same time adding comfort. The original, wooden-legged version of the chair was soon replaced by another with metal legs and spine. Although the all-wooden "Eames chair" displays a classic aesthetic unity of form and material, Eames himself preferred the metal-wood combination, as it better expressed, he felt, the separate functions of the parts.

In 1957 Eero Saarinen introduced his equally well-known and elegant "tulip" chair, whose basic form stemmed from his earlier work with Eames. The body of the chair, a molded fiber glass-reinforced shell shaped to fit the human body comfortably, fuses arms, back, and seat into one organic whole.

Yet Saarinen was disappointed that the base could not be cast as part of the fiber glass body. Instead, it had to be cast in aluminum with a fused plastic finish to blend in visually. His disappointment echoes Frank Lloyd Wright's desire to create harmonious, integrated interiors that would epitomize—in fact lead—the industrial spirit of the day. Saarinen wrote: "The undercarriage of chairs and tables in a typical interior makes an ugly, confusing, unrestful world. I wanted to make the chair all one thing again. All the great furniture of the past from Tutankhamen's chair to Thomas Chippendale's have always been a structural total. With our excitement over plastic and plywood shells, we grew away from this structural total. As now manufactured, the pedestal furniture is half plastic, half metal. I look forward to the day when the plastic industry has advanced to the point where the chair will be one material as designed." Saarinen abandoned the traditional idea of a chair having four legs for support. His innovations blazed the trail for new forms now made possible by experiments in molded fiber glass and plastics. Saarinen and earlier furniture pioneers inspired future generations of designers to carry on the creative enterprise of seating America. □

Accommodating America's large middle class has ever been a goal of the nation's furniture makers, as seen in the easeful library chair below, with pull-out footrest and reclining back. The Smithsonian recently acquired the well-padded lounger of TV character Archie Bunker, above. Opposite, the classic Saarinen chair, an example of how, by clever design and bold engineering, comfort can be achieved without kitsch.

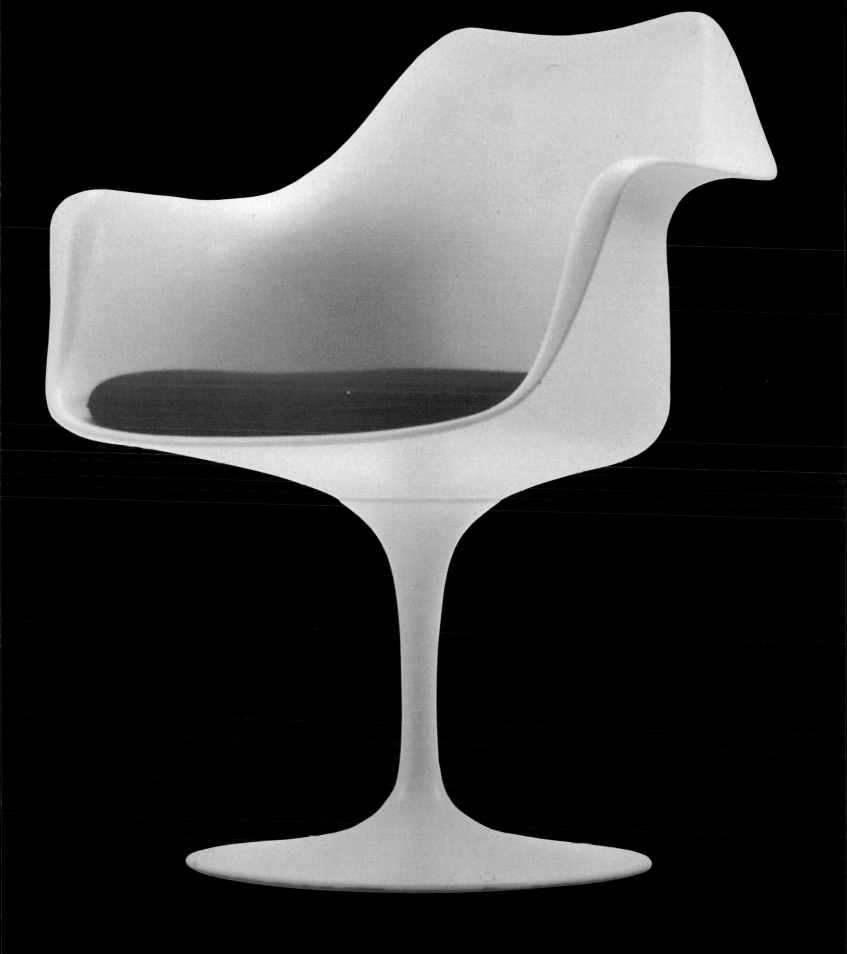

Spare Parts

The pace of modern medical treatment in our society closely parallels the general trend of technological development. Even mankind's least fortunate technical practice—warfare—has served as a powerful catalyst to medical progress: it has only been in the last century, when victims of major extremity trauma have commonly survived their wounds, that there has been development of modern artificial limbs.

The accompanying illustrations present some of the elegantly simple solutions to certain problems in human suffering—replacement of faulty or worn-out parts. The examples provided are those that are not only feasible but also now available as standard medical practice. They do not include artificial organs such as a kidney dialysis machine to which one is connected temporarily. These are permanent prosthetic or replacement parts that are implanted within the body. Fabricated of nonliving materials, they are different from organs or parts transplanted from other persons.

While many materials and designs are available through modern engineering science, there are severe limitations on those that may be used within the body. First, the materials must be biologically inert, so that the body cannot recognize them as "foreign" and unleash its deadly antibody reaction to reject them.

Second, the design must duplicate body function without causing damage. Heart valves must open and close without harming blood cells, which could cause death by triggering excessive blood clotting. Joint replacements must move in a way that does not cause damage to the surrounding bone or put undue strain on surrounding tissues.

Additionally, the components of the replacement part must be extremely durable because overhaul would require subsequent surgery that is in some cases life-threatening.

In spite of these restrictions, prosthetics have been developed which can save lives, as in the case of heart valves and arterial replacements; they reduce disability by replacing destroyed joints and clouded eye lenses; they lessen the physiological and psychological trauma of such potentially mutilating surgery as radical breast resection.

All indications point to continued invention in this field. One day, in future editions of this book, the person depicted here will be even more saturated with better prosthetics, reflecting a consequent decrease in human suffering and disability.   □

Walter Abendschein, M.D., F.A.C.S.

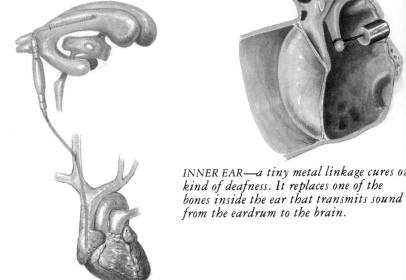

BRAIN—*high fluid pressure can cause death. A plastic tube attached to a one-way valve drains fluid from the brain into the blood stream.*

INNER EAR—*a tiny metal linkage cures o kind of deafness. It replaces one of the bones inside the ear that transmits sound from the eardrum to the brain.*

ARM—*special cables control a jointed artificial limb. Power comes from movement of the opposite should*

ARTERY—*Dacron tube, complete with accordion ple replaces a section of the aorta, largest blood vessel in the body, right, below kidneys.*

HAND—*crippling arthritis can at last be combatted by surgic replacement of wrist and finger joints.*

BREAST—*silicone plastic gel in a bag can replace breast tissue removed in potentially disfiguring cancer surgery.*

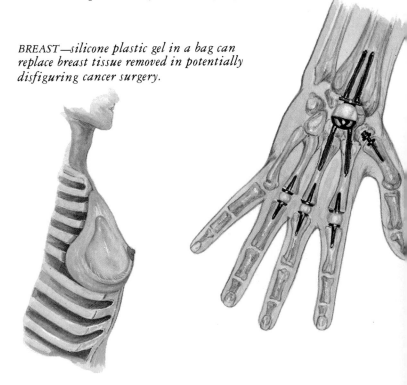

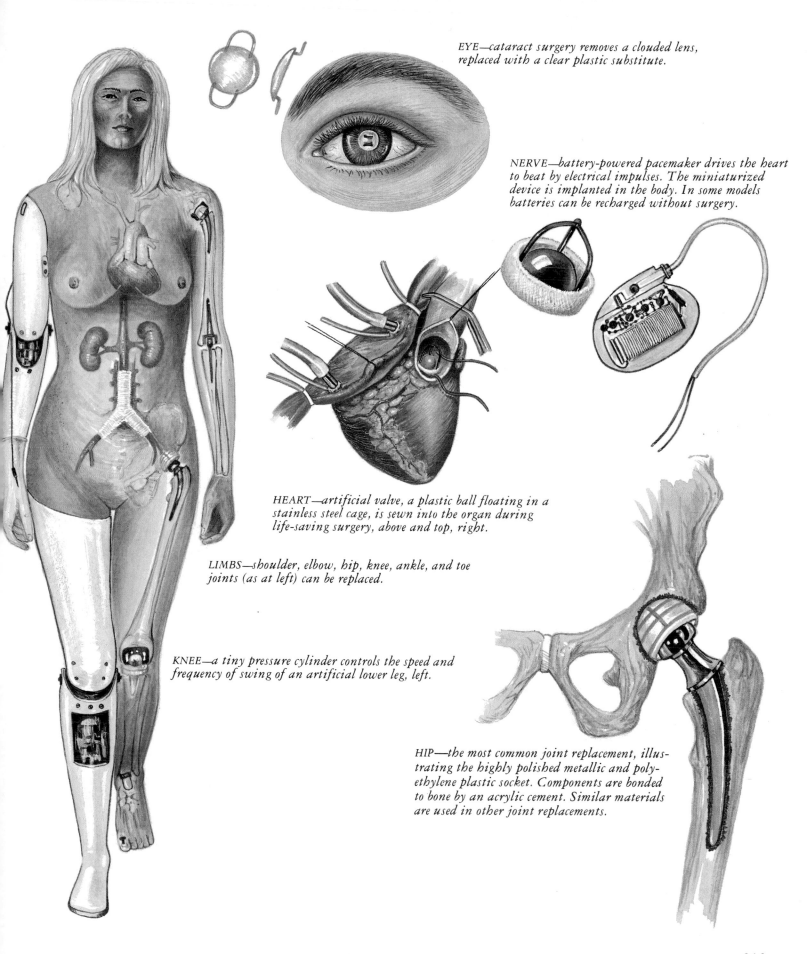

EYE—cataract surgery removes a clouded lens, replaced with a clear plastic substitute.

NERVE—battery-powered pacemaker drives the heart to beat by electrical impulses. The miniaturized device is implanted in the body. In some models batteries can be recharged without surgery.

HEART—artificial valve, a plastic ball floating in a stainless steel cage, is sewn into the organ during life-saving surgery, above and top, right.

LIMBS—shoulder, elbow, hip, knee, ankle, and toe joints (as at left) can be replaced.

KNEE—a tiny pressure cylinder controls the speed and frequency of swing of an artificial lower leg, left.

HIP—the most common joint replacement, illustrating the highly polished metallic and poly-ethylene plastic socket. Components are bonded to bone by an acrylic cement. Similar materials are used in other joint replacements.

213

7
PART

The Summons of the Future

As a scientist gingerly lifts a beaker of DNA in solution, he holds the means to control heredity. So the inventor, like the first man to flake a rock's face to a sharp edge, creates a new set of possibilities and probabilities for all who follow into the future. But how might the inventor best proceed in the coming century: where is the profound challenge and where the real need?

For those who would follow the high technology route—a yellow brick road that has taken us into such diverse realms as space colonies and artificial human bodies—the essential problem is how to transfer enough benefits to industry and society to justify the astonishing costs of research. Quirks of human nature play a major role in the success of the transfer.

For those who would follow the alternative, an equally sophisticated but less centralized approach, the problem is also people. Inventors can devise the most ingeniously efficient machines and techniques, but need to turn the mind of the nation to new directions before their proposals will educe a new reality.

For those who harbor justifiable fears that such progress, however won, will still exclude those millions of Earth's peoples who live in overpopulated poverty, scientists are exploring a strange variety of flora and fauna. Ranging from jojoba beans to the water buffalo, these locally well known but neglected food sources are viewed as harvests for tomorrow.

Civilizations have made innovative adjustments before in history. We appear now to be going through yet another threshold. . . .

The Labyrinths of High Technology

Melvin B. Zisfein

For a revealing glimpse of today's high technology and the almost unbelievable world of microelectronics, let us look at the watch I bought last May as a Mother's Day gift. Actually, I was shopping for a handbag or umbrella (or anything else that didn't come in sizes) when I noticed a sale of ladies' electronic watches with LED (Light Emitting Diode) displays. Two or three years earlier such a watch would have cost between one and two hundred dollars, but now it was listed at about $20. The watch was an excellent example of high technology. At the press of a button it displayed the hour and minute. A second press gave day of the week and date. A third press gave seconds. This brilliant piece of equipment was powered by a miniature battery, and its brain was a tiny MOS, a Metal Oxide Semiconductor or "chip." The chip is a very thin slice of silicon crystal that typically measures about a quarter of an inch square. On this chip can be implanted electronic circuits with thousands of tiny components like resistors, diodes, transistors, amplifiers, adders, and so forth. In action the circuits inside the watch (mostly those on the chip) take a miniscule current from the battery and generate a set of timekeeping signals that can be read on the LEDs as glowing red numbers any time the button is pushed. One hundred years ago such a device would have exceeded the wildest dreams of all but the most adventurous visionaries. Today such devices are commonplace and their prices are falling rapidly. However, the subsequent history of my mother's watch illustrates one of the reasons why a certain disillusionment with high technology is presently felt in some circles.

I visited my mother at her home, and in the middle of one of her gestures (mothers will be emphatic) the watch literally came apart before my eyes, sending pieces of 20th-century technology all over the place. This brings us to the low technology of the watch case. Obviously, in his zeal to market an inexpensive futuristic dream—a small share of the thrilling world of business tycoons, lawyers, and submarine commanders—the watch manufacturer hadn't worried very much about the construction of the watch's case.

The research and development necessary to advance from conventional electronics to the microelectronics inside my mother's watch is, on reflection, staggering, and mass producing them to make a precision timepiece at a manufacturer's cost significantly less than 10 dollars is a miracle of our age. My mother's watch was great while it lasted; too bad that particular manufacturer didn't worry very much about the relatively simple technology of making ladies' watch cases.

I phone my mother regularly and scrupulously avoid asking the time or mentioning watches.

What is high technology? C. E. K. Mees, formerly the articulate director of the Eastman Kodak laboratories, defined it approximately as follows: basic research, he wrote, is the examination of materials and phenomena to discover fundamental properties, relationships, and trends. Applied research combines basic research with existing technology to yield new technology.

But what about this technology is "high"? That, it turns out, is a matter of time and place. To an Australian aborigine, the typewriter could serve as an example of incomprehensibly high technology. To a child of the next century, the development of a data processor based on microelectronic chips and integrated circuits might be a fascinating project for a rainy weekend. Let's avoid too precise a definition by classifying as high technologies those engineering applications that are so advanced that they are exceedingly difficult for most people to understand and apply. We all know more or less what high technology produces: transistor radios and TV, giant computers and pocket-sized calculators, airplanes and spacecraft, nuclear power plants and bombs, advanced structural materials like beryllium and carbon-epoxy composites, microwave and fiber-optics transmission lines, radar, and many

Melvin B. Zisfein, Deputy Director of the National Air and Space Museum, was Associate Director of the Franklin Institute Research Laboratory.

Ideas venturing forth face a maze of problems.

other complicated processes, materials, and devices, including my mother's watch.

Modern high technology has had a unique image and history. At times the high technologist has been a hero, the darling of the industrialists and investors, and the envy of his fellow citizens. On the other hand, during the late 1960s and early 1970s the technologist's image deteriorated markedly, and the period was characterized by massive unemployment. During the same period, beginning then and still true to a lesser extent, it became fashionable in some quarters to regard technologists as bestial enemies of society who are all zealously working to destroy civilization by war, massive pollution, or ideological subversion. Actually, the product of the high technologist is rarely an unmixed blessing or a curse.

The oxygen lance that allows better steel making, for example, can be a terrible polluter if it is not carefully controlled. The rocket-powered booster is able to propel a weather satellite into orbit or a nuclear warhead against an enemy city. The new chemical intended to boost food production can have horrible side effects on animals and humans. The key issue ultimately is how the institutions of society use and regulate science and technology. And so the ringing battle cry of Pogo, the lovable comic strip possum, "We have met the enemy and they is US!"

Yet high technology has produced some supreme moments. The Apollo program that brought men to the moon and knowledge back to Earth also sent the human spirit and imagination soaring as have few programs before. The first moon landings in 1969 rivaled such previous feats as the completion in 1914 of the Panama Canal or the joining by rail of the North American coasts in 1869. Interestingly, in 1869 much of the process of railroad and rolling stock design and construction was a part of the high technology of that era. Which suggests one of the most important features of today's high technology: without a doubt it will be tomorrow's low technology.

One of the most frustrating phenomena of modern technology is that the people who create it are generally not those who performed the basic research leading to it and generally not those who will be called upon to perform the developmental programs from which a product or process will result. For instance, many discoveries come out of military or space programs; but how are they applied in, say, housing or medicine? Exactly how is technology transferred? Moreover, it is a constant suspicion of high technologists that their achievements, comprehended in depth by only a small "in-group," could be applied in other fields "if only others really understood it." Two such interesting transfers are personally known to me. I present them as discrete, successful examples of a

The road to the marketplace is beset by devils.

poorly understood and somewhat haphazard process. If the technology transfer process is ever really analyzed, and if transfers can then be "orchestrated," we'll be much closer to that desired great world of the future. Some years ago, in order to gather and transmit satellite data efficiently, an electronic "multiplex" system was designed by an electronics contractor. This multiplex system sampled each of the satellite's many data channels, converted each signal into a series of numbers, encoded each of the numbers and transmitted these back to Earth in different "time slots" over the same transmission channel. Once the signals were received at the satellite's Earth station, the process was reversed and the many channels of data were re-created and modified for further processing. Quite an advantage. Transmit over only one channel instead of many and send the signals down through "smart" encoder and decoder circuits in such a way that noise and spurious signals are actually minimized. The speed and accuracy of such multiplexing are good enough to transmit even music and television in this manner.

The capability to multiplex a set of electronic signals isn't that great a novelty. The first machine I ever saw perform such an operation was shown to me in 1961. The trick is in handling a great many separate channels of data and in being quick enough in each operation that even a set of TV signals can be sampled, transmitted, and all channels reconstructed without impairing picture quality. That takes the response of modern "chip" electronics.

In any case, the company that produced the satel-

lite multiplex system wanted to transfer the technology it had developed to other areas, and decided to try to use it to transmit many channels of music through one cable to all the seats in a new wide-body jet airliner. The company won a contract and was able to install the system handily, saving the weight of an enormous amount of copper wire. It was next challenged by the prospect of using its system to distribute the audio, video, and command signals in the Smithsonian's new National Air and Space Museum, while at the same time sampling the outputs of hundreds of diagnostic sensors on the exhibits to signal any breakdown to the museum operating crew. The company won the competition and successfully installed the system now in use.

I once worked with some excellent chemists who specialized in surface physics. They had successfully completed a number of government contracts, working in such areas as making more efficient steam condensers by treating the surfaces of the condenser tubes. A large paper-products firm sponsored some applied research by this same group to improve, if possible, the paper hand towels the company sold. The chemists correctly perceived that what was important was the rate at which the towel drew water away from moist hands. A towel that absorbs water quickly is regarded as a very efficient towel. The chemists therefore developed a new kind of towel by designing a novel configuration of the paper surfaces to draw water away at an astonishing rate. They used their knowledge of surface physics and applied it to the simple paper towel. The product they created is now a popular brand of paper towel, available in virtually any supermarket or grocery.

The utility of such research, while limited, is undeniable. And would it not be a most desirable goal for a society if research teams could improve all aspects of life through the brilliant application of theory to reality? Perhaps, but it couldn't happen soon.

If a common thread weaves between these examples, it is that it is difficult to anticipate where the lightning of technology transfer will strike next. In each case the scientists or high technologists learned a great deal about a specific subject while being sponsored under various contracts. Then, by some process still not clearly understood, an outsider learned of this expertise and suspected that it could be applied to another problem far removed from the field in which the original work had been performed. I am disquieted to think that for every case (such as those here) where a match was made, there have been many where nothing happened, where no gaps were jumped.

Seeing high technology out there stepping high can be thrilling, especially when the whole process moves right along with a full head of steam, pacing a strong economy. Just such innovative brilliance provides half of a pretty good definition of high technology. When it's good—like the girl with the curl right in the middle of her forehead—it can be very, very good. But when it is bad—the economy, that is—times are horrid indeed. In fact, high technology can be characterized as that which retrenches and sometimes folds first when a recession hits, sending its Ph.D practitioners out into the real world as cab drivers and door-to-door salesmen.

Ironically, that highly educated hawker may be pushing today the advanced product he discovered only yesterday. Remember the days of Teflon skillets? Yesterday's glamor material is today's household word. And a certain economic resilience lies in such rapid transformation of high research into product development, and into new consumer products at your very doorstep.

The world of today's high technology is, however, far wider and deeper than a skillet or even my mother's wrist watch. For example, many advanced structural materials receive much study. Composites, materials in which super strength is supplied by imbedding fibers of glass or carbon in a matrix, are already finding use in such products as bicycle frames, fishing rods, and golf clubs. Turbine engines for automobiles may employ remarkably specialized pottery for the turbine blades, elements subjected to intense heat and stress. Glass technology—an outgrowth of the ancient potter's art—has come a long, long way lately. Very thin glass fibers will soon begin to replace heavy copper cables for the transmission of pictures and sound. Pilot operations have demonstrated a potential for sending more information down the same line with such fiber optics than is possible with any other competing system, including microwave transmission.

And the winner-of-winners in the high-technology sweepstakes, the laser, is at heart a rod or tube of synthetic ruby, sapphire, or a specialized glass. And it is that same laser that led engineers to investigate the savings in money and resources that could be realized through the use of glass fiber optics.

It is, in fact, almost commonplace for one high-technology tool to help shape another, even more advanced high-technology tool. Technological leapfrogging and parlaying create the new far frontiers, suddenly leaving behind a whole trove of old advanced materials and processes just waiting for manufacturers to turn into consumer products.

The name of this exotic game is spin-off. And in its classic form, the opening plays begin between government agencies and private contractors. Object: solve problems by study, analysis, and application of innovative tools and techniques.

The late 1960s were lean years for those of us in contract research. Sponsors were elusive, Federal funding was sluggish, and nearly every opportunity brought at least 10 hardpressed competitors vying for the privilege of spending precious overhead to write a proposal which only one would eventually win. In the spirit of leaving no stone unturned, I regularly checked the State Department for opportunities and once secured a briefing from an expert on certain North African countries.

He told me that a major impediment to the development of the North African countries was an acute scarcity of construction materials, and therefore the provision of simple shelter consumed an inordinate amount of most people's time. I learned further that there was almost no clay for bricks, few trees suitable for construction lumber, and little readily available dolomite for Portland cement and concrete. On the other hand, sand and sunshine were abundant. Why not, I asked myself, design simple solar furnaces for the North African people so that they would be able to sinter, or heat-bond, sand in brick-sized molds to yield glazed blocks about as strong as our bricks? But, I was told, sand sinters at a temperature beyond what practical solar furnaces can achieve. However, it might be possible to find an additive that, in trace amounts, would lower the sand's sintering temperature markedly.

Spending a bit of precious

A fixed idea runs its course.

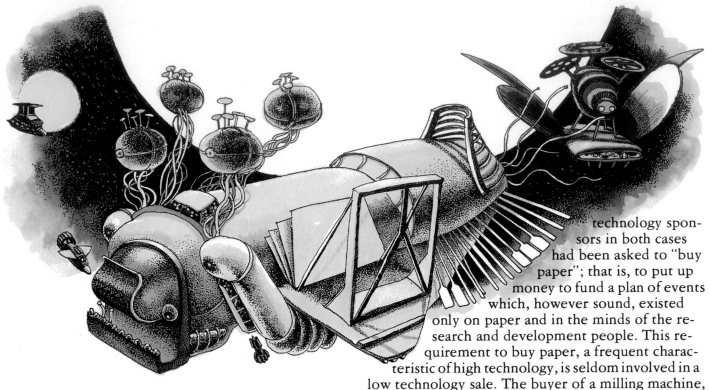

Mining the moon.

overhead money, we experimented with a few possible additives and quickly found one which actually lowered the sintering temperature of the sand, though not quite enough. Nevertheless, we had made surprising progress considering how few avenues we had explored. We put together a convincing proposal and waited. To the best of my knowledge my former associates are still waiting. We seemed to be in the position of not being able to convince anybody that we could do something until we actually did it. Naturally, if we could just walk into the lab and succeed, we wouldn't need a research grant at all. But in this case we found ourselves in a kind of Catch-22 situation.

This attitude—caused in part by skepticism, in part by penury—is not uncommon when low- or no-technology people dabble in high technology. I remember a clothing manufacturer who approached us to develop a chemical spot-bonding process to enable him to bond rather than stitch pieces of cloth together. He wanted an assembly of cloth that felt and lasted as though sewn but which could be produced more economically. My chemists were positive they could develop such a process after a relatively modest $10,000 to $30,000 research program. However, our prospective sponsor insisted we guarantee success, something we could never afford to do.

In these examples, a basic communication mismatch, which I have always called "buying paper," lies at the heart of the problem. The prospective high

technology sponsors in both cases had been asked to "buy paper"; that is, to put up money to fund a plan of events which, however sound, existed only on paper and in the minds of the research and development people. This requirement to buy paper, a frequent characteristic of high technology, is seldom involved in a low technology sale. The buyer of a milling machine, for example, can go to a showroom or demonstration area, turn one on and cut metal. Surely, only a little faith is required, certainly less than the faith required of one who sponsors a high technology research and development program.

Moving high technology from research to development requires a good idea, a real need for the end product, someone who is willing to develop the idea as far as is needed to make a practical device, and, of course, the money to accomplish all this. High technology literature is filled with good ideas whose time has not yet come, or may never come.

The ballistic missile race during the late 1950s and 1960s produced frantic activity on both sides of the Iron Curtain. The so-called "re-entry" problem proved difficult to solve during the early portion of this period. Briefly stated, the problem was how to bring a missile's warhead back through the Earth's atmosphere to the target without the warhead burning up like a meteor.

The shock tube was an important tool in the research effort that tamed ballistic re-entry flight; it was invented by aerospace research people around 1950 to create a high-speed gas flow with just the right energy qualities for simulating the expected aerodynamic heating loads of a re-entry flight.

However, the usable flow from a shock tube lasted for only a few thousandths of a second, demanding measuring instruments of fantastic sophistication to get any data at all. The obvious thought was to try to produce a shock tube flow that would last, say, for a few seconds, giving data of at least some precision.

At one of our great nonprofit research centers, a few very capable technologists invented a new kind of test facility in which multiple shock tubes were used to form a continuous stream of good flow.

This shock tube invention was formally known as the Wave Superheater but was generally referred to as "Little Rollo." Little Rollo's success led to the development of Big Rollo, a test facility which ran productively during the 1960s and generated an abundance of the desired information. Here was an invention so specialized and sophisticated that only a few thousand people (at most) in the United States knew why it was needed at all!

But here is the point of this story. Some historical research showed the space flight people that they hadn't really invented it. They had *re*invented it, possibly for the fourth or fifth time. The first shock tube appears to have been invented in France around 1880 to simulate the travel of explosions through mine shafts. The shock tube was later reinvented to simulate the formation and passage of shock waves through air lines, such as those connecting the braking systems of railroad trains. Later, yet another reinvention of the shock tube seems to have been stimulated by the need for a facility in which to study certain kinds of physical and chemical interactions in gases.

Isn't there an important high technology lesson here? All of the inventions of the shock tube were well documented and published in the appropriate trade journals. But consider the inventor's problem. If you were trying to simulate the aerodynamic heating of air flows at very high speeds and altitudes, would you go to the mine safety literature, or to railway engineering journals? Of course not. The needs were vastly different in each case as were most of the researchers' basic areas of interest.

However, they all invented shock tubes to solve their respective problems. As technology grows (some say explodes) in the future, should we try to prevent this sort of duplication? How might we do so?

The mass of literature can swamp researchers, especially in interdisciplinary work. But high tech may come to its own aid, as with SCORPIO, the computerized search system at the Library of Congress.

Some recent high technology proposals have spanned a scope of almost unbelievable dimension. One of the most ambitious of these was put forward several years ago by Gerard K. O'Neill to begin the colonization of space. More recently, Dr. O'Neill has championed a closely related plan directed at solving the Earth's energy problems. I include his stupendous plan here because it represents the most "mind stretching" example that I know of the numerous high technology proposals in today's literature.

Basically, Dr. O'Neill proposes going again to the moon, mining it, refining the ores in space-based factories, then fabricating, in Earth orbit, a family of solar collecting power satellites that would each hover over a fixed point on Earth and beam down enormous power via microwave links. Dr. O'Neill envisions building and provisioning a giant moonship in Earth orbit, transporting the needed materials and workers via the space shuttle (scheduled to be operational around 1980). The material sent into orbit would be assembled into 1) a huge solar power generator, 2) a giant moonship to be powered by the electricity from the solar power generator, and 3) the moonship's cargo, tons of things and materials needed for the duration of the mission. The moonship would be made of some 2,000 tons of material, all of which would be brought up into Earth orbit by space shuttle flights. Dr. O'Neill states his requirement as a few dozen shuttle flights per year for several years. Once this enormous moonship reached the moon it would go into a low lunar orbit and detach descent modules (something like Apollo's LM's) to establish a lunar colony. Actually, hundreds of tons of material would be sent down to the lunar colony in about 20-ton increments. An important part of this transported mass would be mining machinery for cut-

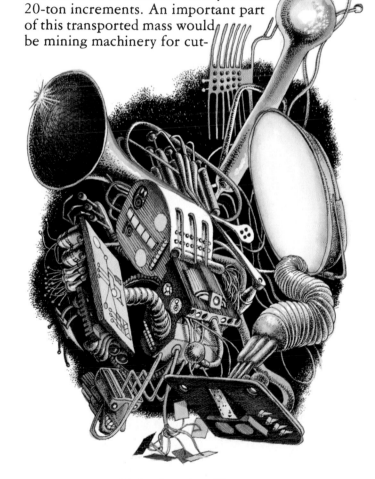

Technological traffic jam.

221

ting up some of the moon and using it as ore. Another major part of the equipment sent down to the moon would be assembled into a "mass driver" for hurling chunks of moon ore into a giant catcher positioned in space behind the moon. The ore catcher would feed the moon ore into a giant refining plant in high Earth orbit. This plant is supposed to produce silicon, aluminum, steel, oxygen, and other materials obtainable from the moon. These materials would be manufactured into huge solar power-generating satellites, positioned at fixed points above the Earth's surface. They would receive energy from the sun on their primarily silicon solar cells, convert sunlight into electricity, and then beam this power over microwave links to fixed receiving stations on the surface of the Earth. Total cash outlay is expected to reach the vicinity of 50 to 70 billion dollars before power revenues turn the curve back toward profit. By the 12th year of the project, 3,000 workers are expected to be in orbit.

Say what you will about Dr. O'Neill, he's no piker! We are discussing here a proposal for what may be the greatest technological effort conceived to date for the ultimate benefit of an advancing and increasingly sophisticated human race. Remembering the history of past prophecy, who among us is smug enough to say that it will never happen? Moreover, this is merely one of many fantastically ambitious proposals aimed at taking us into space to solve a human need as important as the need for energy. Will any of these really happen, and if so, when?

I have stated that high technology is difficult to define and even more difficult to understand. I have also predicted that with our current rate of progress in fields such as microelectronics, advanced materials, electronic transmission systems, and satellite systems, today's very high technology will become the lower technology of some era in the not too distant future. Will this better-understood technology find its way into many things made for our greater good? Despite efforts by agencies such as NASA, there seems to be no wide-ranging organized system in our society to bring this about in some orderly fashion. I have presented some examples of the technology transfer process and described its haphazard nature in each

As high technology replaces old technology, early devices are replaced with more sophisticated models producing the same item.

example. Clearly this is an area deserving far more serious study. We must develop better ways to move from basic research to production and better systems for the exploitation of our future technological gains in fields not well known to the original researchers. In order to succeed at any of this we must develop better communication tools and procedures.

I reject as nonsense the argument so attractive to many people 10 years ago that all technology is bad and that the more technology is introduced into our lives, the worse off we will be. Such thought would reject all improvements from the bicycle to modern life-support systems, would in practice drive our average life expectancy down by 20 or more years, and reduce our average standard of living to that of Colonial America or lower.

But there is no doubt that we have not become as proficient as we might at benefiting from technology or for rejecting or modifying that technology which produces harmful side effects. To be sure, there is an appalling general lack of knowledge and sophistication in these areas.

The march of technology appears to be inexorable. New processes, materials, and products appear continuously. How do we ensure that these are predominantly good with minimal bad side effects? As a bare beginning we had better learn more about high technology. As a civilization, we don't know enough about how to sponsor it, how much to sponsor it, how to control it, how to measure it, and how to maximize its potential for good. Our present ineptitude and wastefulness in moving basic research through applied research and through developmental research into technology is a striking example of this need. Our lack of an organized and effective large-scale approach to the transfer of high technology to all of the areas that can benefit from it stands as further testimony. □

Neglected Riches of Nature

Noel D. Vietmeyer

Man's inventiveness has already been wondrously applied to agricultural development, but in selecting the plants we use for crops we have been appallingly parochial. Of the 500,000 known plant species, only about a hundred have been domesticated, or genetically changed to make them more useful for man. Even fewer species, about 30 in all, provide 85 percent of the weight of food eaten by human beings and 95 percent of the calories and protein. Three-fourths of all human food energy comes from a mere eight species, all cereals: wheat, rice, maize, barley, oats, sorghum, millets, and rye. This is a dangerously small larder from which to feed the world.

Our lack of inventiveness is graphically demonstrated by the fact that not a single major food crop has been domesticated in modern times. For 4,000 generations we have traded on the brainpower of Neolithic man. But can this limited food system sustain the world much longer?

I grew up thinking that the crops we produce had somehow been judged and selected long ago because they were the best; that some sort of scale had indicated, for example, that potatoes were more desirable than other root crops. In 1966 I became aware that this all-wise selection probably had not occurred, that indeed there might be alternative food, fiber, and oil crops as good or better than the few we rely on now. As a graduate student at the University of California, I visited Nicholas Mirov, a pine tree expert in the geography department. After an hour's discussion of pines, he reached into a desk drawer and pulled out a few seeds, a small bottle of oil, and a block of white wax— all products from the remarkable jojoba (pronounced ho-*ho*-ba) plant.

For 30 years, off and on, Dr. Mirov had tried to interest industry in jojoba *(Simmondsia chinensis).* Isolated in North America's Sonoran Desert, jojoba has followed its own peculiar evolutionary route; its cells and enzymes form a vegetable oil possessing unique

Noel D. Vietmeyer, born in New Zealand, is a professional associate with the National Academy of Sciences Commission of International Relations.

molecular shape and size and unusual properties. Why a plant should leave the mainstream of evolution to produce a different fat (one of the basic building blocks of life) remains a mystery. Nor is it known why jojoba oil is virtually identical with the oil of the sperm whale—one of nature's greatest coincidences.

Millions of jojoba bushes dot the slopes and flats of perhaps 100,000 square miles of Arizona, southern California, and Mexico. Each shrub struggles for existence in a barren, inhospitable area where rain may not fall at all during some years, and where summer temperatures sometimes top 115° F. in the shade. In the

Seeds, oil, and crystalline wax obtained from the jojoba plant, a desert bush that grows in the American Southwest and Mexico.

spring, male jojoba plants fling pollen into the wind to pollinate the inconspicuous leaf-like flowers on the female bushes, which then swell into green ovoid fruits that, in the heat of summer, mature, dry out, and drop their peanut-sized seeds onto the ground. The soft, wrinkled, dark-brown seeds are half oil; simple refining produces a clear oil with almost no smell.

In 1970 I moved to Washington, D.C., and told Dr. Mirov's story to William Miller at the Office of Economic Opportunity. A Cherokee and former Olympic javelin champion, Miller directed OEO's Indian Economic Development Program. He became interested in the jojoba primarily because it suggested a rare chance to provide jobs for Indians on desolate reservations in the Sonoran Desert. Miller exhibited the spirit, drive, and influence required to move Dr. Mirov's jojoba idea forward. In meeting after meeting, he and I questioned botanists, agronomists, chemists, and representatives of industry and government, probing for any problems that might doom a jojoba project. None appeared.

As a result of the specialists' optimism, OEO provided funds in 1972 for Indians to harvest tons of jojoba seed from bushes growing wild on reservation lands in Southern California and Arizona for sale to several hundred industrial companies at home and abroad. The harvests have created such demand for jojoba oil that the wild stands produce only a tiny fraction of industry's current demands.

We have made a strong start toward domestication of jojoba during the last three years. Government development programs in California, Arizona, Mexico, and Israel total about 10 million dollars. Indeed, jojoba now appears so rewarding a crop that in 1977 about a dozen companies planted almost 2,000 acres. Jojoba grows slowly, however, and plantation-grown oil will not enter the marketplace for another three or four years. Jojoba and sperm whale oil share unequaled lubricating qualities for certain industrial and cosmetic uses. Jojoba may soon rescue whales.

The discovery that jojoba faced no serious barriers to its domestication suggested that other plants might also be suffering neglect for no good reason. In 1973 at the National Academy of Sciences we began searching for unexploited species with which to expand the world's agricultural base. Our prime targets were species overlooked by our Neolithic forerunners. Such species now deserve to be domesticated because, like jojoba, they possess inherent value for farmers, industry, and consumers—especially for developing countries.

Fortunately, nature provides a huge reservoir of plants on which to draw. When my colleague Mary Jane Engquist and I first began the search for such plants, we queried about 150 botanists for their ideas.

An Indian woman picks the oil-rich seeds of a jojoba shrub growing wild in the desert of Baja California.

In their responses they recommended over 400 different species that now are under-exploited or neglected entirely but show promising economic potential. A subsequent questionnaire turned up another 400 nominees for future crops from *Leguminosae* alone, the botanical family that includes vegetable legumes as well as many potentially useful shrubs and trees. In our latest search, several hundred foresters and botanists have nominated more than 1,000 fast-growing trees and woody shrubs for raising in plantations to help relieve the terrible firewood shortages now besetting most developing countries.

But our project's objective is to go beyond identifying useful, obscure plants, and actually to select the few that have the greatest merit—a task involving careful decisions, diverse opinion, and much debate. For this process the National Academy of Sciences appoints panels of distinguished experts who weigh the relative merits of various species and nominate those deserving immediate attention.

Our first such panel was co-chaired by Edward S. Ayensu, then Chairman of the Smithsonian's Department of Botany. He and 19 panelists from nine different nations sorted out 36 potential "superplants" from the 400 nominated in our first questionnaire, including jojoba and most of the plants described below.

Many of the plants chosen had been ostracized from wide use because of their association with a particular ethnic group. Indeed, for more than two centuries after African slaves brought the peanut to North

225

America the crop was spurned as a suitable food. It was this very neglect that stimulated George Washington Carver to take up peanut research. He and his peanut products gave the crop the momentum to break through cultural barriers until, in less than a century, it became one of the top 30 crops of the world.

Cultural discrimination against worthy crops still continues, as seen in the tale of the amaranths. Centuries ago in the highlands of Mexico, Guatemala, and Peru, amaranths (*Amaranthus* species) were staple crops. Rich sources of vegetable protein, food energy, and fiber, they were highly valued in Aztec and Incan cultures and featured prominently in religious ceremonies and in tributes to native rulers. Subsequently, the victorious conquistadores, in order to crush the pagan religions, banned all cultivation of amaranths and substituted barley instead. Thus for purely political reasons the amaranths were deliberately suppressed; as a result they have remained obscure, half-wild plants for the past 400 years.

Amaranths belong to a small group of plants termed C_4, all of which utilize sunlight more effectively than most other plants. Fast-growing, vigorous, and tough, scientists regard them as self-reliant plants that require very little cultivation. C_4 plants germinate and grow well under adverse conditions, adapt to a wide range of climates, and thrive in very poor soils.

Resembling cereals, amaranths grow as tall as a man and are topped by full, fat, pink or brilliant crimson seed heads. The carbohydrate content of the small but numerous seeds is comparable to that of the traditional food grains, but in protein and fat amaranths surpass those cereals. And in 1973 Australian nutritionist W. J. S. Downton found that amaranths contain high levels of lysine, a protein substance vital to human nutrition. It appears that the Spaniards cultivated the Indians' souls at the expense of their bodies.

In 1977, in a far-sighted research venture, Rodale Press, publishers of *Organic Gardening and Farming,* distributed 14,000 packets of *Amaranthus hypochodriacus* seeds to gardeners across North America. The positive responses of these gardeners affirm that this once suppressed crop has important potential and that scientists, like the Spaniards before them, have neglected the amaranths. With more testing and research the amaranths may soon add important nutrition to our breakfast cereals and breads.

The need to exploit nature's wealth is most pressing in developing countries, many of which lie in the tropics, an area with a desperate food problem. The wealth and variety of tropical plant species are staggering, but most agricultural scientists do not realize the scope of their potential because the major scientific research centers are located in temperate zones. The long neglect of tropical botanical and agricultural

Almost every part of the winged bean, sold above in a Bangkok market, provides nutritious food—including the protein-packed tuber, below.

226

possibilities is a disgrace to modern science.

For this reason many of our studies at the National Academy of Sciences are now focusing on tropical plants. One of our most exciting finds has been the winged bean *(Psophocarpus tetragonolobus),* which could literally become a tropical counterpart of the soybean. Prior to 1970 only three or four researchers had ever seriously considered working to develop this obscure poor man's crop from New Guinea and Southeast Asia. But in 1972, after reading a promising report written by Geoffrey Masefield of Oxford University, I began collecting all available knowledge on the plant. In 1974 the National Academy of Sciences convened an expert group of nine plant scientists from five nations to review the evidence. The panel's report proved so optimistic and so popular that we have since had over 20,000 requests for it. The plant is now under commercial or experimental cultivation in more than 70 countries, and scores of researchers are working on its development. Many see it as a kind of "wonder plant" to provide protein to the most malnourished areas of the world.

The winged bean grows easily and quickly in tropical climates and yields profusely. Bacteria in its masses of root nodules, many hundreds of which have been counted on a single plant, convert nitrogen from the air into nitrogenous compounds that the plant uses to build protein. Indeed, protein pervades virtually every part of the plant. Every bit of the winged bean plant can be eaten—leaves, pods, shoots, and flowers all go into the cooking pot. When the season is over the villagers in Southeast Asia dig up the fleshy, tuberous roots and roast them. Any remaining stems are fed to livestock.

The plant looks like a bushy pillar of greenery with viny tendrils and blue or purple flowers. From the tendrils hang succulent green pods, as long as a man's forearm in some varieties. The pods, oblong in cross section, are green, purple, or red, and have four long flanges or "wings" along the edges. When picked young, the green pods are chewy and slightly sweet. Raw or boiled briefly, they make a crisp and snappy delicacy. Pods are produced over several months and a crop can be collected every two days, providing a continuous supply of fresh green vegetables.

If left on the vine the pods harden, but the pea-like seeds inside swell and ripen. When mature, the seeds appear brown, black, or mottled. In composition they are essentially identical to soybeans, rich in protein and in polyunsaturated vegetable oil. The protein in turn contains a considerable amount of the nutritionally critical amino acid lysine. In addition to the pods and seeds, the winged bean's leaves and tendrils make good spinach-like potherbs. Furthermore, its flowers, when cooked, are considered to be a delicacy,

Extremely versatile leucaena wood serves as cooking fuel in Los Banos, the Philippines. Foliage is tasty for cattle.

with a texture and taste reminiscent of mushrooms.

But surely the most startling feature of the plant is that it adds up to a combination soybean-potato plant. For, in addition to the foods it produces above ground, it also can grow fleshy, edible tuberous roots that have firm, ivory-white flesh and a delicate nutty flavor. Not all types produce tubers big enough to eat, but those that do are potentially important as root vegetables in the humid tropics where sweet potatoes, yams, and cassava (manioc), are already staples. Protein abounds in winged bean tubers; they can contain 10 times the protein of potatoes and the other root crops.

Early in 1978 about 200 researchers from six continents attended an international winged bean conference held in the Philippines. Most had come to report on their winged bean research; almost 1,000 pages of technical reports were presented. Their evidence clearly demonstrated the usefulness and efficacy of modern research in developing new crops and the extent to which farmers and scientists have been blind to the wealth of potential crops that nature offers.

The winged bean with its soybean-like seeds and potato-like tubers, and jojoba with its unique oil, exemplify how radically different our future crop plants may be from those which Neolithic man cultivated. Perhaps the most revolutionary species yet studied in my program is leucaena. *Leucaena leucocephala,* which is variously pronounced as loo-*see*-na, loo-*kee*-na, or loo-*kay*-na, is a sort of "schmoo" of the tree world that offers extreme versatility and a range of useful products which could change our whole approach to farming in much of the tropics and subtropics. One of the fastest growing plants yet measured, it provides forage, timber, fuel, paper, and fertilizer, and can be used to reclaim barren soils. It may take the form of either a tall, slender tree or a rounded, many-branched bush. It can be cultivated in many soils now lying idle, too barren for conventional crops. It fixes its own nitrogen, resprouts from stumps, survives drought, tolerates the salt of coastal areas, and resists many pests and diseases.

Although almost entirely overlooked in modern times, leucaena, a native of Mexico and Central America, was widely used by the Mayan and Zapotec civilizations. Indeed, the name Oaxaca, Mexico's fifth largest state and a prominent modern city, is derived from a pre-Columbian word meaning "the place where leucaena grows."

Leucaena has the potential to increase meat and milk supplies throughout the tropics where animal feed shortages are acute and chronic, for its leaves—similar to alfalfa in digestibility and nutritional value—are particularly palatable to dairy cows, beef cattle, water buffalo, and goats. Under favorable conditions the plant can produce about twice the edible dry matter produced by alfalfa with about the same percentage of protein.

The bushy varieties about five feet high are used for forage. Cattle wander out of sight among the foliage, munching leaves from ground to eye level. They relish them so much that in their eagerness they strip the bushes of all leaves and young stems. Fortunately, new foliage appears quickly; within two weeks the bushes can be ready for browsing once more.

Though the foliage contains an unusual amino acid that, if taken in excess, causes goiter in cattle, two decades of research have shown that leucaena diets supplemented with grass can produce extraordinary weight gains. Cattle browsing on leucaena near Brisbane, Australia, have grown at about twice the rate normally expected; the weight increases approach those usually obtained only in feedlots where animals are stuffed with high-energy, concentrated rations.

In the 1960s University of Hawaii professor James Brewbaker found in Mexico certain varieties of leucaena that grow into tall trees. With their thin bark and light-colored wood, these varieties have a useful commercial future as sources for pulp and paper, poles and posts, lumber and plywood. In equable tropical climates arboreal leucaenas grow so quickly that they can be twice the height of a tall man six months after planting, as high as a three-story building after two years, and as tall as a six-story building, with a trunk cross section as big as a large frying pan, in only six or eight years. Even among the world's champion fast-growing trees, such prolific growth is exceptional!

Small plantations of leucaena trees could greatly benefit rural villages. Firewood for cooking and heating water is as essential as food itself for poor people of developing countries. In some areas a family now spends as much on firewood as it does on food and, as supplies diminish, wood prices continually rise, thus creating "the poor man's oil crisis." Leucaena wood burns well, and the plant supplies fuel continuously because the stumps resprout so quickly they defy the woodcutter. Indeed, tropical countries with their abundant sunshine and year-round growing conditions could exploit leucaena in large plantations to fuel industry and agriculture.

Leucaena belongs to the family Leguminosae, and, like most other legumes, it benefits from a partnership with soil bacteria of the genus *Rhizobium.* The bacteria penetrate young rootlets and can absorb large amounts of nitrogen gas from air trapped in the upper soil layers, producing from it up to 500 pounds of nitrogen-containing compounds per acre per year. This is equivalent to providing about half a ton of ammonium sulfate fertilizer each year. Most of the compounds end up in the foliage, and six bags of dried leucaena leaves contain the same nitrogen as one bag of ammonium sulfate. Thus, small farmers, for whom commercial fertilizers are too expensive or even unobtainable, can grow their own fertilizer.

Long disdained as a nuisance weed, leucaena now promises to become one of the most valuable crops for developing countries, perhaps the greatest agricultural "invention" ever seen in the tropics.

To have participated in the renaissance of such useful new crops as leucaena, winged bean, and jojoba has been enormously exciting. Initially, when Dr. Mirov first impressed on me the importance of helping jojoba's development, I doubted that such a valuable product could have been so long neglected. It seemed that there must be a catch, some technical or economic flaw that Dr. Mirov hadn't seen. But now I've watched jojoba rise in five years from total obscurity to the point where it is well on its way to becoming a profitable crop. I've also seen the recent results with amaranths, as well as the flood of winged bean research all over the world. Although leucaena research remains embryonic, thousands of acres of young plantations are thriving in the Philippines and the plant seems destined for rapid worldwide acceptance. Perhaps a meteoric career, such as that of the soybean, awaits each of these plants.

The soybean, too, lived through its share of ignominy. American farmers ignored the soybean for more than a century after Benjamin Franklin introduced it from the Jardin des Plantes in Paris. Soybean advocates at that time were often thought of as crackpots. Even early in this century, Americans considered the soybean a second-rate crop fit only for export to the "unfortunates" in the Far East; absolutely none was eaten here. But then, in the 1920s, University of Illinois researchers established a comprehensive soybean research program that helped sweep aside this cultural discrimination. The soybean acquired new status as a "legitimate" product, and its development gained so much momentum that today it probably provides the world with more protein than any other plant species. Soybean products are now found in many of the processed foods eaten in the United States.

Predicting the future in detail remains as always a very risky business. Yet scientists and generalists alike can realistically hope and work for solutions to pressing environmental problems in many lands. Agricultural research and application may be a key. For instance, rising production of jojoba oil could help ease the demand for oil from whales. Then sperm whales would be able to live unmolested, free to reproduce until their numbers are once more adequate to keep the species from extinction. Also, new strains of amaranth could improve the nutrition of people in highland regions of South America and Asia. Such under-exploited plants as wingbean and leucaena can help tens of millions of people in the tropics escape from a vicious cycle involving hunger and poverty.

The great advances in the agricultural and biological sciences of recent years could easily produce a cornucopia of new crops, new foods, and new industrial products. They could also extend high-yielding agriculture to vast, previously neglected regions. Indeed, our future depends upon such advances. We must expand the area suited to productive agriculture; we must raise from despair the ever increasing numbers of humans in developing countries who waste away their lives in malnourished poverty; and we must find and cultivate plants to produce raw materials that now come from petroleum. It is crucial to civilization's future that we press on with this exciting variety of inventiveness.

New U.S. Foods

Five native American crops that appear to have the technical merits to make a claim on dinner tables across the nation—and elsewhere in the hungry world:

Groundnut

The sweet, starchy tubers of the groundnut *Apios americana* were much esteemed by Native Americans from Florida to New England; the Pilgrims survived their first few winters by eating them. Little is known about their nutritive quality, though an analysis done in 1938 reports a protein content eight times that of potatoes.

Prairie potato

The prairie potato, the tuber of *Psoralea esculenta,* was once considered a special delicacy by the Plains Indians. Its flesh is firm, chewy, and palatable both cooked and raw. More than three times richer in protein than the conventional potato, it still grows wild from Colorado to Canada.

Tepary beans

A crop of the Papago and other Indians of New Mexico and Arizona, the tepary *(Phaseolus acutifolius)* grows in arid regions along the Mexican border region and requires far less water than conventional beans.

Hogpeanut

Amphicarpa bracteata produces large, edible seeds rich in oil and protein. Amazingly, the plant also produces a flower that blooms underground.

Buffalo gourd

The seeds of this desert melon *(Cucurbita foetidissima)* contain about one third protein and one third polyunsaturated oil. The plant grows an enormous root, packed with starch and as heavy as a man.

The buffalo gourd, a wild melon of deserts in Texas and northern Mexico, produces protein, edible oil, and carbohydrates.

Hoof and Fin

In selecting animal species for domestication we have been almost as parochial as in selecting plant species for crops. Indeed, as is the case with plants, we still rely on the ingenuity of Neolithic man for our animals. Of the Earth's 4,500 mammal species, for example, only 16 have been tamed and domesticated—none of them in recent times.

But burgeoning population growth, increasing hunger and malnutrition, and an energy crisis, as well as environmental and conservation concerns, summon us to re-examine undomesticated and lesser known animals. This is especially important for swamps, deserts, rainforests, and other marginal lands where traditional development is either technically or environmentally unfeasible.

From the Arctic to the tropics, scientists are investigating animal species that might supply additional food and resources. Scattered, little-known, but highly innovative, these projects involve "farming" such creatures as crayfish, snails, butterflies, frogs, toads, crocodiles, turtles, and quail, as well as mammals such as antelope, deer, musk ox, manatee, and capybara.

Breeding novel animals offers hope for feeding our hungry planet. Animal farming will protect some threatened species from extinction, and habitats won't be destroyed if the animals they harbor have economic value. Roast beef of water buffalo, boiled crayfish, and barbecued crocodile tail are just a few of the delicacies that may someday be common fare at dinner. □

Breeding and protecting novel animals offers hope for feeding our hungry planet and for saving threatened species. In Papua, New Guinea, top, farmers rear captured baby crocodiles to marketable size. A harmless herbivore and one of the most endangered aquatic mammals, the manatee, right, feasts on aquatic weeds that clog waterways and foster mosquitoes. Opposite: bottom left, a Louisiana red, Procambarus clarkii, *peers from its den. Farmed intensively in Louisiana, this crawfish appears in gourmet dishes such as "crawfish étouffé." Above, vaqueros round up an Asian water buffalo in its new Brazilian home. The water buffalo has adjusted successfully to locations in Europe and South America and is adapting well in Florida and Louisiana, too. It may one day become a valued source of meat for the U.S. Bottom right, an Indian boy with his catch of arapaima, a giant fish of the Amazon Basin. Recent poor yields caused by relentless overfishing have spawned projects to encourage its farming as aquaculture.*

7
PART

Alternatives: Smaller, Better, Gentler

Wilson Clark

A curious event occurred along the path of technological progress in the 1970s. It took place on Scotland's Outer Hebrides where weavers produce the famous woolen cloth called Harris Tweed. The weavers had been facing increasing economic competition from factory-made tweeds from Britain and other countries. The Harris Tweed Association limits use of the name to cloth manufactured in homes on hand looms producing 29-inch widths, a commodity hard to sell in a world turning to larger sizes, and increasingly standardized by the metric measurement system.

By way of remedy, the Harris Tweed Association, backed by major unions and the government, proposed a modernization plan to standardize Harris Tweeds with other woolen goods in the international market by introducing power looms and changing the standard width. The weavers would work in factories to be built on the islands. When this economic plan was put to a popular vote of the weavers themselves in October 1976, it was overwhelmingly rejected—by 497 votes to 55.

This rejection of modern technology is by no means confined to rural weavers. A former vice president of the National Association of Manufacturers, Richard Cornuelle, challenged the root concepts of efficiency and success in modern business management in his book, *De-Managing America.* Cornuelle tells of an incident in which he interviewed a young woman worker in a Chicago plant. She was operating a plastic-molding machine which produced cake plates. Cornuelle observed an enormous pile of rejected cake plates surrounding the operator. She explained that she had been instructed to discard any blemished plates, and that the machine had not produced a "passable" plate for "ever so long." According to Cornuelle, ". . . the young woman had been subhumanly programmed and was confidently—almost stubbornly— playing out the animal role some impatient production engineer had assigned to her. His conclusion: "In every managed institution in America, millions of carefully programmed people are wasting themselves and their time in aimless and perverse activities."

Technology today is increasingly separated from basic human needs. Frequently considered a means of increasing the flow and conversion of raw materials into useful objects for industrial societies, the development of technology in society is not generally planned as a means of increasing the happiness of the individual or the security of the human community. Technologies are usually aimed at certain limited goals, not at increasing the diversity of choices of experiences for communities, cities, and countries.

Consider the forecast of a leading national science adviser, Ali Cambel, who portrays a future United States of great metropolitan areas (megalopolises) linked to central energy resource pools—hydroelectric, coal, nuclear, geothermal, solar—depending on geography and availability of fuels. Unlike "Adkinsville," the imaginary community seen at right, each megalopolis portrayed by Cambel would be covered by a large geodesic dome partly powered by solar energy; above the dome, "the sky would be clear, clouds having been removed by yet to be developed methods of weather control."

Under the domes, the millions of inhabitants would live in plastic houses, enjoy a constant 74° F atmosphere, cook on radar ovens, and wear disposable synthetic clothes while dining on disposable dishes. To meet the needs of a growing population, food would be produced in "agro-industrial complexes" powered by nuclear breeder reactors producing vast quantities of fresh water from oceanic desalination, and manufacturing fertilizers from fossil fuels such as coal.

It is only a few intellectual paces from domed megalopolises to the wholly artificial space stations of Gerard O'Neill, described on page 221. The technological goals proposed for Earth by Dr. Cambel and for space by Dr. O'Neill may indeed be *achievable,* but this begs the greater question: are such goals important and timely, given the needs of today's world?

Among the major issues vexing the world's lead-

Wilson Clark, advisor to Governor Edmund G. Brown, Jr., of California, on energy, economics, and the environment, wrote Energy for Survival.

Adkinsville is, by all reports, a slow burg, but its energy needs are as low as its energy level. Much of its electricity is generated by its own windmill and by the municipal hydropower plant at Wilson's Falls below. Banks of solar cells on the roof of the Sippican Barge Co. serve the warehouse and provide some electricity for the power net. The holding pond below the windmill is pumped full at night and emptied through a turbine for peak-load power.

It is a matter of local pride that these fields of non-hybrid crops are for our own tables, irrigated by wind-power and fertilized by municipal sewage sludge and by the community compost and leaf dump at the recycling drop.

Solar and earth insulated new homes

Adkinsville is served by freight and passenger rail service for intercity travel, by light rail trolleys for intra-city transport, and by yellow jitney minibusses. Pedestrianism is encouraged by a dense collection of shops, broad sidewalks, and even a footbridge over the river.

solar clothes drying

Older homes retro-fitted with solar panels and insulation, wood stoves, and greenhouses.

solar panels

Barge traffic on the Sippican River.

233

This low-tech energy solution is the Sewca stove, an extremely efficient wood heater made from recycled propane tanks.

ers and thinkers are food for a growing population, finding and exploiting new sources of energy, minimizing the spread of nuclear weaponry, housing expanding populations, and attempting to control boom-and-bust international economies. Until recently the only way we could think about solutions to such questions was to think big; it is my contention that thinking big has been as much a problem-creating curse as a cure.

Through the 1960s, the prevailing scientific and technical wisdom of the West held that world food demand could be met by adapting mechanized agricultural techniques from the United States and other industrialized nations to the rest of the world. In addition, most scientists were confident that nuclear-fission energy would offer a reliable, available replacement for dwindling oil and gas reserves.

In both cases dreams failed to become realities. To accommodate the growing food needs of a global population now estimated at four billion and destined to swell to perhaps 12 billion in a century, agricultural technologists have assumed that a combination of mechanization, genetic improvement of seed stocks, and increased use of chemical fertilizers and pesticides

would assure increasing food supplies. What the technologists did not count on were basic environmental factors, diminishing supplies of fossil fuels to provide the motive power for mechanization and the feedstocks for agricultural chemicals. Yet, according to David Pimentel of Cornell University, "Modern, intensive agricultural practices of the Western world and those proposed by 'green revolution' agriculture will not offer a solution for the world food problem. . . . To feed a world population of four billion while employing modern intensive agriculture would require an energy equivalent of 1.2 billion gallons of fuel per day. If petroleum were the only source of fossil energy and if all petroleum reserves were used to feed the world population using intensive agriculture, known petroleum reserves would last a mere 29 years."

Nor have the ecological effects of big agriculture traditionally been considered by its proponents. A key ecological concept is "carrying capacity," a phrase used to describe the biological and resource constraints on living systems. Human history is fraught with examples of our exceeding the Earth's carrying capacity. We have, many times in many places, despoiled the Earth's forests, "overmined" soils to support intensive agriculture, and overfished the seas. The overdependence of our present form of mechanized agriculture on fossil fuels has been detailed in other chapters. Additionally, agricultural technology has diminished natural seed stocks, replacing them with newer "miracle" hybrid seeds that flourish with increased fertilization and constant irrigation. With the advent of the hybrids, many strains of older stock have been lost—ending a genetic continuity of many millennia.

The issue of genetic vulnerability was confronted by U.S. growers in 1970, when a corn blight wiped out 15 percent of the nation's crop; the situation was corrected only when new seeds not subject to the specific disease were made available. Later, the National Academy of Sciences concluded that many U.S. crops suffer from genetic vulnerability, and that the technological and social forces of uniform, mechanized, large-scale agriculture "pose a severe dilemma for the sciences that society holds responsible for its agriculture." The study noted that, in 1969, over 70 percent of the following crops were dominated by "small numbers of varieties": corn, snap beans, millet, peanuts, peas, and potatoes.

The crop monocultures now dominating Western-style agriculture provide a startling example of the extent to which diversity has been overruled by the increasing mechanization of the fields and the pressures of modern marketing—which demand uniformity. Technological optimism has spawned a variety of problems for modern agriculture in all countries.

Before the OPEC oil boycott of the '70s, little or

no attention was paid to the possibility that cheap energy would become expensive, scarce, or unavailable altogether. Following the Second World War, the promise of nuclear power was seen by government experts as a panacea so bright as to warrant the claim that within a few years it would be too cheap to meter!

Yet the warning signs were already evident in some industrial and academic circles. M. King Hubbert of the U.S. Geological Survey correctly predicted fully two decades in advance the decline of American gas reserves in the early '70s. Dr. Hubbert noted that the global period of industrial growth fueled by cheap energy sources would be short-lived. "It represents," he said, "a brief transitional episode between two very much longer periods, each characterized by rates of change so slow as to be regarded essentially as a period of nongrowth."

The critical failure of technological planners of the industrialized world has been in continuing to advocate heavy reliance on dwindling fossil energy sources and uncertain nuclear sources, rather than charting a prudent course which would ensure that scarce fuels are conserved and technologies implemented to make better use of existing resources.

This should, in turn, call for basic changes in the housing industry, in transportation, in industrial energy use, and in the consumer's use of available technologies. Indeed, it calls for a new way of thinking about progress. According to the American Institute of Architects, "If we adopted a high-priority national program emphasizing energy-efficient buildings, we could by 1990 be saving the equivalent of more than 12.5 million barrels of petroleum per day." Such a national program would involve retrofitting existing buildings with insulation, improved heating and air-conditioning equipment, reducing lighting levels, and other measures. Improving the efficiency of new buildings and houses is considerably easier. One of the most innovative building programs for energy conservation has been undertaken by the State of California. State architect Sim Van der Ryn is planning new state office buildings with the goal of consuming 80 percent less energy than conventional buildings. The proposed state buildings use advanced technologies in air conditioning and heating, as well as climatically sensitive construction techniques for natural lighting, heating with solar energy, and night air cooling.

Consumers can now take advantage of a range of energy-conserving technologies, including energy-efficient appliances such as water-saving toilets, solar devices for water heating and space conditioning, heat pumps and other energy-conserving air-conditioning and heating systems, as well as improved housing designs using insulation and climatic techniques to reduce conventional energy demands.

To make the transition to a more energy- and resource-efficient society demands a close examination of the basic lifestyles and patterns of modern-day America. We might learn from the European experience, where, in countries such as Sweden, energy use is about 60 percent of the U.S. average, although both nations enjoy a comparable standard of living. In Sweden, less energy is used in transportation because of mass transit and smaller, better-engineered cars; less is used in industry because of improved technologies and a greater concern for conservation; less is used in buildings because of the incorporation of basic conservation practices and the official endorsement by the government of conservation through laws and building codes.

In Sweden and other European countries, technologies for "district heating" are in widespread use. District heating plants produce steam and hot water for building heating in local areas through underground pipe distribution systems. Such plants are largely unknown in the United States, although a Brookhaven National Laboratory study indicates that "up to one-half of the U.S. population could be served by district heating at costs that are competitive with the present costs of imported oil." District heating can be accomplished by harnessing rejected heat from electrical power plants, or industrial plants, or by

A low-tech answer for industry, the omnipurpose Garden-Way cart.

burning unconventional fuels such as garbage.

A related approach for energy saving in industry is "cogeneration"—the name given to various technologies employed to use waste heat effectively, and to generate electricity from industrial steam plants. A Dow Chemical Company report concluded that available cogeneration technologies could supply all U.S. industry with half its own needs for electricity by 1985, while saving fuel from conventional sources and eliminating the need for construction of 50 new nuclear power plants.

Although cogeneration is not a household word—certainly not as well known as nuclear power or coal power—it represents a substantial industrial source of energy for the future. Basically, cogeneration technologies allow for the maximum use of heat from a variety of different industrial processes. A simple example is an industrial facility which uses the exhaust heat from a gas turbine or internal combustion engine for additional space heating or for heat for another manufacturing process.

I recently visited a sophisticated and ingenious cogeneration facility at a Weyerhaeuser Corporation paper and pulp plant near Eugene, Oregon. At the timber company's plant, an energy-rich black liquor from the pulping process is burned to produce steam for the production of electricity in a conventional turbine generator. Located in the center of the bustling industrial plant, the "energy center," as it's called by the company, is housed in a small building adjacent to the pulping facility.

The electrical power plant is actually owned by the Eugene, Oregon, municipal utility, but the Weyerhaeuser company operates and maintains the plant by a service contract. The by-product steam from the 51-megawatt turbine generator is used to provide process steam in two stages, for pulp processing as well as pulp drying. In the meantime, all the electricity produced by the cogeneration facility is sold to three California municipal utilities—Pasadena, Glendale, and Burbank—over 800 miles from the plant.

In this situation, everyone came out a winner. The Eugene utility not only found reliable customers to justify the investment in the cogeneration plant, but the California cities found a cheaper source of electricity. And for Weyerhaeuser, the plant provides process heat for existing industrial needs, at high efficiency and low cost.

Reaching the full potential of industrial cogeneration will require more than a few ideal contracts such as this one. In many cases, existing electrical pricing policies and regulatory agencies on the local, state, and Federal level activity discourage innovative cogeneration proposals.

Taking such a decentralized approach to energy development can assist in the introduction of solar energy on a large scale, as well as other *renewable* energy sources for society. Techniques are available to harness solar energy for home and building heating needs, as well as sophisticated solar collector designs which provide cooling. California, Colorado, and Florida have taken the lead in the development of solar energy for housing applications, and new Federal programs are designed to reduce costs by large-scale purchases and heavy investments in solar technologies.

Other than the direct use of solar energy for building, home, and water heating and low-grade industrial heat needs, the sun's radiation can be tapped for higher quality energy uses. Photovoltaic cells convert solar energy directly into electricity, and have been used successfully on thousands of spacecraft and for remote power applications, such as emergency navigation beacons.

Photovoltaic technology has been in use since its initial development in the 1950s by Bell Laboratories. The most common material used in solar cells is silicon, a semiconductor material used widely in the electronics industry (silicon "chips" have helped revolutionize this industry). Silicon cells convert sunlight directly to electricity, typically at about 9-12 percent efficiency. However, due to the precision with which the hand-crafted cells must be made, the production of electricity is extremely costly. At present, the Federal Department of Energy is engaged in a large-scale purchase program to reduce the high cost of photovoltaic electricity by stimulating mass production.

Other specialized approaches utilize concentrating solar collectors to generate intense heat to replace the use of conventional fuel sources in electrical power cycles. The Department of Energy is testing a solar thermal facility in New Mexico at present, and plans to construct a $100 million, 10,000-kilowatt electrical plant near Barstow in California's Mojave Desert for operation in the mid-1980s.

Other renewable energy technologies include wind power, small-scale hydroelectric power, and "biomass" energy conversion—harnessing the energy of biologically derived fuels such as wood, crops, and wastes. The only large-scale use of renewable energy today in the U.S. is hydroelectric power (now about four percent of the nation's energy). Although new sites for large hydro dams are quite limited, studies indicate that sizable amounts of power can be obtained from developing new or already-existing small hydro dams (3,000 to 5,000 kilowatts of capacity), and improving large dams.

The potential for wind power is enormous—the World Meteorological Society estimates that 20 million megawatts of wind-generated electricity can be tapped at good global sites. Using the winds for the generation of motive power has been an important source of energy since long before the Industrial Revolution; by 1850, windmills in the U.S. accounted for 1.4 billion horsepower-hours of work—the equivalent of burning more than 11 million tons of coal. Technologies for generating electricity from the winds have been improved since the early years of this century.

During the Second World War, a massive 1,250-kilowatt wind generator was built at "Grandpa's Knob" in the central Vermont mountains; the plant had two blades 175 feet in diameter. The Grandpa's Knob plant was successfully operated during the war, feeding electricity into the lines of a local utility, until wartime materials shortages forced a shutdown. Finally, a blade cracked, and the nation's largest experiment with wind power ended in 1945.

But within the last five years, a number of critical developments in the United States and other countries have triggered national attempts to reintroduce wind power, using advanced technologies—many derived from the aerospace industry. The Department of Energy is engaged in an ambitious testing program designed to advance the art of wind–powered electricity. Wind machines in this program have been built in Ohio and New Mexico.

Private utilities are also interested. In May 1978, the Southern California Edison Company announced a two million dollar wind energy development program—one million of which is earmarked for purchase of a 3,000-kilowatt wind generator designed by Seattle's Wind Power Products Company. The machine was picked by Edison for purchase after an exhaustive review of wind technologies under development across the nation. According to the utility's representatives, "it was the only one working well enough to say, 'Let's go with it.' "

The Wind Power Products Company was founded by Charles Schachle, an inventor with little patience for Federal programs. In a recent discussion, Schachle explained to me his own review of previous attempts to commercialize wind power. He noted that his wind generator design borrows from many previous successes and incorporates lessons from the past—such as his decision to utilize laminated wooden blades covered with fiber glass. He decided against metal because of stress problems and cracking—a wise decision, in light of recent Department of Energy disclosures that their wind machine in New Mexico is suffering from metal fatigue in the blades.

The Schachle wind generator will be built 4,000 feet above the California desert near Palm Springs, where the winds average 18 miles per hour. Such sites are ideal since they require smaller wind machines and provide a reliable "fuel" source on a yearly basis. A recent study of the potential for wind power in the

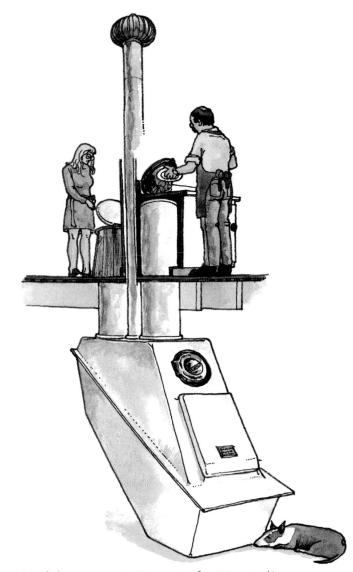

Low technology waste disposal: the Clivus Multrum composting system, utilizing human and kitchen waste.

U.S. concluded that the well planned placement of 100,000 wind generators of 1,000-kilowatt size would supply about 15 percent of the nation's electricity. "There is no problem in producing the machines; a wind generator is less complex than an aircraft."

The energy potential for biomass (non-hydrocarbon organic fuels) conversion is likewise great. Today, just under two percent of the nation's energy is supplied by wood fuel in homes and industry, electric power generation by wood, agricultural and refuse-derived fuels, and process steam in industry generated by biofuels. Two recent reports commissioned by the Department of Energy indicate that wind power and biomass energy may loom larger in the country's energy picture by the turn of the century. The studies project solar energy's share of the market in the year 2000 at six to nine percent, with wind and biomass conversion sources playing a leading role.

Most technical studies of the future role of solar energy (which includes wind and biomass conversion) agree that its potential is enormous, but draw widely differing conclusions about the practicability of specific approaches. According to a recent optimistic survey by the Council on Environmental Quality, solar and related technologies could supply all of our energy needs while using only one percent of our land area. According to the council: "All of these attributes (availability, employment potential, environmental desirability, etc.) of solar energy indicate that it has the potential to be a leading source of U.S. energy supply, not just a supplement. Indeed, from a standpoint of technology and resources, there appears to be no reason why solar energy cannot meet most of our needs, given adequate integrated efforts to increase energy efficiency."

Achieving such a future may be possible from a narrow technological viewpoint, but major obstacles stand in the way of conversion to these approaches and technologies. Compared to $10 billion in Federal funds spent on conventional, cen-

tralized technologies in 1976 (including incentives and subsidies), the various forms of solar energy received only $100 million—one percent of that spent on conventional sources. The Battelle Northwest Laboratory study referred to earlier concluded that: "If it is socially desirable and technologically feasible to increase solar energy's share in the national energy budget, the paramount policy question is one of selecting an incentive strategy and determining the government's level of investment in it."

Already, expenditures to increase the production of energy from *non*renewable fuels are a major national budget item. From 1973 to 1975, the U.S. invested $112 billion in plant and equipment for energy production—about 35 percent of capital expenditures in the entire economy. This could rise to 40 percent in the 1980s. Such major expenditures on centralized energy production tend to "crowd out" alternative expenditures in the economy. To generate a more efficient, decentralized future will require investment in local and community energy technologies, as well as technologies to improve the efficiency of food production and other basic resources. Small businesses will become increasingly important, as these problems cannot be solved by a purely central economic or government approach.

According to government figures, small businesses comprise 97 percent of all businesses

Appropriate technology applied to transportation: the Cannondale Bugger. This particular dog is obviously a low energy item, as well.

in the United States and generate more than half of all jobs, yet ". . . a set of impediments have developed that are preventing smaller businesses from attracting the capital without which they cannot perform their traditional function of infusing innovation and new competition into the economy." Ironically, the lack of capital for small businesses occurs at a time when economists and planners are beginning to recognize that small-scale organizations and individuals may be far more productive than their larger business and government counterparts. *The Sources of Invention,* a comprehensive survey of invention and innovation, catalogs 71 major inventions of this century, noting that more than half were the product of individual inventors, working outside of major corporations or government. Some of these are: E. Armstrong (radio); L. H. Baekeland (Bakelite); F. G. Banting (insulin); L. Biro (ball-point pen); S. G. Brown (gyrocompass); C. Carlson (xerography); S. W. Cramer (air conditioning); P. Farnsworth (television); H. Ferguson (tractors); A. Fleming (penicillin); L. De Forest (radio); L. Godowsky (Kodachrome); E.. H. Land (Polaroid camera—synthetic light polariser); H. von Ohain (axial-flow jet engine); F. Wankel (Wankel engine).

A comment by Brown, the British inventor of the gyrocompass, probably typifies the sentiment of the lone inventor: "If there were any control over me or my work every idea would stop."

Reversing the trends of increasing governmental and corporate concentration in order to assist smaller, more innovative organizations will require analysis of government subsidies, programs, taxes, and other incentives. Already, the recognition of small-scale economics is transforming Western attitudes toward development in the Third World. Since the pioneering efforts of the late British economist E. F. Schumacher (*Small Is Beautiful*) and others involved in technological aid programs, several Western nations have recognized the value of "intermediate" or "appropriate" technologies. Schumacher coined the term "intermediate technology" to describe the kind of small-scale economic and resource development needed in the developing world, as contrasted to the typical aid programs which assume that developing countries need only sophisticated, mechanized industries and power facilities. In his words, "I have named it *intermediate technology* to signify that it is vastly superior to the primitive technology of bygone ages but at the same time much simpler, cheaper, and freer than the supertechnology of the rich."

Solving the pressing world needs for energy,

The PureCycle system begins with an initial charge of 1500 gallons of water and supplies a household with all its water needs indefinitely. Greywater and sewage is pumped into its complex system to be purified beyond all EPA standards and held for re-use, independent of municipal water and sewage. Minor loss from evaporation can be replaced with rain water, snow-run-off or even seawater.

waste water

pure

food, and resources will not be an easy task economically or politically. First we must recognize that resource problems know no national boundaries, and that the technologies which made today's energy-extravagant world possible are not the best approaches to the future.

Proponents of a decentralized, conserving society are often told that their schemes would plunge the world into an economic dark age. Houses and factories would go dark, the stock market would collapse . . . but as the song goes, it ain't necessarily so.

In a recent interview, Francis Kelly, a leading Wall Street economist, said the key to avoiding a depression is "recognition by government that existing technologies are no longer capable of ensuring sufficient growth to maintain present fiscal and social policies." What Kelly sees as the best alternative is "smaller scale technologies, evolutions in existing processes designed to make manufacturing pollute less and use energy more efficiently. . . ."

Such an emphasis, he says, would restore our "perception of the long run" without which there can be no confidence in the future. With that perception restored, says Kelly, "it would be very bullish." ☐

239

Tradition and Progress

Theodore A. Wertime

Because its processes simulate those of the brain, that mighty and troublesome organ of human thought, the computer stands as the critical climactic invention of Western civilization. Even in the mechanical form (below)—predecessor of its electronic apotheosis—the computer successfully rivals the Mediterranean invention of writing dating from 8000 B.C. and even ranks above the Renaissance development of the printed alphabet which sparked the

great and continuing revolution in the modern media.

Furthermore, the mechanical computer, in all its whirling ingenuity, represents our Western preoccupation with coded communications. Like many of our other machines the computer goes back to the earliest Egyptian experiments with rotary grinders for grain and the first wheeled carts, appearing in Mesopotamia about 3500 B.C. It also reflects the cyclic, cybernetic speculations of the builders of Stonehenge in 1900-

The computer, like many inventions, has origins lost in time. "Difference machines" made in the 19th century for logarithmic

computations were one root of the idea. The machine below was made by P. G. Scheutz in 1853.

1700 B.C. In time, windmills, water mills, rotary lathes for Greek coins, Roman windlasses and pulleys, and numerous wheeled devices (including the first reaper—about 400 B.C.) came to dominate the European scene. Piston devices imported from China and crankshafts out of western Asia supplied additional power. Ahead lay the 18th-century notion of the steam engine and the 19th century's automobile.

Until recently our geared-up technology was accepted as an essential component that moved civilization forward. But in the last generation serious doubts have arisen, springing in part from the possible horrors of mass annihilation in high technology warfare and in part from knowledge that the age of fossil fuels and fire is coming to an end with the 20th century. Obviously, our familiar world won't end exactly at A.D. 2000; but, as the carbon dioxide proportion of our atmosphere rises toward 600 or 700 parts per million, and no one knows whether the net effect of such pollution will be a greenhouse or an ice age, the prospect of ending soon is indeed worrisome.

I am a follower of René Dubos rather than of Henry David Thoreau—meaning that I take a practical view of what we can do about the future, rather than a romantic, aesthetic, despairing view. So I decided to try to find a small-scale, personal solution to the problem of adapting to the future's demands. For me, an attempt to build a new kind of solar house of sprayed concrete on Scrub Ridge near McConnellsburg in southern Pennsylvania was less a return to nature than an effort to make a new compromise with her.

In trying to re-create American frontiersmanship in my small corner of the world, I decided that the only way to proceed was to be like any farmer: pick out a plot, plant the seeds, and let the sense of innovativeness spread. One can do this through schools, through business enterprises, or simply by example. But the seed must be a viable one. Solar energy is definitely on the way, but selling the sun is not enough in the rural Pennsylvania hinterland of the great Eastern megalopolis. To make a helpful statement, the new house must be a kind of aesthetic, energy-efficient, material-conserving paradigm. It should itself bespeak the imminent demise of the age of metals as we have known it, even of man's use of fire as we have used it.

My obstacles and failures I will not detail, simply because they are too boring. But my reasons for trying I will elaborate.

Man's innermost doubts about the civilization which inventors have given us—the kind of fundamental questions that computers cannot solve—can be

Theodore A. Wertime, a Smithsonian research associate and editor of books on iron and tin, is currently working to develop alternative technologies.

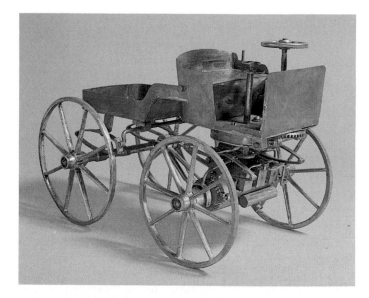

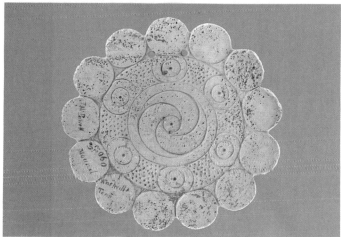

Pre-Columbian Indians of the Tennessee Valley used wheels for decoration, above, but not for transport. Even such a primitive auto as the one represented by the 1895 patent model, top, required a highly advanced technological and industrial base.

traced back to Greek debates about the powers of mankind and to scriptural writings about sin and atonement. These deep-seated dilemmas of human history must be confronted, or at least put in context, before we can deal with the crisis of our technological-economic system that withers even as it blooms.

The thought of invention, contrivance, craft or cunning as the motive power of change has been with us since well before Aristotle. Hesiod, the Greek poet of the eighth century B.C., recorded the myth of the fallen god Prometheus, who stole fire and crafts from the gods and gave them to man, as described in Aeschylus's *Prometheus Bound:*

> *I taught them to determine when stars rise or set—*
> *A difficult art. Number, the primary science, I*
> *Invented for them, and how to set down words in*
>   *writing—*

When Greek mythology's Prometheus, above, gave man craft skills and fire, a wrathful Zeus chained him to a mountaintop, then punished mankind by releasing Pandora's box of evil. The myth reflects traditional societies' uneasiness with progress.

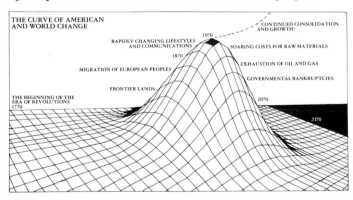

THE CURVE OF AMERICAN AND WORLD CHANGE

CONTINUED CONSOLIDATION AND GROWTH?

1970

RAPIDLY CHANGING LIFESTYLES AND COMMUNICATIONS

SOARING COSTS FOR RAW MATERIALS

1870

MIGRATION OF EUROPEAN PEOPLES

EXHAUSTION OF OIL AND GAS

GOVERNMENTAL BANKRUPTCIES

FRONTIER LANDS

THE BEGINNING OF THE ERA OF REVOLUTIONS 1770

2070

2170

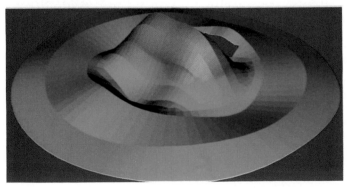

Classic bell curves (from the author, top, and from science text) may chart how civilizations rise and fall. But anyone can play, tracing great eras and dark ages as society lurches along its path toward tomorrow.

The all-remembering skill, mother of many arts.
I was the first to harness beasts under a yoke . . .

A furious Zeus retaliated by chaining Prometheus to a mountain peak and releasing upon humanity Pandora's box of evil and disease. Because of Prometheus men relinquished the golden age of indolence to bear the burdens of the era of iron.

Similarly, for eating of the fruit of knowledge Adam and Eve were banished from the Garden of Eden and sentenced to eternal work—the work which necessarily accompanies technological advance. The Hebrew tradition expresses the curse most vividly in the apocryphal book of *Enoch,* in which the reasons for Noah's flood are expounded at length: Azazel and the fallen angels put the race of mankind under a second condemnation by teaching them crafts; and the Lord, like Aeschylus's Zeus, is determined upon the destruction of man.

The poignancy of this great poetic and Biblical heritage of sin counterbalances the explosive progress that has marked Western civilization since at least 1000 B.C. Western men, hearing the words of their ancestors, sensed that they were loosing two great shadows over the world, population and technology.

The populations and technologies of the ancient Mediterranean interacted vigorously, far more so than in any other contemporary society, including the Han or Tang-Sung dynasty. The Roman Mediterranean and Han China each had about 60 million people heavily clustered about a heartland. Each was a pyramid, capped by a learned and wealthy elite. Each toppled, to be followed by a dark age during which, paradoxically, technology jumped in new directions.

But there the resemblance ends. Because of its unique mix of scientific inventiveness and necessity, Europe went on to found the modern era. Whereas in A.D. 1700 China and Europe may have been on a par in iron and steel production, by 1800 Britain was well into its coal-fired, steam-powered industrial revolution which enabled it to produce in that year more metal than all of China (200,000 tons). The great technology race was on, to be spread over the Earth by migratory waves of Europeans. Europe and the West had been by then long committed to growth wherever technology might lead—a philosophy often confused with rationalism.

The height of scientific rationalism in Western history occurred in 1789 during the French Revolution. It is no mere coincidence that the revolution took place immediately after the discoveries of Lavoisier in

242

Shaking free of traditional restrictions, a seeker of truth—in this drawing of uncertain vintage—ponders the awesome workings of the cosmos. Somehow he sums up scientists' centuries-old efforts to plumb the secrets of the universe.

chemistry, the improvements of Watt in steam power, Franklin's accomplishments in electricity, the adoption of the U.S. Constitution, and the first census of America. This was surely one of the great turning points in Western civilization, when a wood-burning, industrially primitive European society backed into the most explosive period of technological growth in world history, that of the fossil fuel-fired Industrial Revolution. Incidentally, one should recognize that intellectual perception of the time was enriched by the use of statistics, which for the first time enabled thinkers to see quantitatively how the world was expanding and changing.

The two classic modern statements of scientific-technologic optimism and demographic pessimism are derivations from this calculating era. The optimistic verdict was rendered by Marie-Jean Garitat, Marquis de Condorcet, secretary of the National Legislative Assembly and a mathematician with a flair for probability theory. In 1794, while trying to flee from the Terror (from which he later died), Condorcet wrote his *Esquisse d'un Tableau Historique des Progrès de l'Esprit Humain,* presenting a panoramic view of the progress of men from hunting and gathering to pastoralism, agriculture, the inventions of printing, and ultimately the intellectual and political revolutions of the 18th century. Instruments and machines, Condorcet believed, would "add every day to the capabilities and skill of man." Such perfectability would lead men to greater equality, limitless improvement in the expectancy of life, and the ultimate transfer of the new means of livelihood from Europe to the poorer countries of Asia and Africa.

If Condorcet saw nothing but good issuing from the hands of man, he would be brought to book by someone else who foresaw doom in the sheer number of hands. In an *Essay on the Principles of Population,* published in 1798, Thomas Robert Malthus expressed the thought that men reproduce geometrically whereas their means of subsistence increases only arithmetically. In examining the censuses of the American colonies, he found a population doubling every 22 years. Though wrong in thinking that means of subsistence cannot increase geometrically, Malthus was generally right in believing that human societies tend to expand to the carrying capacities of their surroundings. His pessimism, which soured some of the optimism of the 19th century and haunted many 20th-century anthropologists and demographers, has returned in a paradoxical way to the lessons of the ancient writers about the original sins of mankind.

The modern pessimism takes as much strength from the critics of Malthus as it does from Malthus himself. In 1965 Danish economist Ester Boserup, in *The Conditions of Agricultural Growth,* argued that new technologies do not spur population growth. Quite the other way around, she said. Population pressures spur men to adopt new technologies and expand their subsistence; technology and invention become not the results of great innovative spurts in human affairs but desperate holding actions, depending on contrivance to contain the effect of more people. Along with new studies of the relative labor efficiencies of stone-age societies by such anthropologists as Marshall Sahlins, Boserup and her numerous followers have restored the Greek theory that societies grow downwards

rather than upwards. Perhaps the extreme statement of this gloomy view is a book by Nathan Cohen, *The Food Crisis in Prehistory,* which argues that since the days of foraging, human civilizations have been moving steadily down the trophic scale.

To the contemporary, pessimistic student of society, Western civilization is merely an exaggerated form of the organized social life that appeared for mysterious reasons nearly simultaneously in both the Old World and the New some 10,000 years ago. Since then some 5,000 civilizations have come and gone, not all of them marked by the rise of cities, and only a few related by trade in ideas. Many of them, after the initial wave of invention that included the domestication of plants and animals and gave community life its economic base, showed little further development. The Hopewell Indian culture in the United States typifies those kinds of societies in the New World. They developed trade systems but had no urge to employ wheels or to use iron in any but meteoritic form. They had but little idea of mechanism. Their ethic was to cohabit with nature rather than to dominate it.

We of the late 20th century have gone a long way toward dominating nature and perhaps face the most dreadful challenge of any world civilization. The problems we face have been compounded by the lack of any new land frontiers on this Earth to absorb our growing population. We have nowhere to go. Yet the hopelessness implicit in the pessimistic view makes it of little use to history and to humankind.

There is a need to understand how history works . . . whether mankind, freighted with the heavy warnings of its forebears and the shrill cries of contemporary commentators, has had and continues to have the genetic strength to cross new thresholds. At first blush the curve of change in Western civiliza-

Windrow of windmills: earliest design, below, 10th century A.D. Persia; horizontal-shafted Mediterranean mill, Dutch, 12th century; prairie pinwheel (30 feet); electro-turbine, Vermont, 1940s; test model, 1970s.

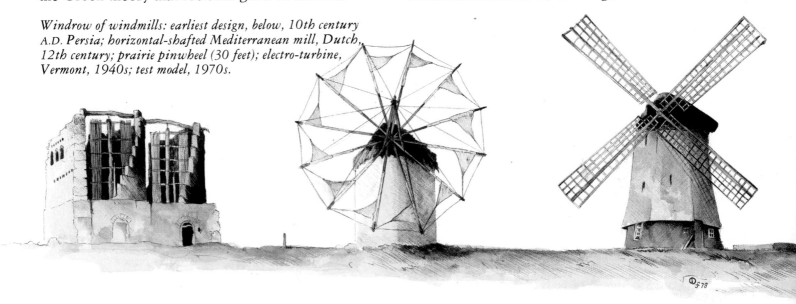

tion appears as a huge S, reaching the top of its curve for the first time in the 1970s and 1980s. But a closer look would show that the curve is composed of a number of minor zigs and zags, each representing a rise or fall in populations and technology. One perturbation occurred toward the year 1100 B.C. at the simultaneous demise of the regimes in Mycenae, the Hittite Kingdom, and New Kingdom Egypt, variously ascribed to overpopulation, drought, or the wanderings of the Sea Peoples. During this moment of interrupted trade in copper and tin, iron became the utilitarian metal in Cyprus, Palestine, and Greece, and inventors and technologists helped those civilizations cross the threshold to a new age of innovation.

Diocletian's Rome of the third century A.D. experienced a similar population decline, in this case, owing to plague and mismanagement, but it saw increased use of waterpower to grind grain. New technologies evolved, providing and utilizing glass, soap, skis, and deep plowing. In the wake of Rome's demise, waterpower was slow to spread across Europe, coming into its own only during the pre-industrial revolution of the 14th and 15th centuries. At that time European agriculture and populations, encouraged by the monasteries, the horse-drawn plow, and the water-powered charcoal blast furnace, invaded many previously forested areas, though the Black Death stilled and even reversed the process for a time.

For anyone trying to diagram the aggregation, dispersion, and reaggregation arising out of the major changes in Western civilization, the simple S curve does not seem to work well. Some historians have therefore turned to the Gaussian or bell curve, a wave that rises then falls, with invention playing a part in the ascending curve.

I prefer to see invention as a mutation in the body politic, analogous to the laws of natural selection as they apply to mutation in the biological organism.

In tune with the seasons, Indians built this dwelling in the great stone cleft at Mesa Verde. Though hidden in shadow from summer heat, the houses are in sunlight in winter. The cliff shields the entire community from storm and cold.

Change in the arrangement of the chromosomes' amino acids, whether caused by internal or external agents, can occasionally lead to the creation of a new species as a kind of caricature or mirror image of the old. New eras and new technologies are precisely this: caricatures of the old. Indeed, perhaps the most appropriate diagram for history is the Watson-Crick DNA double-helix model of DNA.

Having made a positive proposal for how history works, let me suggest yet another way of recovering from gloomy predictions about the end of our civilization. I would point out that we are at the second great climax of scientific thought in history, analogous to the moment of Alexander the Great's conquests and the peaking of Hellenistic science. In an unbelievably rich and short 50 years, scientific minds made tremendous journeys in the exploration of the atom, of life, of tectonic Earth, and of space. In the 1970s we have admittedly come to the end of an *ancien régime,* as global population growth, global farming, and global industrialization have affected nearly every human being on the planet. With the population of the world's cities doubling every 11 years, the number of passenger automobiles every 10.4 years, and electrical generating capacity every 8.7 years, the Earth may indeed be coming to the end of its resources. But with a new scientific awareness now focused on the Earth, can we not learn to live within the limits of our particular garden? This is the question that must be asked by everyone, and I do not exclude myself.

The public is just now being forced by inflation and impending shortages to look at semi-underground sitings and combinations of solar heat, wood heat, and off-peak storage of electric power. Since my own house will not be truly complete until I find a new mode of generating home electricity cheaply, I cannot persuade the public that I have final solutions to this game of adaptations. Neither can I sell any specific new product beyond a formula for spray concrete, a way of uniting concrete and urethane, and a possible new design for a long-burning wood stove (all originated in some respect by others).

As a country-bred lad—and also as an archeologist—I had learned long ago that nature is man's most deadly adversary. She will weed you out as ruthlessly as she will kill a tree or a bird. Two brutal winters and one brutal summer spent in an effort to rediscover an age of sun, stone, and wood sharpened my belief in the desperate need for human inventiveness in the struggle against animate and inanimate forces.

In the end, Thomas Edison did not give us the modern electric system nor did Rudolf Diesel the era of diesel engines. Both merely wandered in the labyrinth of innovative adaptation. Because of the technical complexities of illuminating a new cluster of ideas, they were contributors to a process involving many people rather than just lone inventors. Unlike some of the other essayists in this volume, I do not believe that there is any such thing as a single invention. An electric light bulb has a whole edifice of new technologies behind it. And my spray-concrete solar house (which some say I "invented") is really a molehill of unexplained pitfalls along with a few fairly obvious advances that might be called innovations upon innovations. One must not be fooled as he tries to steer himself and his family toward life in a white, airy, partly self-sufficient and semi-electronic cave; the "inventor" deserves not all the blame.

In the great dialogue in Western civilization between the optimists and the pessimists, modern social scientists have joined the worst pessimists. To them progress is a downward movement, as it was to the Greeks. They do not accept, even as do I, that men back slowly uphill, often blindly, but nevertheless toward the richer life, playing a game of rediscovering others' inventions as they go. □

Michigan schoolteachers perched a wind generator next to a highly insulated wooden igloo. Pupils calculate the energy needed to heat, light, and run shop machines in their geodesic classdome.

Invention Time Chart

Samuel Slater, New England industrialist and inventor, perhaps first hummed that hymn we call Yankee Ingenuity. Soon all of America was singing along. And the whole world likes the tune, to gather from the growth of American-style inventive ingenuity around the globe. Today, many lands in many ways out-invent the nation that in the 19th and 20th centuries achieved a brilliant, and perhaps fleeting, Golden Age of Invention. In this time chart are milestones in the great innovative process we celebrate, with an emphasis on the American experience.

Technology

Hardware is America's glory—whether in nuts and bolts and plumbing or in computers, spacecraft, conveyances, and weapons. Technology receives strength from science and industry and in turn helps support them.

Science

As America aged, a remarkable breed of inventor—the smock-clad scientist working in a university or industrial or federal laboratory—came up with formulas that would profoundly affect our civilization.

Industry

From little inventions have grown vast systems for production and profit. And from these industrial systems have developed even vaster innovations—in transportation, in communications, and how we reckon our place in the universe.

1700s⟶

Technology

			1753 First steam engine assembled in U.S.	1786-1787 John Fitch and James Rumsey operate steamboats	
				1792 Timothy Palmer builds Essex Merrimac Bridge	1795-1803 Middlesex Canal built in Massachusetts
		1726 Press used by apprentice Ben Franklin in London	1776 *The Turtle,* David Bushnell's submersible torpedo boat	1793 Eli Whitney invents the cotton gin	

Science

Benjamin Franklin 1706-1790, by Charles Phillips; Pioneer in American science, industry, technology		1743 American Philosophical Society founded			1794 Joseph Priestley brings European science to U.S.
	1722-1726 Mark Catesby surveys the natural history of the eastern United States			Thomas Jefferson 1743-1826 Naturalist and architect	1798 Benjamin Thompson studies heat

Industry

				1790 Samuel Slater builds first U.S. cotton mill	
1646 First ironworks in North America at Saugus, Massachusetts		1740 Franklin stove marketed			1792 New York Stock Exchange organizes
				1791 Alexander Hamilton writes *Report on the Subject of Manufactures*	

			1826 John Stevens runs first American steam locomotive	1837 Modern U.S. patent system is operating		1845 Elias Howe develops his sewing machine	
1807 Robert Fulton's steamboat *Clermont*	1818 Thomas Blanchard develops a "copying lathe"		1829 Jacob Bigelow finishes his *Elements of Technology*		1843 Norbert Rillieux invents evaporator for sugar cane		1849 Abraham Lincoln invents a boat-lifter
		1825 Opening of the Erie Canal	1836 Alonzo Phillips invents the safety match	1830 Robert Stevens designs T-Rail for trains		1846 Richard M. Hoe introduces rotary printing press	1849 Walter Hunt patents the safety pin
1809 John J. Audubon begins bird banding		1819 *American Journal of Science*, Vol. 1, No. 1 is published		1832 Joseph Henry announces electrical self-induction			
	James Smithson 1765-1829 British chemist and mineralogist		1833 William Beaumont describes digestive process	1841 James Espy publishes *Philosophy of Storms*	1847 Yale and Harvard establish scientific schools	Maria Mitchell 1818-1889, by Vail Brothers; First American woman astronomer	
1812 Benjamin Rush pioneers the study of the mind			1838-1842 The Wilkes Expedition to Antarctica and the Pacific Northwest	1842 Ether first used in surgery			Asa Gray 1810-1888, by J. A. Whipple; *Elements of Botany*
1801 E. I. Du Pont de Nemours and Company founded						1836 Samuel Colt patents revolver	
1807-8 Eli Terry mass produces clocks				1830 First U.S. passenger trains	1834 Jacob Perkins invents first mechanical refrigerator	1840 4,500 miles of canals carry U.S. goods	Cyrus McCormick 1809-1884, by Charles Elliott; Inventor of mechanical reaper
1801 Oliver Evans operates high-pressure steam engine				1830s John Hall and Simeon North mass produce firearms		1844 Mesabi Range discovered in Minnesota	1846 Alexander T. Stewart opens "Department Store"

Technology

1851 William Kelly invents converter for steel production

1870 John W. Hyatt patents Celluloid

1883 Brooklyn Bridge opens

1858 Mason jar patented

1861 Elisha G. Otis patents steam elevator

1866 U.S. Army adopts Gatling gun

James B. Eads 1820-1887, by N. Sarony; Builder of St. Louis Bridge

1870 Margaret Knight patents first of 27 inventions

1884 Ottmar Mergenthaler patents Linotype

1862 The *Merrimac* battles the *Monitor,* foreground, at Hampton Roads

1868 Christopher L. Sholes patents his typewriter

1877 Joel Tiffany patents a successful refrigerator car

1886 Charles Hall patents aluminum process

1890 Construction of the Hudson River Tunnel

Science

1890 Herman Hollerith uses electrical data processing for 1890 census

1853 Charles Ellet publishes flood control study of Mississippi and Ohio Rivers

1859 Massachusetts Institute of Technology founded

1876 Henry Draper takes first photo of solar spectrum

Louis Agassiz 1807-1873, by Louis Mayer; Naturalist, teacher

1886 David T. Day studies petroleum chemistry

1891 Smithsonian astro-physical observatory founded

1863 National Academy of Sciences established

1882 First stethoscope patented

1885 Louis Pasteur successfully vaccinates against rabies

1883 "Edison Effect" presages electronic revolution

1893 Theobald Smith studies Texas cattle fever

Industry

1850 9,000 miles of U.S. railroad, three times European mileage

1852 Daniel Webster wins "Great India Rubber Patent Case" for Goodyear

1864 George M. Pullman designs railroad sleeping car

1872 First Montgomery Ward mail order catalog

1882 Edison's Pearl Street Station lights 83 homes

1892 Labor suffers defeat at Homestead

1856 Western Union organizes

Charles Goodyear 1800-1860, by Schussele; Vulcanization of rubber

1865 Alexander L. Holley begins first Bessemer steel production in U.S.

1884 First public electric railroad in U.S.

Andrew Carnegie 1835-1919, by Jacques Reich; Industrialist, philanthropist

1851 London's Crystal Palace showcases U.S. goods

1859 Edwin L. Drake strikes oil at Titusville, Pennsylvania

1869 Ives W. McGaffey invents vacuum cleaner

1876 Alexander Graham Bell patents telephone

1883 H. R. Towne is developing production engineering

1891 First zipper patented

Samuel Gompers 1850-1924, artist unknown; Founder of American Federation of Labor

George Eastman 1854-1932, by Paul Nadar; Inventor of Kodak camera

	1900 GE founds research lab; Du Pont, AT&T, and Eastman-Kodak follow suit	1903 Wright Brothers fly at Kitty Hawk	1914 Caresse Crosby patents first brassiere	1927 Al Jolson in "The Jazz Singer," first talking motion picture	1954 First nuclear-powered submarine, U.S.S. *Nautilus*	
George Eastman 1854-1932, by Paul Nadar; Inventor of Kodak camera			1914 Panama Canal opens	1928 Vladimir Zworykin develops TV camera	1957 USSR launches Sputnik I	1969 First manned lunar landing
1893 Edison patents "apparatus for exhibiting photographs of moving objects"	1901 Guglielmo Marconi sends wireless messages across the Atlantic	John P. Holland 1840-1914 Designer of first U.S. Navy submarine		1929 Charles Abbot publishes *The Sun and the Welfare of Man*		1961 First golfball typewriter / 1976 Viking spacecraft lands on Mars
	1907 Albert A. Michelson wins first U.S. Nobel Prize	1918 Harlow Shapley measures the Milky Way	1928 George E. Hale begins construction of Palomar Observatory		1958 Edward H. Teller directs Livermore Radiation Laboratory	
Marie S. Curie 1867-1934; Co-discoverer of radium and polonium	c. 1916 Albert Einstein announces theory of relativity		1925 Bell Telephone labs record sound electrically	1948 Palomar Observatory dedicates 200-inch telescope		Gordon Gould 1920- Inventor of the laser / 1978 Princeton announces breakthrough in fusion energy
	1920 Norbert Wiener completes early work on cybernetics	Henrietta S. Leavitt 1868-1921; Law of stellar-period luminosity	1925 R. A. Millikan names cosmic rays	1948 Bell Telephone labs announce invention of the transistor	Enrico Fermi 1901-1954 Nobel Prize winner for experiments with radioactivity	
1901 U.S. Steel organizes	1911 Frederick W. Taylor writes *Principles of Scientific Management*	1920 First regularly scheduled U.S. radio broadcasts	1929 U.S. stock market crashes on Black Friday	1933 TVA established	1942 First flight of a U.S. jet	
1903 Henry Ford begins Ford Motor Company				1938 Du Pont markets nylon	1944 Marki, the first true computer	1957 First U.S. atomic plant for electrical power / Harland Sanders 1890- Creator of Kentucky Fried Chicken
1904 King Gillette patents safety razor	1912 The *Titanic* sinks	1928 Jacob Schick patents first electric razor	Richard G. Drew 1899- Inventor of Scotch tape	1941 First commercial television broadcast		1958 Boeing 707 begins trans-Atlantic service / 1977 Alaskan Pipeline opens

Index

Picture Credits

Jacket: Charles H. Phillips
Front Matter: 1-3. Charles H. Phillips; 4-5. National Palace Museum, Taipei, Taiwan, Republic of China; 6-8. Smithsonian Institution; 10. Charles H. Phillips.

Part I: 14-15. Smithsonian Institution; 16-21. Jan Adkins; 22. Smithsonian Institution: National Portrait Gallery; 24. Smithsonian Institution: Al Harrell; 25. Smithsonian Institution; 26. Smithsonian Institution: National Portrait Gallery; 28. Smithsonian Institution: Henry Eastwood; 30. Patricia Upchurch; 31. Robert C. Post; 32-33 Smithsonian Institution: Kim Neilson; 34-35. Charles H. Phillips; 36. (top) Smithsonian Institution: Dane Penland; (bottom and right) Charles H. Phillips; 38. Smithsonian Institution: Dane Penland; 39. Smithsonian Institution: Al Harrell; 40. Smithsonian Institution; 41. (top middle and right) Steve Altman; (all others) Smithsonian Institution; 43. (top) Henry Eastwood; Courtesy of San Francisco Academy of Comic Art; (bottom) Smithsonian Institution; 44. Henry Eastwood; Courtesy of San Francisco Academy of Comic Art; 45. (left top and bottom) Smithsonian Institution; (right top and bottom) Henry Eastwood; 46. (left) Vahan Shirvanian; (right top and bottom) The New Yorker Magazine; (right middle) Clarence Brown; 47. The New Yorker Magazine.

Part II: 48-49. S. Jonasson/Bruce Coleman, Inc.; 51. Virginia Museum of Fine Arts; 52. Smithsonian Institution: Kim Nielsen; 53. Charles H. Phillips; 54-55. The Bettmann Archive; 56. Edward S. Ayensu; 57. Smithsonian Institution: Kim Nielsen; 58. Ross Chapple; 59. Smithsonian Institution: Freer Gallery of Art; 60-61. (top) David Good; (bottom) Smithsonian Institution: Freer Gallery of Art; 62. Smithsonian Institution; 63. Smithsonian Institution: Dane Penland; 64. The Pierpont Morgan Library; 65. Utrecht University Library; 66. Bibliothèque Nationale; 67. Smithsonian Institution: Dane Penland; 68. British Library; 71. Cornell University, Program of Computer Graphics; 72-81. Ross Chapple; 73. (Wedgwood pyrometer) Royal Scottish Museum; (Portland Vase) Drs. Harold and Caroline Brown; 76-77. Fogg Art Museum, Harvard University, © 1978 by The President and Fellows of Harvard College; 78. The Metropolitan Museum of Art, Bequest of George C. Stone, 1936; 79. The John Woodman Higgins Armory; 83. (left) The Bettmann Archive; (right) Thomas Jefferson Memorial Foundation; 84-85. Charles H. Phillips.

Part III: 86-87. Chuck O'Rear/Woodfin Camp, Inc.; 88. Ross Chapple; 89. The Boeing Company; 90. (top) Courtesy, Burndy Library; (bottom) Briggs Cunningham Automotive Museum; 91. Smithsonian Institution; 93. Newport News Shipbuilding; 94-95. Jan Adkins; 96. Smithsonian Institution; 97. (top) Collection of Lester S. Levy; (bottom) Smithsonian Institution; 98. J. B./Lensman; 99. (left) Peter B. Kaplan; (right) David Plowden; 100. The Panama Canal Company; 101. Linda Bartlett/Woodfin Camp, Inc.; 102. Jill Richards/Woodfin Camp, Inc.; 103. U.S. Department of the Interior, Bureau of Reclamation; 104. The Bettmann Archive; 105. Jeffrey Foxx/Woodfin Camp & Associates; 106-107. Fred J. Maroon; 108. Smithsonian Institution; 109-110. Smithsonian Institution: National Portrait Gallery; 111. (left) Culver Pictures; (right) The Bettmann Archive; 112-113. (left) Courtesy of Eastman Kodak Company; 113. (right) Smithsonian Institution; 115. The Metropolitan Museum of Art, David Hunter McAlpin Fund, 1963; 116-117. Smithsonian Institution; 118. Culver Pictures; 119. The Patent & Trademark Office of the U.S. Department of Commerce; 121. (top) Smithsonian Institution; (bottom) Library of Congress.

Part IV: 122-123. Rob Lewine; 124. Charles H. Phillips; 126. ND - Giraudon, Courtesy, Burndy Library; 127. (top) Courtesy of the Museum of the Jagellonian University in Cracow; (bottom) Smithsonian Institution; 128. Ross Chapple; (manuscript) The Pierpont Morgan Library; (prisms) University of Cambridge, Whipple Museum of the History of Science; 130. Charles H.

Phillips; 132. Ross Chapple; 134-135. Pierre Mion; 136-138. Ross Chapple; 140-142. NASA; 143. (top) NASA; (bottom) Goddard Space Flight Center; 144-145. © Association of Universities for Research in Astronomy, Inc., The Kitt Peak National Observatory; 146-147. Courtesy of Bell Laboratories; 148-149. Cornell University, Program of Computer Graphics; 150. Smithsonian Institution: National Portrait Gallery; 151. (top) Smithsonian Institution; (bottom) The Bettmann Archive; 152. Charles H. Phillips; 153. Christopher Springmann/Black Star.

Part V: 154-155. R. McGill Mackall; 156. Smithsonian Institution: Dane Penland; 157-158. Smithsonian Institution; 160. Smithsonian Institution: National Collection of Fine Arts; 161. Charles H. Phillips; 162. Library of Congress; 163. Smithsonian Institution; 164. (top) Smithsonian Institution: Al Harrell; (bottom) Earl Roberge/Photo Researchers, Inc.; 166-167. James A. Sugar/Woodfin Camp, Inc.; 169. (top) Smithsonian Institution: Al Harrell, (bottom) Ross Chapple; 170. Kenneth Garrett/Woodfin Camp, Inc.; 172. U.S. Army Photograph; 173. Ross Chapple; 175. Charles H. Phillips; 176. Smithsonian Institution: Al Harrell; 177. Henry Eastwood; 178. (top) Smithsonian Institution: Al Harrell; (bottom) Smithsonian Institution; 179. (left) Charles H. Phillips; (right) Steve Altman; 180-181. Robert Lautman.

Part VI: 182-183. Barry M. Blackman/Lensman; 185. National Gallery of Art; 186. Smithsonian Institution; 187. (top) Smithsonian Institution: Al Harrell; (bottom) Charles H. Phillips; 188. Smithsonian Institution: National Portrait Gallery; 189. (top) Dartmouth College Library; (bottom) Courtesy, Burndy Library; 190. Smithsonian Institution; 191. Lowell M. Herrero, Courtesy of the U.S. Air Force Art Collection; 192. Yale University Art Gallery, Bequest of Stephen Carlton Clark, B.A. 1903; 193. Smithsonian Institution; 194. Charles H. Phillips; 195. (bottom left) Smithsonian Institution: Dick Hofmeister; (all others) Charles H. Phillips; 196-198. The Bettmann Archive; 199. General Electric Company; 200. Smithsonian Institution; 201-202. U.S. Army Photograph; 203. General Dynamics Photo; 205. Courtesy of McDonnell Douglas Corporation; 206. The Museum of Modern Art; 207. Charles H. Phillips; 208. Museum of the City of New York; 209. (top) Smithsonian Institution: Al Harrell; (bottom) Smithsonian Institution: John Wooten; 210. (top) Tandem Productions; (bottom) The Metropolitan Museum of Art; 211. Knoll International; 212-213. Peter Stone.

Part VII: 214-215. Christopher Springmann/Black Star; 216-223. John Huehnergarth; 224-229. Noel Vietmeyer; 230. (top) Noel Vietmeyer; (bottom) James Powell, Jr.; 231. (top and bottom right) Loren McIntyre/Woodfin Camp & Associates; (bottom left) Tom McHugh/Photo Researchers, Inc.; 232-239. Jan Adkins; 240. Steve Tuttle; 241. (top) Smithsonian Institution: Al Harrell; (bottom) Smithsonian Institution: Victor Krantz; 242. (top) The Bettmann Archive; (middle) David Good; (bottom) Brigham Young University, Department of Civil Engineering; 243. The Bettmann Archive; 244-245. David Good; 246. Schroeder/Eastwood; 247. Joe Goodwin.

Appendix: (left to right) *Technology* —Smithsonian Institution; Naval Photographic Center; The Bettmann Archive; The Bettmann Archive; Smithsonian Institution; The Bettmann Archive; The Bettmann Archive; Smithsonian Institution: National Portrait Gallery; Smithsonian Institution; Smithsonian Institution: National Portrait Gallery; Courtesy of U.S. Naval Institute, 1966; The Bettmann Archive. *Science* —Charles H. Phillips; The Bettmann Archive; Smithsonian Institution; Smithsonian Institution; Smithsonian Institution: National Portrait Gallery; Smithsonian Institution: National Portrait Gallery; The Bettmann Archive; Harvard College Observatory; The Bettmann Archive; Argonne National Laboratory; Smithsonian Institution; Joe Goodwin. *Industry* —The Bettmann Archive; Smithsonian Institution; Smithsonian Institution: National Portrait Gallery (next four); Smithsonian Institution; The 3M Company; KFC Corporation.